Industrial Sociology
and
Economic Crisis

Industrial Sociology
and
Economic Crisis

JOHN ELDRIDGE
PETER CRESSEY
JOHN MACINNES

HARVESTER
WHEATSHEAF

New York   London   Toronto   Sydney   Tokyo   Singapore

First published 1991 by
Harvester Wheatsheaf
66 Wood Lane End, Hemel Hempstead
Hertfordshire HP2 4RG

A division of
Simon & Schuster International Group

Typeset in 10/12pt Ehrhardt
by Keyboard Services, Luton

Printed and bound in Great Britain by
BPCC Wheatons Ltd, Exeter

British Library Cataloguing in Publication Data
Eldridge, J. E. T. (John Eric Thomas, *1936–*)
Industrial sociology and economic crisis.
1. Great Britain
I. Title   II. MacInnes, J. (John), *1956–*
III. Cressey, P. (Peter)
306.36
ISBN 0–7108–0777–5

1 2 3 4 5   95 94 93 92 91

CONTENTS

FIGURES AND TABLES

ACKNOWLEDGEMENTS

We are happy to acknowledge with thanks the help and advice we have received.

Professor Richard Brown (University of Durham), Dr Harvie Ramsay (University of Strathclyde) and Dr David Worland (Melbourne Footscray Institute of Technology) have commented constructively on various parts of the manuscript.

Mrs Pauline Connelly, Mrs Ann Adamson and Ms Philippa Townsend have given invaluable secretarial support.

Clare Grist of Harvester Wheatsheaf has shown patience and goodwill throughout.

1

INTRODUCTION: CRISES IN AUTHORITY RELATIONS?

Crisis, turn, juncture, emergency, turning point, given time.
(*Roget's Thesaurus*)

The term crisis has its origins in medicine. It refers to the turning-point of an illness. There is danger but there may, at the same time, be hope of recovery. Physicians may play a crucial role since their treatment will be based on judgements about the nature of the disease. There is diagnosis and there is prognosis. The use of the metaphor of the body goes back to Plato and so the appeal of the term for social analysis is understandable. Yet, like many other terms in social science, the concept of crisis is a metaphor and, perhaps for that reason, capable of being used with a great deal of elasticity. In practice it is multi-faceted in its application and extensive in the range of connotations attached to it.

This is a considerable problem. Just as social scientists have cast doubts on the usefulness of other concepts – secularization, for example – so one might sympathize with those who advocate that its plurality of meanings should lead us to discard it, or at least place a moratorium on its use. This is almost like asking theologians not to use the word God because of the multiplicity of meanings it represents. But if James O'Connor is right when he argues that the idea of crisis is at the heart of all serious discussion of the modern world then we cannot really abandon it (O'Connor, 1987). Just as theologians who argue for the death of God still need the term to develop their analysis, so do those social scientists who want to contest the nature or reality of crises which others claim to have identified.

What we have tried to do, within the limits of particular interests delineated in this book, is to recognize the diversity of usage in order to uncover the kinds of diagnosis and prognosis that are on offer. This involves trying to situate accounts of crisis in terms of a range of contexts and differing theoretical perspectives. In other words, we want to think through carefully what the term crisis has come to signify and, through this, to consider its explanatory adequacy. In doing so we take note of O'Connor's comment:

> The word 'crisis' is soaked with social, political and cultural meanings, and the connections between economic crisis, consciousness and social action

are mediated by these social concepts at many different levels of human experience. In particular, the fusion of economic, social–political and ideological concepts of crisis in the mass media means that a kind of permanent crisis consciousness exists independently of classical capitalist economic 'laws of motion'. (O'Connor, 1987)

Industrial sociology, like sociology in general, is subject to internal debates about the object of its inquiry and appropriate theoretical perspectives. The ground may also be contested by some Marxist theorizing, which sees sociology as one expression of bourgeois social science. O'Connor, for example, refers to bourgeois social science as a theoretical house of cards, which explains little or nothing. Accordingly, he throws down the gauntlet when he writes:

> The academic echoes of the roar of international big capital reverberate through the ideological canyons of a terribly feared future. They call for a return to a mythical past of progress and prosperity; the present is not regarded as history in the making but rather history as a reified past. The call to arms is an entreatment simultaneously to work and save *and* borrow and consume; to stay home with the family *and* leave home to fill the ranks of the exploding service economy; to accept uncritically the new international economy and division of labour *and* at the same time 'rebuild America', defend liberty against state regulation and encroachment *and* bow before the imperatives of national security and state imposed order, *ad nauseam*. Bourgeois theory is thus inevitably not part of the solution to the modern crisis but rather a central problem of late capitalist society. (p. 48)

The argument is, as it was with Marx, that bourgeois social science, whether political economy or sociology, deals with appearances and not reality and cannot therefore have a critical function. Intentionally or not, it is part of the process of mystification. But is this necessarily so? When Gouldner wrote *The Coming Crisis of Western Sociology* (1971) he did contend that the discipline had lost its critical function. On the one hand, the dominant structural–functionalist paradigm, strongly influenced by the work of Parsons at that time, was ideologically conservative and tended to support the order of the society in which its theorists were located. On the other hand, other available theoretical perspectives such as exchange theory, symbolic interactionism and ethnomethodology, were treated by Gouldner as symptoms of the intellectual crisis facing the discipline. The solution for Gouldner was not, however, the replacement of sociology by Marxism. Indeed, elsewhere he drew attention to the tensions and contradictions within Marxism in a discussion of its two major paradigms: the scientific and the critical.

> Critical and Scientific Marxists may each be committed to the revolution, but each views the revolution's future as protected in different ways. The Critical Marxists see the future of the revolution as depending on the clarity of awareness and vigour of conscious commitment, on a consciousness that can be imprinted on history like a kind of germ matter. The Scientific Marxists,

however, see the future of the revolution as essentially vouchsafed not by the heroism of the revolutionary but by history itself; by the inexorable contradictions of each society; by the scientific appraisal of these contradictions; and by seeking the political opportunities created by the crises brought about by these unfolding contradictions. (Gouldner, 1971, p. 439)

Whatever else, there is an unsettled debate within Marxism, which makes its privileged claim to go below the level of appearances (the level at which bourgeois social science is trapped) not so straightforward. So the intellectual crisis of sociology is matched rather than solved by the crisis in Marxism. These intellectual crises – paradigm struggles – arise as attempts to make sense of the world are perceived by many academics and political thinkers to be falling short of the mark. The world is not quite as our theories assumed and so the nature of social change remains a problem to be addressed and not a formula to be trotted out with the old sense of certainty. History is on no-one's side and sociologists, like everyone else, will do well to retain the capacity to be astonished at the nature and significance of social change, the continuities and the discontinuities. How, then, can we begin to get some leverage to aid our analysis, whilst remaining open to future possibilities?

Sociologists since Weber have recognized that the analysis of authority relations can offer a fruitful way of discovering how stable or unstable a society is. Weber's own ideal type distinction between traditional, legal and charismatic bases of authority has certainly been influential (Weber, 1978). For Weber, domination – the probability that certain specific commands will be obeyed – can be grounded in a diversity of motives for compliance. But a minimum of voluntary compliance, an interest in obedience, is always implied:

> Experience shows that in no instance does domination voluntarily limit itself to the appeal to material or affectual or ideal motives as a basis for its continuance. In addition every such system attempts to establish and to cultivate a belief in its legitimacy. But according to the kind of legitimacy which is claimed, the type of obedience, the kind of administrative staff developed to guarantee it, the mode of exercising authority will all differ fundamentally. Equally fundamental is the variation in effect. (Weber, 1978, p. 213)

Weber was explicitly aware of the empirical complexity of societies in different times and places, rejecting the notion that concrete historical reality can be exhausted in a conceptual scheme. Nevertheless, his discussions of the ways in which traditional authority relations could be challenged by charismatic leaders (such as religious prophets) and the ways in which charismatic authority could be routinized into bureaucratic legal forms of domination have proved fruitful. Authority is only one form of power – it implies obedience, for whatever reasons or motives, on the basis of something more than fear and coercion. The exercise of power can be based on physical coercion. It can also be deployed manipulatively so that people do not willingly obey for they are not aware of what has been done, even though it may have real consequences for their lives. Again, any concrete empirical situation may reflect a mix of these different kinds of power. Indeed, a crisis in authority relations may lead to these other forms of power being exercised.

Discussions of authority relations and class relations overlap, which is one reason that contemporary sociologists find themselves in continuing debate with the ghosts of Marx and Weber. Why, for better or worse, has there been no socialist revolution in the advanced industrial societies? Does class matter any more? Although much of this book is concerned with Britain – the first industrial nation – we want in this introduction to draw attention to a number of conceptual and analytical matters which are not tied to considerations of the British scene, to which, however, we will return.

According to Edward Thompson:

> Classes do not exist as separate entities, look around, find an enemy class, and then start to struggle. On the contrary, people find themselves in a society structured in determined ways (crucially, but not exclusively, in production relations), they experience exploitation (or the need to maintain power over those whom they exploit), they identify points of antagonistic interest, they commence to struggle around these issues and in the process of struggling they discover themselves as classes. (Thompson, 1978b, p. 149)

This raises questions about the ways in which societies are structured and the kinds of issues struggled over. We may also consider, with the benefit of hindsight, the reasons for the victories and defeats of the contending groups. One instructive attempt to grapple with such matters is Bendix's *Work and Authority in Industry* (1956), a comparative study of managerial ideologies in four industrializing societies: England, the United States, Russia and East Germany. Bendix argues that ideas concerning work, the authority of employers, and the reasons for subordination form the ideological framework in which the day-to-day operations of economic entrepreneurs are conceived. Analytically, he juxtaposes the concepts of social class and bureaucracy. If the first refers to the tendency of people in a common socio-economic position to develop common ideas and collective action, the second represents the development of organizational interests within a hierarchical setting. Thus, for Bendix:

> Ideologies of management are attempts by leaders of enterprises to justify the privilege of voluntary action and association for themselves, while imposing upon all subordinates the duty of obedience and the obligation to serve their employers to the best of their ability. (Bendix, 1956, p. 81)

Bendix's methodological strategy is to compare two societies at the early stages of their industrialization – England and Russia – and two societies in a later stage where large-scale economic enterprises had come into existence – the United States and East Germany. The other leading contrast is between societies where entrepreneurs and managers form an autonomous class – England and the United States – and those where they are subordinate to governmental control – Russia and East Germany.

In the early stages of industrialization, established pre-industrial ways of life were threatened, as Thompson showed clearly in the case of England (Thompson, 1968, 1967). Pre-existing aristocratic ruling groups and the newly emerging industrial workforce could prove hostile to these new developments. The entrepreneurial ideologies at this stage represented an attempt to justify these new social relationships and the role of industry in society. In this respect, for Bendix, the ideologies of the new entrepreneurs and their apologists represent a weapon in the fight to justify industrial activity and hence to establish new patterns of authority relations.

The struggle involved should not be underestimated at this early stage of industrialization even though it takes place in the context of different historical legacies and social structures. For that reason, the break with traditionalism which industrialization represents can be different in substance and outcome. In the case of Russia, for example, the governmental promotion of enterprises, with Tsarist rule as the lynchpin of authority, led to administrative, social and legal controls which not only supported economic activities but assisted in the recruitment and disciplining of the workforce.

For Bendix, the analysis of entrepreneurial and managerial ideologies can be seen as a clue to changing class relationships. If the French Revolution had shown decisively that a break with traditional forms of political subordination was possible, the Industrial Revolution raised parallel questions concerning the organization of social relations in industry – questions about industrial citizenship. An important part of the story in each instance is, in the end, the ways in which in each industrializing society the presence or absence of civil, legal, political and social rights diminished or intensified the experience of exploitation among the working class. Hence he writes:

> The managerial interpretations of the authority relationship in economic enterprises together with the workers contrast-conception concerning their collective position in an emerging industrial society constitute a composite image of class relations which has changed over time and which also differs from country to country. (Bendix, 1956, p. 443)

The early years of industrialization are likely to see the emergence of a crisis in authority relations. This, in general, is consistent with Giddens' (1973) argument that state socialism, as an alternative variant to liberal capitalism has its best chance of coming into being when a society is at a relatively low level of economic development. If the revolutionary outcome does not materialize at the early stages of industrialization, the working class protest is likely to be incorporated and institutionalized through the extension of citizen rights – political, legal and social – to the whole population (cf. Marshall, 1950).

From this perspective, whilst Marx can properly be credited with identifying the processes of concentration and centralization in the development of capitalist economies, he was mistaken in assuming an interrelated rise in revolutionary working class consciousness:

> What Marx caustically referred to as 'a whole system of swindling and cheating by means of corporation promotion, stock insurance, and stock speculation' becomes, not a transitory phase intervening between 'classical capitalism' and socialism, but the characteristic form of the developed capitalist economy. (Giddens, 1973, p. 152)

A parallel argument was put forward by Mann at about the same time (Mann, 1973). He made an analytical distinction between four elements of working class consciousness:

1. Class *identity* – the definition of oneself as working class in the production process and in common with other workers.
2. Class *opposition* – the perception of capitalists and the agents of capital as enduring opponents of the working class.
3. Class *totality* – class identity and opposition are seen as the defining characteristics both of one's total situation and of the society in which one lives.
4. The concept of an *alternative society* towards which one moves in struggle with the opposition.

In commenting on these four interlinked elements Mann argues:

> True revolutionary consciousness is the combination of all four, and an obviously rare occurrence. Marxism provides a theory of escalation of consciousness from the first to the fourth. Consciousness grows (some Marxists say it 'explodes') as the worker links his own concrete experience to an analysis of wider structures and then to alternative structures. It is in this sense that Marxism is a materialist theory: contradictions within the sphere of production and the growth of collective power are experienced by the worker before he generalises a theory of socialism. (Mann, 1973, p. 13)

As far as class relations in mature capitalist societies are concerned, the position as Mann outlines it may be briefly indicated here. Industrial conflict has been institutionalized and consists largely of aggressive economism and defensive control. At its most developed, this is found in the business unions of the United States, but in any event this form of unionism, in practice, becomes much more prevalent than trade unionism orientated to workers' control, not least because the idea of managerial prerogatives pivots on issues of control. Whilst trade unions can be militant in pursuit of their goals, and even contain some revolutionary rhetoric, they do not challenge the overall class structure. They do not seriously pursue the goal of workers' control of industry and society, which a more revolutionary form of class consciousness would embrace. In this book the chapters on trade unions and industrial democracy explore these matters much more fully in the British context.

One of the more promising exceptions from a Marxist point of view was France in 1968. Mann does not lightly dismiss this and he was writing close to those events. There was evidence of class solidarity and action together with the construction of alternative conceptions of society. Yet the goals of workers' power and *auto-gestion* were not achieved. It is true that issues of industrial participation have remained on the political agenda but the energy and spontaneity of 1968 have long since subsided. Rather, there have been attempts by the state to improve participation at enterprise level, notably through the Lois Auroux which made management–worker consultations at enterprise level a large requirement. (For a useful discussion of these issues see the special issue of *Sociologie du travail*, vol. 28 (1986), no. 3, Retour sur l'enterprise.) The level of trade union membership in France is not high; more generally, by the late 1980s the role of the Communist party in France had much diminished.

There has, of course, been a great deal of discussion about the emergence of the 'new' working class, especially in France (see, for example, Mallet, 1963; Touraine, 1966; Gorz, 1969; Gallie, 1978). The issue revolved around the role of workers in the advanced, automated sector of industry: in process industries such as chemicals and oil refining. Mann expresses doubts as to whether the conflicts that exist between the 'new workers' and their employers amounts to a major contradiction. He draws attention to a paradox: although it is possible to find evidence of *totality* and alternative concepts of society, their sense of *identity* and *opposition* is relatively undeveloped, which is the reverse of the traditional working class. The overall effect, however, is the same: the failure to translate mixed consciousness into a consistent series of radical actions. None of this means that class does not matter any more, which was the general stance of those who wrote of 'the end of ideology'. 'Overall, it seems safer to expect intermediate forms of class relations rather than either revolution or near harmony' (Mann, 1973, p. 69). This expectation has not been upset in the years that have followed.

How, then, are we to approach the subject of industrial conflict? If managerial ideologies are attempts to legitimize authority relations, which are typically class-based, is not industrial conflict an expression of a challenge to such relations? We know that strikes are only one form of industrial conflict but, partly because of the greater availability of strike data they have been much used as an indicator of social unrest (see, for example, Knowles, 1952; Kerr, 1964; Eldridge, 1968; Hyman, 1988). From time to time strikes are seen as indicators of societal crisis, especially when they are widespread and long-lasting, or, of course, at the time of a general strike.

There are strikes and associated forms of unrest which, when related to particular social situations can reasonably be held to have wide social implications, with a potential for national crisis. For example, in July 1989 strikes took place in the Siberian and Ukrainian coalfields. These were described as being the most serious expression of labour unrest in the Soviet Union since the 1920s (John Rettie, 'Miners' Strike Spreads to Ukraine', *Guardian*, 18 July 1989). Over 100,000 miners were involved. According to observers this has not simply been about pay and conditions but includes demands for greater democracy and workers' control over state enterprises and for more of the fruits of industry to be ploughed back into the coal-producing regions. This represents an anti-Moscow, pro-decentralist view. This event can certainly be seen as an aspect of what happens when the Soviet Union, under Gorbachev, seeks to achieve economic and political reform. Protest becomes more visible. *Perestroika* – economic restructuring – is seen to be a potentially painful process that implies a struggle for control as new systems of authority are emerging in the Soviet Union.

This tension over the relationship between the political and economic spheres and between central and local control of enterprises was indeed present in Russia at the time of the 1917 revolution. S. A. Smith reminds us that Lenin believed that socialism could be built by developing large-scale industry (Smith, 1983). This would necessarily involve using capitalist methods of labour discipline and the social organization of labour to improve productivity. This was contrary to the emerging philosophy of the factory committee:

> Implicit within the movement for workers' control was a belief that capitalist methods cannot be used for socialist ends. In their battle to democratise the factory, in their emphasis on the importance of collective institutions by the direct pro-ducers in transforming the work situation, the factory committees had become aware – in a partial and groping way to be sure – that factories are not merely sites of production but also of reproduction – the reproduction of a certain structure of social relations based on a division between those who give orders and those who execute them, between those who direct and those who execute. . . . Inscribed within their practice was a distinctive vision of socialism, central to which was workplace democracy. (Smith, 1983, p. 261)

In the wake of *perestroika* these issues of authority and control are reappear-ing. In the 1920s the solution was to institutionalize massive bureaucratic and centalized control from above, allied to the use of coercive power. In the late 1980s, the reformist Gorbachev government is seeking another way. It is a time of crisis – a significant moment in the history of the Soviet Union – and no-one can predict the outcome with confidence. Modernization and increased productivity are still central to the state's agenda; it is the method of achieving it that is now to be determined and worked through.

We have used the example of the Soviet Union as a dramatic example of the liberalization process in Eastern Europe. Other examples are readily to hand in Hungary and Poland. The case of the Solidarity movement in Poland is remarkable (see Ascherson, 1981; Touraine, 1983). The movement can be seen as a response to crisis: the crisis of a society which by the mid 1970s had run into a debt problem that was getting worse by the year, with low wages and increasing food prices and shortages. Solidarity was a trade union organization but it was also a wider social movement, with strong support from the Catholic Church in Poland and, of course, a Polish pope, and heterogeneous political elements. Ascherson described it as a self-limiting organization in the early 1980s, meaning that it was not attempting to supplant Communist rule but to come to a working compromise that would improve the wages and conditions of the Polish people. At the end of 1981, Poland was taken over by a military coup and Solidarity was driven underground with many of its leading members imprisoned or under close surveillance. Yet those who proclaimed either the limits of Solidarity or even its demise in the wake of the coup, have now to come to terms with the political triumph of the movement in the 1989 elections and the appointment of a member of Solidarity as Prime Minister. The economic crisis has, in this instance, led to the breakdown of the one-party bureaucratic state although, of course, the Communist Party remains a strong presence. But these examples underline the point that, whilst there may be good grounds for referring to capitalist societies as being in crisis, state socialism is also in crisis.

In the case of Eastern Europe, Davis and Scase have pointed out that the issue does not centre, as in capitalism, on declining profitability, but on the organization of investment and the allocation of the surplus. Both threaten the wages and conditions of working people. The crises in the Eastern European countries are affected by the inefficiencies of the central planning system – a crisis of administration – and intensified by the international pressures of the global economy. In a perceptive comment, written in 1985, Davis and Scase observe:

> There is every indication that these problems will continue and crisis tendencies become more acute until the state socialist societies implement reforms for making the party apparatus more responsive to the needs of the population. The evidence so far suggests that such reforms initiated from 'the top' are strictly limited because of bureaucratic inertia and the party's reluctance to give up the monopoly of political power. The alternative, which has all the uncertainty and risks of earlier mass movements under state socialism, is for workers, together with other social groups, to build organisations – including trade unions – which can reconcile the goals of increased accumulation, the fulfilment of personal needs and greater democracy. (Davis and Scase, 1985, p. 164)

This, as they point out, would constitute a 'cultural revolution' of the kind outlined by Bahro (1978). It is this revolution that is now in progress with all its uncertainties and dangers, hopes and possibilities for a new social order. It is a crisis – a 'turning point', a 'given time'.

What about Britain, the main empirical focus of this book? The Conservative Party has been in office since 1979 and there are already a number of books about what are commonly described as the 'Thatcher years' (Hall and Jacques, 1983; MacInnes, 1987; Kavanagh, 1987; Riddell, 1983; Hall, 1989b). From the standpoint of the New Right, which the Thatcher years inaugurated, the 1980s might be said to represent a response to what they had defined as the crisis of consensus: the post-war compromise between Labour and Conservative, which from the New Right perspective represented both economic stagnation and a steady drift to bureaucratic socialism. The result, according to government supporters, has been something approaching an economic miracle – with fast growth rates, increased productivity, Treasury surpluses (much helped by a series of privatization measures) and control of that 'over-mighty' subject, the trade unions. The enterprise culture has been encouraged and nurtured and now flourishes.

There are other ways of looking at it. In 1988, the current account deficit on the balance of payments was £14.7 billion. This heavily exceeded the Treasury forecast of a deficit of £4 billion. The balance of trade in manufacturing goods since 1983 has been in deficit, the first time in Britain's recorded industrial history. Inflation, which the government had aimed to reduce to zero has been steadily rising and by mid 1989 was nearly 10 per cent, more than double most of its Common Market partners. Interest rates, the chosen weapon of monetary policy, had risen to 15 per cent.

The election of a Conservative government in 1979 was widely attributed to the 'winter of discontent' that preceded it – a series of strikes against the Labour government's pay policy. In the four years that followed, unemployment rose from 5 to 12.5 per cent, which was more than twice the average increase for all members of the OECD. As Sir Alexander Cairncross pointed out:

> The rise in unemployment by 1.5 million in the two years 1980 and 1981 is accounted for almost entirely by the fall of manufacturing employment over the same period. So complete was the collapse of manufacturing, following on an earlier but more gradual reduction in employment in manufacturing between the mid 1960s and 1980, that it has since failed to share the recovery in the service sector of the economy. (Cairncross, 1989, pp. 6–7)

The year 1989, with its high interest rates and high inflation saw a spring and summer of discontent. Industrial action of various kinds was manifest: the National Union of Seamen were in a long-running dispute with P&O Channel Ferries; the National Union of Railwaymen engaged in a series of one-day strikes and an overtime ban over wages, working conditions and the use of procedures. The Transport and General Workers, like the Railway workers, went through a difficult legal situation before they were able to call a strike. This was against the government's decision, supported by the Port Employers, to abolish the Dock Labour Scheme. In both these cases an underlying issue was how to resist attempts by the employers to move away from national bargaining. Construction workers employed on North Sea offshore oil platforms engaged in a series of 24-hour strikes over pay and safety conditions, where the Piper Alpha accident in 1988 caused heavy loss of life. Members of NALGO (the national and local government employees' union) were similarly involved in 24-hour stoppages in a dispute over pay and working conditions, which had direct effects on nurseries, day care centres, housing and rates departments and libraries. The broadcasting unions were in dispute with the BBC over a pay offer, which, while it lasted, led to television and radio schedules being upset as a result of lightning strikes. The government, represented by the Health Minister, Kenneth Clark, met fierce opposition from the British Medical Association and many other professional and trade union groups within the National Health Service, following the White Paper proposals on the reform of the NHS.

Miracle or crisis? This book looks at post-war Britain (sometimes in a comparative context) and shows how the concept of crisis has been used and applied to specific collective actors, notably government, management and trade unions. This involves structural considerations, both at the societal level and at the institutional level within industry. Politically, of course, one group's crisis may be another's opportunity. The political dominance of the Conservative Party in the last decade can certainly be traced in part to divisions on the left of British politics. This dominance has provided the crucial context for discussions about industrial relations and enterprise in the 1980s. So there has been a good deal of comment, led from the right, on the need for a 'new realism' in industrial relations. But it has also resulted in provoking the left to rethink its position, as well evidenced by the discussion of 'New Times' in the pages of *Marxism Today* (whose readership extends well beyond the limited confines of the Communist Party).

It is true that we do not read about post-capitalism in the New Times perspective, but we do hear much about post-Fordism, post-Taylorism and post-modernism. Thatcherism is seen as a project which, in some respects, appealed to many people in the Britain (or, at least, England) of the 1980s. The task of the left is seen as a cultural struggle over the central concepts for defining and evaluating society: individualism, freedom and citizenship are key examples. The challenge of identifying and relating politically to these New Times is certainly a challenge to well known versions of Marxism, as Stuart Hall, a leading exponent, recognizes:

> Classical Marxism depended on an assumed correspondence between the 'economic' and the 'political': one could read off our political attitudes, interests and motivations from our economic class interests and position. This correspondence between 'the political' and 'the economic' is exactly what has now disintegrated – practically and theoretically. (Hall, 1988a, p. 25)

This gives a new and unexpected twist to Marx's view that in modern societies all that is solid melts into air, for it includes Marxist theory. This book, therefore, comes at a time of intellectual crisis in politics and social science, and at a time in our own society which many, whether in political, economic or ecological terms, see as critical. In what follows we aim to look at some of the continuities and discontinuities which have led – for better or worse – to turbulent times.

2

THE BRITISH ECONOMY IN CRISIS?

INTRODUCTION: USING THE TERM CRISIS

Many uses of the term crisis have their roots in the Marxist analysis of capitalism as a set of social and economic relations or a 'mode of production'. Marx argued that in earlier forms of society, such as those founded on slave labour or on feudal obligations, social relations tended to remain fixed and stable. Similarly, Weber argued that one important aspect of such societies was their domination by 'traditional' social action: the force of tradition alone was one of the main determinants of social relations. By contrast, both these observers saw industrial, capitalist or modern society as characterized by pressures for incessant change and development, whether this came from the anarchy and unpredictability of the market or the rapid development of productive forces including technology. These pressures manifested themselves through conflict on the market and also within those institutions which dealt with the market: within units of capital and nation states as well as between competing traders, companies or nations:

> The bourgeoisie cannot exist without constantly revolutionising the instruments of production, and thereby the relations of production and with them the whole relations of society. Conservation of the old modes of production in unaltered form was, on the contrary, the first condition of existence for all earlier industrial classes. Constant revolutionising of production, uninterrupted disturbance of all social conditions, everlasting uncertainty and agitation distinguish the bourgeois epoch from all earlier ones. All fixed, fast-frozen relations, with their train of ancient and venerable prejudices and opinions, are swept away, all new formed ones become antiquated before they can ossify. (Marx and Engels, 1968, p. 38)

In short, there would be a permanent crisis. But if crisis is such a fundamental and permanent aspect of capitalist or modern society, it ceases to be a useful concept with which to examine changes in such societies over time. Moreover, such a contrast between the dynamic nature of capitalism and the static nature of pre-capitalist societies can be rather overdone. It would be better if we could reserve the term for more specific developments which made sense of the degree of crisis, of acuteness of contradictions, of the rapidity of change, of historically important choices being made. But such an exercise is difficult because the factors which precipitate profound change may not themselves be acute but chronic. They may develop over a period of many decades or centuries, but surely still deserve to be seen as part of the crisis. For example, many people argue that the competitiveness of British industry is a major problem, and component part of any current crisis. Yet it would be difficult to pinpoint just when British industry 'became' uncompetitive. Rather, it seems to be a problem which has been developing for over a century at least. Just as crises can mature slowly they may also throw up tensions with cannot be resolved quickly. Although they may appear to demand a resolution to bring about change, it may transpire that things are more tractable and tension endurable.

> Countries don't fall over cliffs. Decline can continue indefinitely. Look at other countries and other centuries. (Rutherford, 1983, p. 44)

The idea of a state of health raises another fundamental problem with the idea of crisis, again related to the term's roots in medicine (refer back to page 1). In cases of physical illness, what constitutes a state of health, and consequently the changes desirable to achieve that state of health, are not always contro versial issues. In societies, on the contrary, people of different classes, races or genders, supporters of political parties or inhabitants of different regions may all have diverse and contradictory ideas about what constitutes a state of health and these ideas may change over time. In turn, the significance of the same set of ideas may change as circumstances change. For example, Nove (1983) argues that leaving most economic change to be determined by the market was probably the best way of maximizing increases in living standards for everybody in nineteenth-century Britain, but that in the late twentieth century much more state intervention and regulation of economic activity is needed to secure the same ends.

Different groups in society may also have different ideas about how to move towards a state of health. They may diagnose quite different problems and prescribe different courses of treatment. Conservative thinkers may see the root of the trouble in permissiveness and creeping socialism. Socialists, on the contrary, may blame the outmoded survival of feudal vestiges of deference and hierarchy (see, for example, Anderson, 1964, 1987). Considering 'solutions' to a crisis highlights such divisions even more sharply. What may be a solution for some may be seen as the problem by others. For example, some writers have argued that Britain's poor economic performance since the war has been due to the weakness of state intervention, direction and support for industry (Barnett, 1984). Conversely, Thatcherite analysts have argued that just such sorts of government intervention were a part of the *cause* of the crisis itself.

In turn, such different analyses are bound up with the way crises or their resolution imply different outcomes of costs and benefits to different groups. For example, high unemployment, a prominent aspect of the crisis throughout the 1980s, may be seen by the Labour movement as the illness that needs to be cured; whilst for the government, as we discuss later in this chapter, it was part of the cure itself. Workers in secure internal labour markets in expanding industries may not face any threat from rising or high unemployment. Women workers may have different feelings about a demand for full employment if the opportunity for more employment still leaves them with the bulk of unpaid domestic labour to do as well.

Once we consider these factors we can see that in this sense there is no such thing as a crisis, but a whole range of perceived crises of quite different and contradictory character faced by different groups in society at different times. However, this need not mean that social science should avoid the term altogether, but that it needs to define its use more precisely and be prepared to explore aspects of what is commonly understood as the crisis without trying to reduce them all to one central decisive phenomenon. Rather than using crisis to mean poor economic performance or any specific acute set of challenges or changes facing a particular social group, crisis could be thought of in a more general sense of periods in which a particular society becomes less able to maintain previously established social relations or social action in the old way, to reproduce itself as it has done in the past, whilst groups within that society struggle over the construction of new patterns of social relations. As such, crisis becomes a period of change, of turning points between different stages of social development. By social relations we include both direct economic relations, such as those in the workplace or in the domestic economy, and class relations, political forces and culture. Sociology can examine how, historically, social constraints in the sense of the impossibility or undesirability of old ways of living led to the construction of new social relations, but it cannot demonstrate the inevitability of these processes (people might still have chosen differently) or predict how they might repeat themselves in the future. Nor should it produce too rigorous an analysis of the logic of social relations found on either side of critical turning points: for to do so can also produce rather deterministic accounts of social change which underestimate the potential for other developments found at any point in a society which contains a heterogenous mixture of structures and forces. It cannot, therefore, tell people how crises ought to be resolved but it can use empirical evidence or theory to examine more clearly the constraints upon social action, enabling the processes of crisis to be better understood, inform the choices people make and illuminate the connections between means and ends (Gerth and Mills, 1970; Weber, 1949).

If we reserve the term crisis for conveying the idea of such turning points in the nature of an entire society (whilst bearing in mind the inevitable continuities as well as breaks in history) and focus our attention on industry and the economy, then two such periods stand out in the recent past in Britain. The first is that of the Second World War; the second is that of the dramatic rise in unemployment in the late 1970s associated with the abandonment of government economic policies established during and after the war. The remainder of this chapter, therefore, considers some of the aspects of the development of the British economy since the war which have been seen as relevant to the crisis, concentrating on economic performance. It thus provides a general framework for the detailed discussion of aspects of the crisis in social relations in industry which is the concern of the rest of the book.

THE BRITISH ECONOMY AND THE POST-WAR SETTLEMENT

After almost two decades of slump and mass unemployment Britain was in a poor condition to face Nazi Germany. Until the end of 1941, when Hitler's invasion of Russia seemed set to fail, defeat for Britain was a real possibility. Only in 1942, at El Alamein, did the allies secure their first military victory. An important part of the response to this national crisis were attempts to steer the economy away from the traditions of *laissez faire* individualism – the idea that ultimately the market itself, without interference from the government, was the best guarantee of economic progress. These traditions had been strong in a country which had undergone the first industrial revolution and become the world's leading economic power with much less intervention from the state than found elsewhere (in domestic matters at any rate).

The needs of a wartime economy, the mobilization of millions in the armed forces and the search for means to fulfil the social and economic promises made to boost wartime morale (homes, full employment, better education and health services) all pointed towards the need for more state involvement in the running of the economy, together with more direct consultation between the government and the representatives of the employers and the trade union movement about what needed to be done and how. Such consultation was not just a question of the extension of citizenship rights or industrial (as opposed to political) democracy, but a fundamental part of the new social order if it was to function properly. If the economy was not to be left at the mercy of the market, it would need, at least, the co-operation of the main 'social partners' to guide it in the future. The government might pass legislation on such matters as the rights of employees at work, and it might try to steer the economy, through public expenditure, taxation and other instruments, in such a way as to generate full employment. But it could not simply legislate for desirable economic ends without the co-operation and participation of those at work.

The war posed new economic problems whilst removing the traditional means used to solve them. The war cost a great deal; this was paid for largely by selling off the country's overseas assets. These had previously allowed

Britain to run a deficit on the balance of payments which now had to be made up by increasing the drive to export goods to gain foreign exchange, despite the competing claims of domestic demand enlarged by the need to rebuild a war-damaged economy and provide the new public services of the welfare state.

The set of economic and social relationships which emerged out of the war has been described as 'the post-war settlement' or 'Butskellism', after two leading figures of the Conservative and Labour parties of the day whose policies were identified with its development: Hugh Gaitskell and R. A. Butler. From 1945 to 1951 the first ever majority Labour government built the post-war economic order, not so much by revolutionary innovation as by maintaining in a form suitable for peacetime the controls on the economy established in wartime, such as more steeply progressive income tax, distribution of industry to depressed areas, the nationalization of industries which had been neglected by private owners or which were natural monopolies or indispensable to the country's overall economic effort such as transport and power. Measures such as the introduction of the National Health Service and reform of education had been prefigured by wartime White Papers and Acts. The Conservatives did not oppose many of the government's main measures, neither did the Conservative governments which followed for the next thirteen years reverse any of the major pieces of legislation passed by the first Labour government, nor challenge the principles on which they were based. Only the nationalization of the steel industry proved controversial. Morgan argues that:

> No stronger confirmation could have been found of the broad wisdom of the policies pursued by Atlee and his colleagues than in their Conservative successors' respectful affirmation of them. (Morgan, 1985, p. 495)

The government's new commitment to underwriting full employment in the economy was fundamental. The White Paper on Employment (1944) began by stating: 'The government accepts as one of their primary aims and responsibilities the maintenance of a high and stable level of employment after the war' (Cmnd 6527, p. 1). Its confidence in proclaiming such an objective came from the triumph of Keynesian economic ideas in the government during the war. One of Keynes's arguments was that there was no reason why the main markets in a capitalist economy should balance, or find 'equilibrium', at the most desirable level. Markets might balance at levels of economic activity – and therefore employment – far below what the economy could in fact sustain: there was no reason why high unemployment should be self-correcting if left to market forces. Instead, governments could improve on the free operation of markets by intervening to regulate the level of demand for goods and services in the economy. If the government injected more demand into the economy by public expenditure than it took out by taxation, it could increase the level of economic activity, boost the demand for labour and reduce unemployment. This would imply that the government borrowed to finance its expenditure rather than continuing to aim for a 'balanced budget' as governments had done in the past in order to maintain confidence in the value of the currency. Conversely, if employment looked like it might become too full, if demand in the economy threatened to exceed supply and so produce inflationary pressures, governments could cool off the economy by increasing taxation above the level of public expenditure.

The post-war employment record was impressive, as Figure 2.1 suggests. The millions of servicemen and women released at the end of the war found jobs. In contrast to the 1920s and 1930s when unemployment was always above 1 million and often nearly 3 million, under the Atlee government it fell to well below half a million, and in 1955 the rate of unemployment dipped below 1 per cent during the summer. Apart from the severe winter of 1963, unemployment remained below half a million until the end of the 1960s. The adoption of a strong regional policy, which restricted the development of industry in the more prosperous areas of the country and pushed investment towards assisted areas, meant that even in Scotland, Wales and the north of England unemployment usually fell below 3 per cent and rarely topped 4 per cent. Northern Ireland remained the one blackspot, with about double this rate. At the same time the number of people in employment increased by some 3½ million – evidence of the unprecedented growth of the economy in the post-war period. Productivity (output per person-hour) in manufacturing doubled between 1950 and 1970. Investment ran at about double its pre-war rate. British industry's exports more than trebled in volume between 1950 and 1975. This robust economic performance meant that the government had the

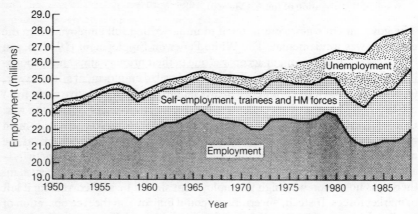

Figure 2.1 Employment and unemployment in the United Kingdom, 1950–88

Source: *Department of Employment Gazette.*

resources to fund the new services to be provided by the welfare state whilst still leaving private individuals dramatic increases in their personal spending power. Manual workers' real earnings (i.e. taking account of inflation) doubled between the end of the war and the end of the 1960s. Such statistics, as Phelps Brown has commented, give a picture of 'a time of outstanding betterment' (1983, p. 208).

In its essentials, economic policy was common to both Labour and Conservative governments. Both attempted to regulate demand by control of taxation and public expenditure, within a framework of progressive income tax and public spending aimed at providing services to all citizens regardless of ability to pay. Rather than legislating to regulate the inevitable pressures between different interest groups, both parties sought to consult, persuade and cajole employers, trade unionists or small business people to act in 'the national interest'. Underwriting such an approach was the room for manoeuvre provided by steady growth. The Conservative prime minster Harold MacMillan could say, without exaggerating, 'You have never had it so good', while the Labour Party's leading theoretician, C. A. R. Crosland, could write his book *The Future of Socialism* starting from the proposition that the main problems besetting capitalist economies had been resolved and brought under the control of the much more powerful modern state. No longer was private ownership of the means of production of central importance because of the threefold developments of nationalization, the divorce of ownership from control, whereby manager-employees ran private corporations and government control over a range of economic instruments which affected the way in which the private sector ran itself:

> The government can exert any influence it likes on income distribution, and can also determine within broad limits the division of total output between consumption, investment, exports, and social expenditure. (Crosland, 1956, p. 27)

This led Crosland to argue that it was no longer sensible to think of the British economy as fundamentally capitalist. The latter sort of society had as its essential features:

> First the veneration of individualism and competition: secondly, an insistence on the absolute and unconditional rights of private property: thirdly, an intellectual belief that the unfettered exercise of private rights must, by 'the invisible hand' of economic competition, maximise the welfare of the community. (p. 64)

All these essential features had disappeared, argued Crosland:

> Nor does anyone now much believe in the overriding rights of private property. . . . As for the dogma of the 'invisible hand', and the belief that private gain must always lead to public good, these failed entirely to survive the Great Depression. (p. 65)

The limits of the post-war settlement

There were limitations to the post-war settlement (which was, after all, rooted in a wholly market-based economy) despite the ideological changes Crosland emphasized. The right to work, implied in the commitment to full employment, was not developed into the principle of rights at work. Whilst unions might be consulted at national level about the course of economic policy, employees had little say in the running of their workplaces or companies. Thus whilst state intervention in the form of macroeconomic direction of the economy was accepted, its impact upon social relations at workplace level was more limited: the state might 'hold the ring' between employers and unions, but they were left to themselves to determine the rights people enjoyed in the workplace, as well as how they negotiated the terms of their relationship. This reflected not only reluctance on the part of managers to concede such rights but ambivalence on the part of trade unions, who preferred to exert influence through more traditional methods of developing workforce organization and collective bargaining, whilst letting managers 'get on with their job'. They often feared that a greater role for the state in setting minimum rights for all could undermine the importance of an independent role for unions. Only in the 1970s did industrial democracy or participation become more of an issue, with the recognition in law of a series of basic rights for employees concerning job security, discipline and health and safety.

Nor did full employment, increased public services and progressive taxation add up to the abolition of poverty, the arrival of equality or even of equality of opportunity. The millions of new jobs and the shift towards white collar and professional employment created a substantial increase in *absolute* upward social mobility, but the new social order did not do much to increase relative social mobility. That is to say, whilst all classes had more chances of upward mobility because there was now more 'room at the top', it was still the members of the lowest social classes who had least chance of getting there. Conversely, there was little *downward* social mobility (Goldthorpe, 1980). Whilst there was some redistribution of income and wealth away from the richest, its extent was controversial. In 1962, R. M. Titmuss published what was to become a famous study suggesting that the raw statistics on income distribution gave a misleading account of the changes, and argued that what redistribution had taken place was not substantial. An article in *The Economist* of January 1966, entitled 'The indefensible status quo', used data on investment income to estimate the distribution of wealth. It concluded:

About 84 per cent of wealth seems to be owned by the top 7 per cent of taxpayers. . . . And the reason for this extreme concentration is not that a few have such vast wealth. It is that so many have virtually no wealth (*The Economist*, 15 January 1966)

Nor was the problem simply one of 'gaps' in the network of support provided by the welfare state. For example, Coates and Silburn (1970), in a study of poverty in Nottingham, concluded that low wages were still a major source of poverty. The post-war settlement was still a society with tendencies towards inequality as well as greater affluence and opportunity. Small business people or professionals or high-earning white collar employees might be taxed more, but their opportunities to earn more or increase their wealth were greater still. There were also aspects of welfare state provision, such as the education system, which appeared to serve them better than they did the working class.

The post-war settlement was also one made mostly by and for men rather than women. The welfare state was founded on the concept of the family wage. Male earners in a household were assumed to support their female partners. Child care provision for working mothers was not seen as part of the welfare state, nor was it seen as a tax deductible expense for either employer or employee. Only in the 1960s were the principles of equal pay and non-discrimination in employment accepted and legislated for in the Equal Pay Act, 1970 and Sex Discrimination Act, 1976. Even then occupational segregation and other factors meant that in the decade after equality legislation women's hourly earnings only increased from 63 to 74 per cent of men's. Men continued to work substantial amounts of overtime (around eight hours per week per person in manufacturing) leaving women to do the bulk of unpaid domestic labour and often confining them to part-time employment opportunities. But full employment opened up some new job opportunities for women as employers unable to recruit men sometimes revised their stereotypes of what was men's and women's work. Some traditionally male occupations, such as clerical work in banks, became feminized. The problem for women was that such feminization was often accompanied by a downgrading of pay and status too. By 1970 there were 2 million more women workers in the labour force than two decades earlier – an increase of almost 25 per cent. Much of this increase was accounted for by married women working: in 1951 only one in five married women had a job, and in many occupations women who married would be expected to leave their job. By 1971 the proportion of married women working had doubled, and by the end of the 1970s had passed 50 per cent. As Figure 2.2 shows, all the employment growth in the economy after 1965 was in the growth of women's employment.

Comparative British economic weakness

Perhaps the most serious 'limitation' of the post-war settlement was the question of how sustainable was the apparently virtuous circle of rising living standards, higher employment levels, wider public provision and slowly decreasing social inequality, and how important the role of the state had been in achieving it. Economic growth was certainly good by British historical

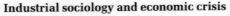

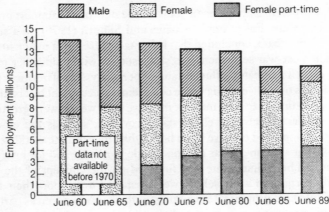

Figure 2.2 The rise in women's employment in Great Britain, 1960–89
Source: *Department of Employment Gazette.*

standards, but it was less impressive than that achieved in other industrial capitalist economies. The rapid expansion of world trade, the economic confidence engendered by full employment and expansionist economic policies by governments elsewhere brought higher rises in productivity and output in those countries than that experienced by Britain. This not only implied that earnings and living standards in Britain started to slip behind those enjoyed elsewhere, but also low growth bred a productive system which was undynamic, less able to respond to changes in world markets, less able to compete in domestic markets and less able to grow in the future because of the resultant balance of payments constraints. Britain's share of world trade declined steadily.

Low productivity growth in the export sectors of the economy made British exports less competitive, whilst imports became relatively more attractive. This in turn put pressure on the value of the pound, since devaluation could help make British exports relatively cheaper, but by making imports more expensive, increased the rate of domestic inflation. Alternatively, governments could try to restrict domestic demand (by curbing public expenditure, increasing taxation and tightening credit) in order to encourage producers to try to export, but at the cost of dampening the overall level of activity, increasing unemployment and possibly slowing longer-term productivity growth by encouraging firms to delay or revise investment plans. The succession of small-scale crises which beset the economy gave rise to what came to be known as stop–go policies. In the stop phase, governments would try to avert balance of payments or currency problems by cooling the economy and restraining demand. In the go phase they would seek to avoid increasing unemployment by doing the opposite. As Massey and Meegan (1981) show, job losses occurred both as companies failed to remain competitive and pulled out of production, and as companies responded by introducing labour-saving techniques or intensifying labour effort in order to try to maintain competitiveness. By the mid 1960s this started to lead to absolute falls in the level of manufacturing employment, often referred to as 'deindustrialization', as British capital failed to remain productive enough in international terms to sustain employment levels. Measures of profitability are not easy to make because of the problems of calculating depreciation and the effects of tax, but from the mid 1960s, too, profits declined sharply in manufacturing.

As well as suggesting that Keynesian full employment policies were somehow working less well in Britain than elsewhere, these economic difficulties posed a basic question about the nature of the post-war settlement: how far was this 'time of outstanding betterment' actually brought about by the intervention of the new welfare state? Was it possible that these policies had simply coincided with a general boom in capitalist economic activity which had other causes? If it was the latter then these new economic policies might be less effective in preventing the return to the problems of pre-war capitalism if these other underlying conditions for economic boom disappeared. Those who are more sceptical of the importance of state activity in producing the conditions for post-war growth argue that, in practice, most state intervention took the form of restraining demand to prevent 'overheating' and inflation. But others point out that the commitment to full employment fundamentally altered the expectations and behaviour of enterprises: the boost to business confidence became a self-fulfilling prophesy underwritten by the state.

THE POST-WAR SETTLEMENT AND INDUSTRIAL RELATIONS: BRITAIN'S 'UNION PROBLEM' AND THE SUPPLY SIDE

Dissatisfaction with British economic performance in the 1960s came to focus on the labour market and on industrial relations between employers and unions at workplace level: what came to be known as Britain's 'union problem'. Advocates of full employment policies had recognized that such policies would change the balance of bargaining power between workers and employers, in so far as the threat of high unemployment could no longer be used to discipline workers' demands. On the one hand, greater economic security might be thought to contribute to less conflictual relations at work, greater flexibility in the labour market and therefore higher productivity. For example, redundancies or redeployment can be easier to introduce if the workers involved know they have other job opportunities. But in so far as workers used their new bargaining power to bid up wages faster than increases in productivity, or used restrictive practices to bargain over wage demands, thus slowing productivity increases, then full employment could be seen as dangerously inflationary. It was possible to envisage a worst case scenario in which powerful workgroups used their bargaining power to win wage increases which other groups then tried to follow. The resultant increase in the wage bill could threaten export competitiveness either directly through higher prices or indirectly by reducing funds available for investment, but there was nevertheless a pull for government committed to the principle of full employment not to use its macroeconomic policy to squeeze companies to resist such wage increases in case this resulted in higher unemployment. To the extent that higher wage increases fed through to higher prices, fuelling inflation and so precipitating further demands for wage increases, an inflationary 'spiral' could be established.

There might be a collective interest for the labour movement in holding money wage increases to a level which maximized long-term real increases by underwriting faster productivity rises and economic growth, whilst safeguarding full employment. The problem was that for any individual group of workers there could be no guarantee either that other groups would also respect the limit or that the resources thus made available to private enterprises would indeed go towards domestic investment rather than shareholder dividends, investment abroad or larger increases in managerial salaries. In what was still fundamentally a market system it would be unrealistic to expect workers with skills in short supply not to ask for the higher wages they could command in the market. Thus most Keynesians argued that planning the level of employment also meant planning the level of wages: full employment meant incomes policies, and possibly controls on prices and dividends too. As early as February 1948 the Atlee government introduced the first incomes policy which lasted three years. There was a short 'voluntary' freeze in 1956 and from 1961 to 1979 there was a succession of twenty different pay policies, usually with price controls too, and usually depending heavily on the voluntary co-operation of unions and employers rather than legal regulation (Fallick and Elliott, 1981).

Because of these pressures interest began to focus on the condition of the supply side of the economy rather than just on the control of demand by the government. By the supply side, economists referred to the way in which firms and individuals responded to changes in demand. For example, how far did increases in demand result in increased output and employment in the economy and how far in increased prices for the same output? In the 1960s, political debate came to focus on the trade unions and the development of industrial relations at workplace level during the 1950s and 1960s. Full employment and increased bargaining power had brought with them changes in the structure of the industrial relations system: the way in which unions and employers bargained over terms and conditions. In private sector industry, national deals covering entire branches of industry were becoming less significant and bargaining at plant level was becoming more and more important. Often this bargaining was conducted in an informal manner at plant or workgroup level by lay officials, commonly known as shop stewards (i.e. unpaid officials of a union who were employees of the company concerned). This could be a flexible and quick arrangement for the parties at local level, but there were less desirable possible effects. One was that it encouraged disorder in industrial relations: a plethora of local deals could set up leap-frogging claims for improvements in wages and conditions, creating anomalies for the future and boosting inflation in the process. A second criticism was that it encouraged industrial conflict particularly unofficial, 'wildcat' strikes by the groups of workers involved pressing for a quick resolution of their claims. In the popular press and in political debate the shop steward became a symbol of trade union irresponsibility, and workplace conflict came to be seen as *the* major problem underlying poor productivity performance and Britain's economic problems. The Donovan Commission, appointed by the government to examine the problem concluded that, in practice, stewards were a lubricant rather than an irritant, that the problem often lay with a poor management approach to industrial relations and that the best solution lay in formalizing and deepening collective bargaining between unions and management at plant and company level rather than moving to a more formal structure of legal regulation. The Labour government accepted the spirit of many of the Commission's proposals but still sought a legal solution to the problem of wildcat strikes. Its Conservative successor also tried to regulate industrial relations by using the law with a comprehensive Industrial Relations Act. It was bitterly and successfully opposed by the trade unions, and fell with the Heath government in 1974, but many of its measures which gave employees particular legal rights in the workplace came to be included in the employment legislation of the Labour government.

Whilst it was possible to see the link between full employment and the changing structure of workplace industrial relations in Britain, what was far from certain was just how important such industrial relations factors were in explaining Britain's relatively poor economic performance. There was a whole range of possible explanations. Among the possibilities were the quality of the technology in British firms: was it as modern as their competitors, were enough resources devoted to innovation, and in turn to research and development? Were the products well designed and marketed? Was such technology used effectively: was the workforce sufficiently well trained, how effective at its job was management itself? In turn, many of these issues could be inter-related and lines of cause and effect could go either way. Thus if investment was low, was this a question of management myopia or a matter of resources being diverted to pay higher wages, or innovation being delayed by the prospect of union resistance to its introduction, or the disruption of invest-ment plans by market uncertainty caused by stop–go economic policies? How important was the historical nature of British economic development? Had its early leading role, followed by its concentration on empire markets, left British industry with the wrong sort of structure: firms of the wrong size or in the wrong sector of production? Did the economic strength of the City help or hinder the development of industry in Britain? Other factors included the education system: did enough people have access to the right level and type of education and training? Or more generally, was there a cultural problem of the attitudes towards industry in Britain, or a lack of entrepreneurship? Given the variety of possible explanations, the empirical evidence used to argue that the organization of labour or attitudes of trade unions were the fundamental factors behind poor productivity growth was not very convincing (Nichols, 1986).

THE 'OIL SHOCK' AND THE 1970S

Whatever the precise causes of Britain's supply side weakness, problems became much more acute in the 1970s. The importance of the interdependence of growth-orientated policies in different countries was underlined by the shock delivered by the deterioration in the international trade environment. Since 1945 world trade had expanded much more rapidly than ever before and played an important role in generating full employment. This expansion had coincided with a favourable move in the terms of trade for the industrial capitalist economies. That is to say the relative prices of the raw materials they imported from the underdeveloped countries had been falling. In the early 1970s this process reversed sharply: between 1972 and 1974 the volume of exports needed to pay for the same volume of imports increased by around one-quarter. The price of imported oil quadrupled. This coincided with an attempt by the Conservative government to reflate the economy to combat rising unemployment by a 'dash for growth' which it was hoped might increase the supply capacity of the economy more than it boosted inflation or worsened the balance of payments. The result was accelerating inflation and a badly deteriorating balance of payments which in turn precipitated another collapse of confidence in the pound. In 1976 Britain secured a loan from the International Monetary Fund of £3½ billion and agreed to cuts in public expenditure as part of an anti-inflation package: thus abandoning, at least for the short term, the post-war commitment to full employment. As Figure 2.3 shows, unemployment rose steeply, but as Figure 2.1 confirms, this was not so much due to a collapse in employment as its failure to rise fast enough to absorb increases in the size of the labour force driven by demographic trends: by 1980 there were 1 million more people of working age than in 1973.

In a famous speech to the Labour Party conference in 1976, the prime minister James Callaghan appeared formally to abandon the principles of Keynesianism:

> It used to be thought that a nation could just spend its way out of recession and increase employment by cutting taxes and boosting government spending: I tell you in all candour that option no longer exists.

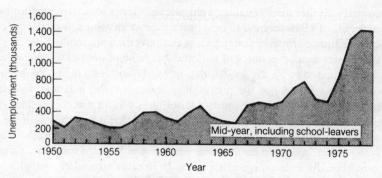

Figure 2.3 Unemployment in the United Kingdom, 1950–78
(including registered non-claimants).
Source: *Economic Trends*, Annual Supplement, 1980.

The 1970s appeared to be a miserable decade for economic performance. After
the rapid expansion of the 'dash for growth' manufacturing output fell and productivity growth slowed down. Pressure on the pound and balance of payments
difficulties forced Britain to ask for a loan from the IMF whilst government
statistics appeared to show that half of the country's economic activity was now
controlled through the public sector. The scale of government intervention in
the economy over such matters as prices, incomes and subsidies to protect and
promote investment and employment were such as to promote some observers'
fears that collectivism (through the twin evils of rising state expenditures and
price inflation) was about to stifle democracy, individual freedom and the
market economy itself. Samuel Brittan, a prominent economic commentator
of *The Financial Times* warned in 1975 that: 'on present indications the system
is now likely to pass away within the lifetime of people now adult'.

In an effort to restrain inflation the government used monetary as well as
fiscal policy. Public spending programmes were cut and a tight incomes policy,
the Social Contract, was adopted: this held real earnings virtually steady until
the final year of the government, as the incomes policy disintegrated and was
followed by the 'winter of discontent'. Public sector workers with low pay took
widespread strike action, angry at the prospect of private sector workers
gaining increases unrestrained by pay policy whilst the government continued
to press for low settlements. The disruption undermined the credibility of the
government's corporatist approach to dealing with economic affairs.

However, the image of a country on the verge of economic breakdown in
the 1970s which some commentators have since conjured up does not stand
up to more sober scrutiny. The 1970s saw much poorer economic progress
throughout the industrial capitalist world as it adjusted to the oil shock.
Indeed, in relative terms Britain's position improved, in the sense that its
growth and productivity performance worsened less than other OECD

countries. Rather than signalling a chronic imbalance in Britain's trade position the events of 1976 seemed to be a more short-term and acute crisis. Revised statistics showed the position to be less alarming than originally thought. Public expenditure as a percentage of national income had not been rising as fast as it had appeared to be. By 1978 inflation was falling fast, as Figure 2.4 shows. North Sea oil held out the potential to transform the balance of payments position as well as increase industrial output: by 1985 it accounted for over 6 per cent of GDP. Whilst it has been suggested that it was the events of 1976 and the attention paid to monetary targets by Labour's chancellor Dennis Healey which launched government economic policy on a monetarist strategy, it would be difficult to argue that it was 1976 rather than 1979 which marked the decisive break in government policy. Unemployment at over 1 million was certainly not 'full' employment, and public expenditure had been cut: but the government still believed it was responsible for the level of employment and could intervene through its macroeconomic strategy and consultation with employers and unions to bring both unemployment and inflation down.

Meanwhile the focus of industrial relations conflict had started to shift towards the public sector. Since the government was either the employer or the major paymaster, bargaining had remained more centralized here than in the private sector, and embraced consultation with the unions concerned over broader issues than wages and conditions of employment. Governments were committed to recognizing and dealing with unions in the manner of a 'good employer' and to promoting 'good industrial relations'. Pay was often determined by the principle of 'comparability': negotiations often followed the rates of pay being offered to comparable jobs in the private sector. These features together with the public service element in much public sector work (for example, health care or education) had meant that there was little pressure for open conflict, and little professional organization of personnel and industrial

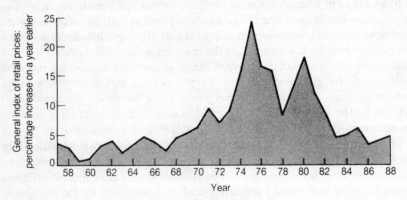

Figure 2.4 Inflation.
Source: *Economic Trends*.

relations issues. This changed dramatically from the early 1970s onwards. Governments applied pay policies more energetically in the public sector, both to control public expenditure directly and to set an example to the private sector. This undermined comparability and increased a significant problem of low pay. Meanwhile, pressure to reduce public expenditure also led to more demands for higher productivity and reductions in employment, increasing workloads and reducing job security or promotion prospects. Thus if the stereotypical striker in the 1960s had been a car worker, in the 1970s it became miners, power, transport and local authority workers, firemen and health service workers. The outcome of the two general elections (in 1974 and 1979) were strongly affected by public sector strikes immediately before them: those of the miners in 1974 and the range of local authority and health service workers who struck in the 'winter of discontent'.

In the 1979 general election the Conservative government which was elected was one no longer committed to the post-war settlement, which, it argued, had come unstuck anyway. Its campaign slogan 'Labour isn't working' summed this up: there was no longer full employment and the system which both Labour and Conservative governments had run since the war could no longer provide it. Although the group around the new leader of the Conservative Party had spent the years of opposition in the 1970s preparing a new set of policies which emphasized the role of market forces and took a thoroughly negative view of what the state could do in economic matters, it was not at all clear to begin with how great the break with previous policies would be. The 'Thatcherites' were by no means in a majority in the Conservative Party, and Conservative governments in the past had usually combined a strong rhetorical appeal at the level of principle to the virtues of the market and private enterprise and the dangers of state 'interference' with a deep commitment in practice to the development of the welfare state and the mixed economy. Since the outgoing Labour administration had paid some attention to 'monetarist' ideas and emphasized the importance of reducing inflation, there were apparent similarities in some aspects of the two parties' approaches, just as in the years of 'Butskellism'.

THATCHERISM: SQUEEZING INFLATION, ROLLING BACK THE STATE AND MAKING MARKETS WORK BETTER

According to the Thatcherite analysis, the fundamental problem of the British economy was the rigid and uncompetitive supply side. Attempts to halt rising unemployment by increasing demand through adjusting the level of public expenditure and taxation would result only in inflation rather than in higher output and employment. This was not just a problem caused by the nature of the supply side in Britain, but a question of the proper balance between state intervention in the economy and the role of market forces. The Thatcherites believed that Keynesian policies corrupted the proper operation of market forces, chiefly by removing the potential discipline of unemployment and fuelling inflation by doing so.

Thatcherites saw Britain's 'union problem' as central to wage inflation and poor productivity growth. For some this union problem had a specifically political dimension, apart from the implications of its economic effects. They were alarmed at episodes of militant solidarity during some disputes and wished to destroy its basis. This union problem was sustained by government's commitment to full employment policies which insulated unions from the consequences of their actions in the short term only to weaken the economy in the long term. The argument was that unions or other pressure groups could always make out a politically popular case to governments for the need to increase public spending to provide more services or to maintain the level of demand in the economy to safeguard employment. This meant there was less pressure on employers and workers to be efficient and contributed to low productivity. It also produced inflation since governments were continually creating more demand in the economy than the sluggish supply side could respond to; in effect, governments were too tempted to print money to respond to the demands put upon them.

Inflation was thus seen as the symptom and symbol of all that was wrong with the Keynesian commitment to full employment. In turn, it was aggravated by the continuing accumulation of government intervention in the economy which was seen as frustrating the free operation of market forces. This inflation needed to be 'squeezed' out by making it clear that the government was no longer going to take responsibility for the level of employment, by restricting the growth of the money supply in order to deflate demand and subject the economy to the full force of the market. The public sector borrowing requirement (PSBR) was to be reduced by reducing public expenditure and raising indirect taxes (VAT). Exchange controls were also to be abolished to increase the force of international competition. In addition there was to be a series of moves to help 'markets work better' and to encourage enterprise. Most of these centred on legal restrictions on the way trade unions could organize, increases in inequality of incomes (to reward 'enterprise') and expanding the role of the private sector. Although the justification for preferring the private to the public sector was that the force of competition was what mattered, in practice little attention was paid to this point. This became clear in the choices that the government faced in privatization exercises in which parts of the public sector, including telecommunications, gas, steel and British Petroleum, were transferred to private ownership. This was a policy developed quite late on and which had the twin aims of reducing the size of the public sector directly as well as reducing public expenditure figures by being counted as negative public spending. Clearly, the less subject to competition were the newly privatized industries the more they would be worth when sold. The government's desire to ensure the success of the privatization sales and the profitability of the new corporations seemed to be greater than any desire to enforce stronger competition. From 1983 onwards employment in the public sector started to fall quite sharply because of the effect of transfers into the private sector, whilst employment in the latter grew strongly. As Figure 2.5 shows, employment in public sector corporations had fallen by almost 1 million by 1988, whilst the size of the private sector had grown by over 2 million.

In response to these changes, the government envisaged that employers and workers would adjust their expectations to the new economic environment: encouraging them to organize themselves more efficiently and in particular to moderate wage demands. As Sir Ian Gilmour put it (1988, p. 1):

> This is the first government since the war to base its economic policies on attempts to improve supply potential rather than on the manipulation of demand.

The reduction of inflation was thus to be the overriding priority of all economic policy. Between the general election of 1979 and February 1981 sterling was allowed to rise by 19 per cent. This was a function of the tight monetary policies of the government, the hike in interest rates from 12 to 17 per cent and the coming onstream of North Sea oil: all of which made sterling a more attractive currency. Meanwhile the domestic cost in money terms of raw materials and fuel for industry rose by 31 per cent because of continued

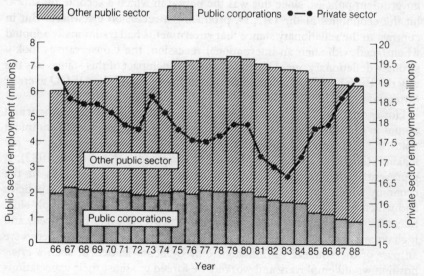

Figure 2.5 Private and public sector employment in the United Kingdom, 1966–88.
Source: *Economic Trends*.

price inflation, which had been given a boost by the rise in indirect taxation. The net result of these two moves was a deterioration in the competitiveness of British industry of nearly one-half. This macroeconomic shock delivered to the economy in the name of letting market forces rule led to a fall in domestic expenditure on manufactures of one-fifth, a fall in manufacturing output of one-sixth (by 1981) and a fall in manufacturing employment of almost one-quarter (by 1983). In short, it led to the sharpest recession ever recorded in British economic history. As a result of this, unemployment rose sharply from around 1¼ million to over 3¼ million, despite the fact that the collapse in employment opportunities led to a fall in the size of the workforce. Precise comparisons of unemployment became progressively more difficult to make because of the many changes which were made to the way in which the unemployment statistics were calculated. In particular, only claimants were counted after 1982, and then all people under the age of 18 were excluded. The Unemployment Unit, an independent pressure group on the issue of unemployment, estimated that by mid 1988 as many as ¾ million people who would previously have been recorded as unemployed came to be removed from the register. However, Figure 2.1, which uses government figures from 1971 onwards on the same basis as used in 1989, still shows clearly the rapid rise in unemployment associated with the fall in employment, and after 1982, the continued rise in the population of working age.

Not all of the dramatic slump of 1979–82 can be attributed to Conservative government policies, since this was the period in which a second 'oil shock' hit the economies of the OECD, producing a recession elsewhere. But in contrast to the reflationary stance that governments had traditionally adopted when faced with such an international recession, the Conservatives took a strongly deflationary one. One indication of the impact of this stance was the way the British unemployment rate moved from around the OECD average throughout the 1970s to a level half as high again in the 1980s.

However, it was the Thatcherites' case that such a crisis in employment and output in the short term was inevitable, so that one minister could comment that: 'the high level of unemployment is evidence of the progress we are making' (Nicholas Ridley, 26 March 1981, quoted in Keys *et al.*, 1983). It represented the necessary clear-out of artificially sustained jobs in the economy which had accumulated through the years of Keynesian policies and which only obstructed the development of a more efficient supply side. Secondly, the adverse trading conditions which employers now faced, and high unemployment and threat of redundancy which confronted workers were all part of the squeeze on inflation: only by being landed in such a crisis position would employers and workers be forced to adjust their expectations and learn to work more effectively. Thus 'digging a hole' in the country's manufacturing base would be worthwhile in the long run since the resultant 'leaner, fitter' supply side would be so much more efficient. This would provide the basis for sustained, non-inflationary growth because it was no longer promoted by government reflation but by the flourishing of market forces and entrepreneurship in the private sector, better able to compete with international competition. To continue the metaphor, the supply side would climb out of the 'hole' by its own efforts, and then keep advancing at a faster rate than it had been capable of in the past, thereby creating higher employment in the long run.

There has been considerable debate, among both academics and those more directly involved about whether economic performance has or has not been fundamentally changed by the Thatcherite shock. Although it might appear to be a fairly straightforward matter of comparing indicators of performance before and after the slump of 1979–82, there are a number of complications. Firstly, comparisons need to take into account changes in the international economic environment. The 1970s was a very difficult decade because of the oil shock and the recession which followed throughout industrialized countries, so we might expect performance to improve in the 1980s regardless of changes made by the government. We therefore need to try to draw comparisons of British performance relative to the rest of the industrial capitalist countries. There are also one-off events to consider, such as the discovery and development of North Sea oil which have made a substantial difference to the country's economic position, but whose impact is difficult to evaluate precisely. Secondly, much can depend on choices of periods over which comparisons are made. It makes sense to try to draw comparisons at comparable stages of the business cycle, but these need neither coincide with political changes nor are the cycles themselves similar in character. For example, the upswing in economic activity following the slump of 1979–82 peaked around 1988, so that the latest cycle has been almost twice as long as its predecessors. In effect, if 1982/3 is taken as the base year from which statistics are measured, then some impressive figures can be recorded as we measure the 'recovery' from the slump. By contrast, if we take 1979 as our base year, and therefore include the slump, the figures look a lot worse.

In turn, it is important to bear in mind that what is at issue is not just technical comparisons of performance in the sense of faster or slower growth or lower or higher inflation but the political issues bound up with what 'performance' represented and the ways chosen to change it. Thus the reduction of inflation for the Thatcherites was more than just the question of producing good economic statistics; it meant also reversing the erosion of the power of private property and individualist values which Crosland had assumed the post-war settlement had rendered extinct. Thus it is important to look also at the hows and whys of changes in economic performance.

The government itself sees the proof of the efficacy of its cure in the high rates of growth of output and productivity recorded from 1982/3 onwards (particularly in manufacturing industry), in the high levels of employment creation which has followed this, and the low levels of price inflation. The government has also pointed to the substantial increases in earnings which have occurred for those in work, which together with cuts in some elements of direct taxation have led to substantial increases in disposable income. This last element can be seen as either positive or negative: affluence *per se* may either be evidence of 'markets working better', but it may also be evidence of the opposite: markets producing inflationary earnings increases.

Thus in the six years from 1982 to 1988, UK gross domestic product (that is the value of goods and services made in the economy as a whole) rose by 22 per cent whilst manufacturing output grew by 26 per cent and exports by 28 per cent. Productivity in manufacturing rose by some 40 per cent. Employment grew by 1.1 million and self-employment by 0.7 million. As Figure 2.1 illustrates, unemployment did not start to fall until 1986 because of the expansion in the size of the workforce, due to both demographic trends (more young people leaving school combined with fewer people reaching retirement age); after 1986 it fell rapidly. Using the government's definition, it had fallen by 1 million by the end of 1988. The rate of price inflation fell from a peak average annual rate of 18 per cent in 1980 to 3 per cent by 1986. By 1988 there were clear signs that recovery had increased the volume of demand in the economy so much that 'overheating' was becoming a problem. The balance of trade plunged into the red as imports increased rapidly in response to increased demand, and the rate of inflation started to rise substantially whilst it remained low elsewhere in Europe. But the government took the view that these problems represented only a 'blip' in the steady path of economic progress and were symptomatic of too much success rather than economic failure. Total personal disposable income increased by 21 per cent in real terms but, following the emphasis on 'incentives', not only were tax cuts concentrated on those with higher incomes, but those high earners also found their earnings increasing much faster than did lower earners, since it was those workers with the least skills and qualifications whose bargaining power was worst affected by higher unemployment. Thus while the average earnings of middle aged white collar workers increased by just under 40 per cent in real terms between 1979 and 1988, young manual workers in the same period had a 4 per cent increase.

The different regions of Britain fared differently too during the slump and recovery. In broad terms, the southern half of the country lost many fewer jobs than the North, Scotland and Wales, whilst the vast majority of new jobs created after 1983 were in the South, as Table 2.1 shows. It is such indicators, particularly the productivity figures, which give a positive picture of economic performance and provide support for those who believe that the underlying performance of the economy has been transformed. Thus in the previous cycle, from 1975 to 1979, GDP grew by 14 per cent, manufacturing output by about 8 per cent, exports by 27 per cent. Employment had grown by ½ million, but self-employment stayed at about the same level. Unemployment fell only

Table 2.1 The regional distribution of employment change, 1979–89

Region	Jobs lost 1979–83	Jobs gained 1983–89	Net change
South East	391	622	231
East Anglia	14	97	83
South West	83	205	122
W. Midlands	299	101	−198
E. Midlands	129	138	9
The South	916	1,163	247
Yorks and Humber	238	13	−225
North West	374	95	−279
North	191	27	−164
Wales	146	80	− 66
Scotland	203	27	−176
The North	1,152	242	−910
Great Britain	2,068	1,405	−663

Source: Department of Employment Gazette.
Figures incorporating revisions from the 1987 Census of Employment results.

by 100,000, again because the size of the working population was rising, as Figure 2.1 shows. The Thatcherites believe that these figures reveal the way in which they have transformed class relations in Britain, unravelled the creeping socialism of the post-war settlement and replaced the language and institutions of 'national interest' and 'public welfare' with those of individual freedom and market choice. The unions have been disciplined and their power regulated whilst the state has been stopped from 'interfering' with industry. Incentives have been restored and the crisis has been resolved by producing an economy driven by the pursuit of individual interests freed from the restraint of more collective forms of control whether they be taxes to pay for public provision or regulations laying down rights that have to be observed.

Alternative perspectives: the costs of crashing the economy

Those who are more sceptical of the degree of change in the economy realized by Thatcherism interpret the same figures in a rather different way, and point to other evidence. They argue that although the performance of the 1980s is better than that of the 1970s, this is not a fair comparison because of the special problems the British economy faced then along with the other OECD economies as world economic growth slowed down. In turn they argue that if longer-term trends are examined, then recent performance looks only to have returned to that trend, rather than establishing a new one. On unemployment, the performance of the government looks very weak indeed. In the 1970s the level of unemployment in Britain was usually close to the OECD average, but in the 1980s it rose steeply to more than half as much again as the OECD figure, and recovered only to a level about 25 per cent higher by 1988. In terms of output growth, British GDP has kept pace with that of the OECD since 1982, but such a comparison misses the important point that in the period prior to 1982 GDP *fell* about 4 per cent in the slump, whilst growth had continued elsewhere. The comparison of industrial output growth is even more miserable. Inflation in Britain certainly fell, but not to the levels found elsewhere in the OECD. The discussion of performance in terms of jobs created or output recorded is certainly important, if rather inconclusive; though it might be thought that given the claims made by Thatcherism about the scope of the changes it was seeking to create, and given the scale and costs of the shock delivered to initiate these changes, then we might have expected a rather more dramatic transformation. But more significant in the debate are arguments about how the economic performance of the 1980s has been achieved, and flowing from this, the prospects for the future. For although those sympathetic to the government accept that it has altered the nature of the British economy, others have argued that the growth of the past few years has occurred for much the same reasons as it has done in the past – a government spending led boom – and has brought with it similar problems to those which Thatcherism attributed to the post-war settlement: inflation and balance of payments problems.

Firstly, behind Thatcherism's rhetoric of public parsimony, council house sales and cheap privatization shares have counted officially as negative public spending but in practice have increased private sector wealth, borrowing and consumption. Secondly, rises in earnings in both money and real terms have been substantial both within manufacturing, where productivity has risen fast, and in the service sector where it has not. Even in the bottom of the 'hole' average gross earnings in manufacturing rose by one-third in money terms: between 3 and 4 per cent short of price inflation. Once the slump was over, earnings moved ahead strongly: rarely below 8 per cent in money and 4 per cent in real terms. (These figures on earnings should make us sceptical about the degree to which fear of unemployment has in fact changed bargaining behaviour, although it would be rash to conclude they are an index of union strength: profits moved ahead even faster after collapsing during the slump.) These earnings increases, together with asset sales, have helped the personal savings ratio fall from 13 to 5 per cent and fuelled a tremendous rise in personal consumption of about 4.5 per cent per annum in real terms since 1981, which Figure 2.6 illustrates. Observers as far apart on the political spectrum as Wynne Godley (*Observer*, 26 June 1988) and Sir Ian Gilmour (1988) have likened this reflation to that engineered by the Barber/Heath

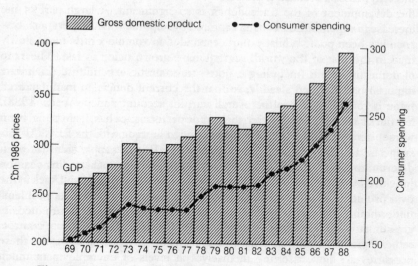

Figure 2.6 Growth of GDP and consumer spending, 1969–88.
Source: *Economic Trends*.

regime of the dash for growth. In a recent paper using unpublished data from the Commodity Flow Accounts, Wells (1988) has estimated the growth of domestic expenditure on manufactures to be about 6 per cent per annum from 1981 onwards: reflation on a dramatic scale. In turn this reflation reflects a good deal of covert pragmatism in the Thatcherite programme in contrast to its public emphasis on high principle. It has never been very clear just what the main economic objectives of the government have been in pursuit of its overall aim of reducing inflation. Thus at different times the money supply and the sterling exchange rate have been the main targets, very different goals for the PSBR and public expenditure have been proclaimed; finally interest rates have come to be the main 'instrument' of government intervention in the economy. Within this range of indicators and targets it has been possible for the government to pursue a macroeconomic strategy and in effect intervene in the development of the economy whilst at the same time maintaining that it has in fact held back.

Once we take this into account the performance of the supply side does not look so good. Rather than being self-generated and responding to international competition, it has been rooted in old-fashioned government manipulation of demand: not through direct public expenditure but by asset sales and direct tax cuts. In addition, monetary and exchange rate policy helped the recovery of British industry: after the dramatic hike in the value of the pound, up to 1981 it was allowed to devalue steadily by one-fifth as monetary policy became less tight. It could be argued, however, that such government 'encouragement' was only possible because of the new dynamism of the supply side. This is why the development of the trade deficit is so significant. A large part of the increase in expenditure has been captured by imports, whilst export perform-ance has been poor. Whilst exports expanded in volume a little more slowly than in the rest of the world, imports have grown twice as fast. The ratio of domestic output (including exports) to domestic expenditure (including imports) has declined steadily, so that the current deficit on manufactured trade is roughly equal to the overall current account deficit (Wells, 1988). Services have not filled this gap (their trade performance has, if anything, been worse). Since 1980 a £10bn+ gap has opened in trade with the EEC. All this suggests that the relative performance of the British supply side has been deteriorating in the 1980s, so that once the rather exceptional trading position provided by North Sea oil passed, the British economy found itself back in the twin problems of inflationary pressures and balance of payments problems undermining the expansion of the economy and long-term productivity growth: stop–go has returned, albeit under a regime of interest rate controls rather than tax changes. There is one major difference, however: these pressures are now asserting themselves at levels of unemployment much higher than in the past. When the squeeze was applied in 1966, unemploy-ment was a little over ¼ million, in 1979 at 1.3 million, but in 1988 at 2 million. In turn this reflects the shrinkage of Britain's manufacturing base: the process of deindustrialization. It has been fashionable to see manufacturing as an 'old' industrial sector which has steadily become less important compared with services. Government ministers have often argued that manufacturing does not deserve any special treatment and that rapid employment decline there is of no special concern. The problem with this perspective is, firstly, that there is little evidence to suggest that as economies become more affluent the share of manufacturing output declines: this appears to be a specifically British problem and represents the comparative international weakness of British manufactur-ing. Secondly, much more of manufacturing output is traded between countries than services: thus to avoid balance of payments problems it is important to have a healthy manufacturing base.

Another way of understanding the trade gap is to consider the volume of output of British manufacturing rather than to concentrate on productivity. Only in 1987 did it recover its 1979 level, and only in 1988 did it finally pass its previous peak of 1974. This would not be a problem if this ex-perience was typical of other countries, or if the British economy had developed a specialization in non-manufacturing activities which could take their place: but neither has happened. Whilst all OECD countries suffered low manufacturing output growth in the post-oil-shock trough of the mid 1970s, they resumed growth in the late 1970s and 1980s whilst output in Britain was stagnant for much longer then grew more slowly than elsewhere, as Figure 2.7 shows. Continued deindustrialization in Britain has been a

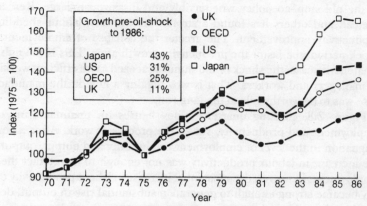

Figure 2.7 Industrial production: OECD 1970–86.
Source: *National Institute of Economic and Social Research Bulletin.*

matter of the *increasing* relative weakness of the supply side in the 1980s, not a shift to some post-industrial economy. In turn this weakness is directly related to the 1979–82 slump. The trade gap, as the Aldington Report made clear some five years ago, shows just how disastrous it was to use North Sea oil to send sterling to a level in 1979–81 that closed one-sixth of manufacturing. Export and domestic markets were lost that could not simply be 'replaced' when better economic circumstances came along.

Lastly, we might question whether the shock treatment applied to manufacturing industry and its aftermath were qualitatively new or just the 'stop' phase

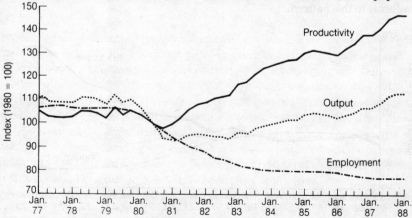

Figure 2.8 Manufacturing labour productivity in Great Britain, 1977Q1–1988Q1.
Source: *Economic Trends.*

of the old stop–go policy writ terribly and disastrously large. Research by Metcalf and others has found a strong link between labour shedding and productivity improvement. The greater the collapse of employment in the shock period, the faster the productivity growth after. This is the nub of the Thatcherite case: the shock of the slump squeezed more efficient working out of managers and workers. That is why digging a hole in the manufacturing base was to be worthwhile in the long run.

Figure 2.8, charting quarterly index figures for manufacturing output, employment and productivity, shows the process at work. After a period of stagnation in the level of employment productivity and output, output fell as the increase in labour productivity was not enough to counteract the fall in employment. However, the substantial increase in labour productivity eventually became strong enough to generate a substantial rise in output, despite a continued fall in employment.

Figure 2.9 is remarkably similar. It covers the period 1969Q1–1973Q2 and the boost in labour productivity that occurred during the 'Barber boom' after the 'U-turn' during the government of Edward Heath. Under Mrs Thatcher's administration, there have been steeper falls in employment and output, faster and longer productivity growth, but much slower recovery of output because of the large size of the 'hole' that was originally dug. In the past, British manufacturing has frequently enjoyed periods of rapid labour productivity growth. The years 1963–5 showed a jump of 18 per cent; 1971–3, 17 per cent; 1967–9, 14 per cent. These jumps usually followed a period of sluggish or negative output growth and labour shedding, and took place in the context of rapidly rising demand, the most spectacular of which was the Barber boom. In many ways the performance of labour productivity under Thatcherism conforms to this pattern.

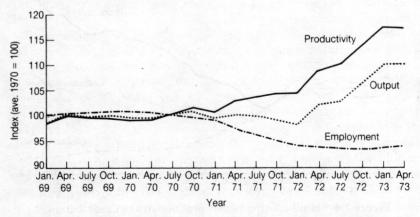

Figure 2.9 Manufacturing labour productivity in Great Britain, 1969Q1–1973Q2.

The conclusion could be that although productivity has looked impressive as manufacturing has been pulled out of the 'hole', this has not compensated for the loss of markets incurred in digging the hole itself. If digging a hole contributed to 'curing' some of the problems of the supply side by boosting labour productivity it simultaneously exacerbated them by wiping out large areas of manufacturing capacity. From this perspective the boom itself is the 'blip'; the twin problems of inflation and trade deficit being rooted in the failure of Thatcherism to transform the performance of the supply side and in the way its hostility to manufacturing industry has weakened the economy as a whole.

The Economic Effects of Thatcherism

The trade gap takes us back to the question of why the macroeconomic shock fell almost entirely on employment and output in industry rather than on wages, and in turn to the question of the mechanics of the effect of Thatcherite policies on the supply side. It seems inconceivable that the government in 1979 expected its policies to more than double unemployment and take it beyond 3 million, when its level then was already seen as unacceptable. The Thatcherites (in so far as there were more than a handful in the cabinet then) must have expected wages to take a good deal of the squeeze, and thus reduce inflation without such a collapse in employment. They rejected incomes policies because they are an aspect of state intervention, and preferred to see employers set wages unilaterally or in free collective bargaining with unions, but there has hardly been a single month since 1979 when ministers have not complained about the level of pay settlements. It is, therefore, important to consider why wages did not at first adjust more to slow the rise in unemployment, and why after sustained high levels of unemployment, earnings increases have been so high as to give substantial increases in disposable income and consumption.

Firstly, in the dramatic events of 1979–81, with the value of sterling increasing and British domestic inflation higher than elsewhere, many firms were placed in a situation where no wage adjustment could have ensured survival. Secondly, wage reductions approaching anything like the level needed to slow the loss of employment in the face of the slump in demand would have been highly unlikely because of many of the features of the way the British labour market and industrial relations operate at workplace level. This is a topic which later chapters in this book explore, but a few comments are useful here. Unions and management believe in principle in their counterparts' legitimacy, whilst preserving in practice their determination to resist any action which threatens their interests. This encourages a focus on substantive rather than procedural agreement, and deals which are short-term, local and focused on *money*: for unionists the surest proof of progress and for employers the most reliable motivator. Given this tradition, the biggest ever slump in economic history was not the sort of bargaining environment to encourage employers and unionists to throw overboard decades of such established relationships and pursue *either* a long-term wages/productivity/ employment security deal *or* an anti-union offensive and wage reductions.

What about the 'spectre of Saltley': solidarity? Why did workforces unable to resist unemployment at individual workplace level, not link up with work-forces in a stronger position elsewhere? Or, to pose this question another way, if full employment was the cornerstone of the post-war settlement and central to the 'time of outstanding betterment' which followed the Second World War, how could a government dismantle this structure in a matter of months without serious opposition? The rise in unemployment did provoke a response, which given the traditional division of activity in the Labour movement was directed through the Labour Party at changing government economic policy. In December 1980, Labour held almost 50 per cent of the vote in the opinion polls. The problem was what was the alternative that solidarity in action was to produce? It was a return to 'ramshackle corporatism': to some other economic strategy worked out between the unions, the employers and either the Labour Party or Conservative 'Wets'. But it was just this economic order which had recently self-destructed in the 'winter of discontent'. And it was just at the time when Thatcherism's economic and political fortunes were at their nadir (1981) that the powerful conflicts within 'ramshackle corporatism' broke out and the Labour move-ment almost dismantled itself as it battled over the lessons of 1979. Thus behind the desire for full employment lay an absence of an agreed strategy or the political or economic structures to pursue it. The meaning of 'full employment' had become less clear as the level had risen above ½ million in 1967, 1 million in 1975 and was still around 1¼ million in 1979. There was, therefore, a small grain of truth in the assertion that 'There is no alternative', which accompanied the destruction of industry and employment. Thus in order to understand the actual impact of Thatcherism we need to go beyond the economic statistics to examine the sociology of the crisis in industry and ask how and why employers, workers and trade unions responded in the ways they did to the new environment created by the government. It is a range of issues flowing from this that we take up in the later chapters of this book.

CONCLUSIONS

This chapter began with some discussion of the use and abuse of the term crisis. In the light of our discussion of the economic context of the crisis in Britain it becomes possible to see the potential insights offered by a more careful use of the term. Firstly, the crisis in the British economy seems to be a chronic rather than acute state of trouble. Many of the problems which governments have faced have remained similar throughout the post-war years, even if the precise forms in which they manifest themselves have not. Secondly, appreciating these persistent economic problems should be complemented with some idea of real economic progress throughout this period: crisis *and* progress have both been part of the economic context in which people have lived their lives. Thirdly, such crisis and progress have, at different times, been crisis and progress for different groups in British society, rather than some global experience of betterment or decline. Both the economic and political dimensions of conflict have focused on the absence of any consensus over the proper obligations that different groups might have to subordinate aspects of their immediate economic interests to wider goals such as higher growth and employment or fairer distribution of resources between classes or regions. Nor has there been much consensus over the institutions or procedures which could undertake such a task. Thus white collar workers in the private sector in the more prosperous regions of the South have certainly not experienced much of a crisis in the 1980s in terms of their employment and career opportunities or level of income and wealth. Shareholders of British-based international companies which have been less dependent on the fortunes of the domestic British economy have seen a substantial increase in their profits and dividends. In general, those in work have enjoyed a sustained and substantial increase in their personal disposable income. Conversely, those who have experienced more unemployment than they would otherwise have faced, who have seen relative earnings decline, who owned or were employed in businesses hardest hit by the slump, who work in or consume public services which have been cut back, will be more aware of a crisis in the economy. Fourthly, if we return to the idea of crisis as one of decisive turning points then it seems important to understand the profound changes which were wrought in the operation of the British economy during the Second World War and its aftermath, and again by the impact of Thatcherism in the 1980s, but also important to bear in mind the historical continuities too. In turn we can only evaluate the balance between continuity and change by looking behind the story told by economic statistics and examining in much greater depth the actual development of social relations in the workplace and the labour market. Such is the focus of the rest of this book.

3

WHAT DO MANAGERS DO?

Managers appear to wield tremendous power. Economic life, both East and West, in the private as well as public sectors, is dominated by the process of management. The proficiency of management can have a decisive impact on the economic performance of a company or an entire country. The way in which managers constitute and legitimate their power and authority determines the regime under which people spend their working lives. The economic position and political outlook of managers as a class is important for the structure of social relations in society as a whole. This is true not only for issues that might immediately concern them – such as the organization of industry or the structure of industrial relations – but for the political character of society too. This is all the more true in modern industrial capitalist societies where managers are also usually the employers of most of the working population. Conversely, the nature of management reflects the character of society in which managers find themselves.

Yet social science has had great difficult in analysing just who managers are and what management is. In much economic literature, for example, management appears as a 'black box'; by definition it is almost impossible to analyse. Rather it is assumed that managers must act in certain ways (e.g. to maximize profits or turnover of a company), but how and why they are able to do so is less clear. In the work of Marx, managers appear as 'agents' of capital: mere ciphers who must follow the dictates of market forces; yet they also appear in the workplace as the all-powerful masters over a powerless proletariat. For Weber, in his theory of bureaucracy, managers also appear as a people dominated by the rules of the office which they occupy.

This chapter looks at what managers do and what management is. It begins by reviewing some of the important classical debates about what management consists of, then considers the problems posed for such 'classical' conceptions of management by empirical studies of what managers actually do, and proposes some other ideas about the nature of management. Lastly, we look briefly

at British management and consider how its distinctive nature may have
played a role in the crisis.

WHAT IS MANAGEMENT AND WHO IS A MANAGER?

The answer to this question might seem obvious. Many management text-
books have offered pat definitions of what management is about; one oft
quoted formula is that of the classic management theorist Henry Fayol. For
him the role of management was 'to forecast and to plan, to organise, to
command, to co-ordinate and control' (Watson, 1986, p. 39). At first sight this
seems to be an uncontentious definition, yet it is at once too general and too
specific. It is too general because it says nothing of the social relations within
which these activities are carried out. Slave owners might forecast and plan,
and command their slaves, so too might the head of a domestic household, but
we do not normally think of them as managers. It is too specific in that it
excludes the activity of many technical specialists who would normally be
regarded as managers but who do not themselves directly control or co-
ordinate others, or plan or organize in a strategic way. There are engineers in
industry who would regard themselves as managers but whose time is spent
mostly on technical problem-solving or the development of technology: they
would hardly recognize themselves in Fayol's definition. It seems that management embraces a wide range of skills, from the highly specific to the
very general and from the purely technical to the social and psychological:
those concerned with the management of people. We thus need a working
definition which illuminates both management's structural position in society
(their power resources and social relations to other identifiable groups or
classes) and its behaviour or way it responds to a changing environment and
helps shape that environment itself (ideologies or norms that shape management action).

THE ORIGINS OF MODERN MANAGEMENT AND THE DIVORCE OF
OWNERSHIP FROM CONTROL

The origins of modern management lie in the development of the modern
joint stock, limited liability corporation. Management is quite a recent
phenomenon. Well into the nineteenth century it was usual for the owners of
capitalist enterprises to direct them personally. There was, in effect, no
distinction between the role of owner, director and employer. Enterprises
could often be family property inherited in much the same way as land or other
material wealth. Indeed, such enterprises are common today, particularly
smaller businesses. But as enterprises became larger and more technically
complex it became more usual for them to take the form of joint stock
businesses in which the enterprise came to have an existence separate from

that of its owners or shareholders. This allowed greater concentration of capital and resources whilst spreading the risk of failure from the owners of the enterprise to its customers and employees as well. Firms could fail without the shareholders losing all their wealth and enduring unlimited liability to those who had lost out from the adventure. Enterprises incorporated under company law consisted of shareholders in the enterprise, who appointed the board of directors with responsibility for the running of the company. Such a board might include directors who were also manager employees of the company. This development of corporate status split the roles of owner and director, and also emphasized that economic enterprises had an existence beyond the particular individuals or institutions of which they might be constituted at any point in time. This separation opened up the development of the manager as a paid employee of the corporation whose role was to direct it on behalf of the board and owner shareholders. Thus day-to-day control of corporations passed into the hands of paid experts who occupied their positions by virtue of their capacity to direct rather than the fact of their ownership of the property. As the size and complexity of enterprises increased, so ownership became less concentrated. There came to be progressively greater numbers of shareholders with progressively less expertise and detailed knowledge of the workings of the enterprise(s) they owned in comparison to the managers they charged with their everyday running. This led to the potential for these managers to develop their own aims and goals for enterprises rather than simply subordinating themselves to the interests and objectives of the owners. There thus arose, synonymous with the genesis of management, the potential divorce of ownership from control.

Indeed, it was just this divorce which led no less a commentator than Adam Smith to be highly suspicious of the potential of the joint stock enterprise and hostile to the notion of managers or 'paid agents' precisely because it would be hard for the owners of the capital they managed to police effectively their activities unless they were of a routine and simple character:

> Being the managers of other people's money rather than their own, it cannot well be expected, that they should watch over it with the same anxious vigilance with which the partners in a private copartnery frequently watch over their own. . . . Negligence and profusion must always prevail, more or less, in the management of the affairs of such a company. . . . (Pollard, 1965, pp. 12–13)

Pollard's seminal study of early British management provides ample evidence from the eighteenth century to support Smith's view and comments:

> Altogether, examples of dishonest, absconding or alcoholic managers who did much damage to their firms abound in this period. (1965, p. 21)

In contrast to Smith's expectations and their inauspicious beginnings, professional managers now dominate economic activity, in both capitalist and centrally planned economies. The growth of management has usually been explained in terms of the growing scale and complexity of economic life. This has eclipsed individual, family or partnership control of all but the smallest and least complex of enterprises because only professional management possess the skills needed to run modern giant corporations. Kerr *et al.* (1973, pp. 150–1) describe the transition in developing industrial societies as one of a shift from 'patrimonial' (i.e. family) to 'professional' management:

> In the early stages of industrialisation the family enterprise is a simple and logical instrument of business activity. Loyalty and trust within the hierarchy are assured . . . where trained skills are scarce and the sons of the wealthy have much of the training, nepotism may be relatively costless. . . . When the family enterprise expands, its patrimonial form is undermined. To find technicians, engineers, and adminstrators with the requisite knowledge, training and skill it must go beyond blood relatives. (1973, pp. 150–1)

Kerr *et al.* also point to the growing complexity of enterprises as the scope of markets and trade grow from the local to the international level. Market research and analysis become highly skilled and specialized activities. Technology grows more complex and sophisticated too, requiring more planning of both technical and human resources and scientific knowledge both to use technology and develop it further. The political and social environment also becomes more complicated: lawyers, tax specialists, professional lobbyists and so on all become part of the management team. The views of Kerr and his colleagues have to be treated with care since it is easy to overdo the contrast between the alleged simplicity and stability of social relations in traditional society and complexity and innovation in modern times: but the link between professionalization and management does seem to be a strong one.

As Adam Smith's complaints about 'negligence and profusion' suggest, accountability in principle may be a far cry from subordination in practice; just as the formal right of an employer to order a servant about may be a very different thing from his or her actual ability to do so. Thus many social scientists have argued that the divorce of ownership from control also meant power passing from the owners or shareholders to managements because the latter had such a monopoly of experience and knowledge of the corporation's affairs that in practice it became impossible for owners to exercise much control over them. This enabled managers, whilst formally remaining the agents of the shareholders, to pursue their own distinct objectives in practice.

There were good reasons that managers should wish to push through this separation of ownership from control. Firstly, managers could have their own distinct interests which they could serve in directing the enterprise in certain ways. For example, it might suit managers' career aspirations and desire for power to prioritize the long-term growth of the enterprise in contrast to shareholders who might have more interest in high dividends and short-term profitability. Secondly, in directing the enterprise managers come into conflict with the aims of other, more subordinate employees. It could be that the ability to modify the aims of the organization so as to embrace some of the concerns of these other groups would make management's job easier, lessening resistance and increasing its power as the arbitrator between the competing claims of different subgroups within the enterprise. Again this would tend to make managers act in different ways from the owners or shareholders.

The separation of ownership from control also opened up the possibility that managers could become a distinct social group in the sense of having their own collective interests. It also highlighted the contradictory roles of management. Moreover, the legitimization of those roles was an important contributor to that ambiguity in that there could always be questions, from both owners and subordinate employees, about the nature of the exercise of management's power. In different contexts managers may find it useful to stress one or the other of the foundations of its authority. At one time it may want to stress its technical role, arguing that its authority stems from its expertise; at other times it may emphasize its role as delegate of the owner, and at others its position as simple salaried employee of the corporation.

Theories of the divorce of ownership from control therefore offer both an explanation for the rapid growth of management as an activity in industrial capitalist countries, and an analysis of the basis of managerial power and the objectives to which such power could be applied. In this view the basis of managerial authority and the role of management becomes not so much power delegated from ownership, as power rooted in management's own expertise in technical and organizational matters. The more proficient that managers become in developing the growth of the organization, the more their power will increase.

One of the most powerful expositions of the managerialist case was that made by Crosland:

> The contemporary business leader does not want high profits primarily as a source of high personal income or consumption; since he does not own the business he cannot as his capitalist predecessor often used to do, withdraw large sums from it for his own enjoyment. Nor does he seek high profits primarily in order to maximise the reward of his shareholders. He seeks them – partly of course, because in the long run his own remuneration depends on the success of the company; but mainly because his social status, power and prestige depend directly on the level of profits. This is both the conventional test of business performance and the source of business power. It determines both the strength and prestige of the firm and the power and social status of its executives. The implications for the distribution of income, as the shareholders champions well realise, and the figures on dividend payments demonstrate, are of course profound. . . . A further result of this change is a less aggressive pursuit of maximum profit at all costs. . . . This explains the

almost obsessive contemporary emphasis on co-operation, participation, communication, democratic leadership. . . . The old style capitalist was by instinct a tyrant and an autocrat, and cared for no-one's approval. . . . (1956, p. 35–6)

Crosland concluded the ownership of the means of production was irrelevant to the distribution of power in society: what mattered was how management was organized and how the much wider economic intervention by the government was used to shape how management acted.

J. K. Galbraith has argued that the rise of management to independent economic power can be seen as the rise of what he calls the technostructure: the range of management experts in such areas as engineering, production, marketing, science, research and development, lawyers and accountants who take part in decision-making by virtue of their specialized knowledge. The monopoly of knowledge is the source of the technostructure's power over the shareholders and the board:

> No owner, large or small who isn't part of the technostructure has access to the information that allows of useful judgement on decisions. . . . The board of directors in large corporations . . . is appointed by management. That tells something of its independence. . . . In fact, the directors of modern corporations are treated with ceremony and respect and allowed to ratify decisions that have already been taken. . . . The truly giant corporations . . . are independent republics of their own management. As it is difficult for the stockholder to have information that affects decisions, so it is difficult for taxpayers to have information that allows of influence. And as the board of directors is denied real power, so also the legislature. (Galbraith and Salinger, 1981, pp. 70–1)

Galbraith's ideas about the technostructure have been influential both in the West and in the centrally planned economies of the East, where advocates of *perestroika* have envisaged the development of a management responding to market pressures and have quoted Galbraith's ideas approvingly.

Thus the idea of management as a body of people with an independent source of power, as a distinct social group with a particular role hinges, to a substantial degree, on the idea of the separation of ownership from control. In the absence of such a separation, management remains a cipher of the power of ownership of property. However, the separation of ownership from control which gives management the space to act, does not tell us how that space is used or the nature of management activity itself. Thus while Smith saw it as space for management to indulge itself and insulate itself from pressures to develop the business and maximize returns and profits, Galbraith, Crosland, Kerr and his colleagues saw it as space for meritocratic economic management to develop free from the ties of family obligation or the pursuit of profit for personal aggrandizement.

The merits of the theory of the separation of ownership from control are discussed presently. Meanwhile it is useful to consider what sort of 'definition' of managers and management it leads us to. We could say that management is the process of directing an organization, in return for a salary, on behalf of those who nominally have the right to control it, using various forms of technical and organizational expertise. Such a definition gives us the two main components of management activity – expertise and authority – whilst also suggesting that the position of managers is a contradictory one, liable to involve arguments about management legitimacy which management itself will justify in different ways.

The problem with our definition is that it suggests just how pervasive the activity of management is. For if we reflect for a moment it seems that:

> In a sense, everybody in a work organisation 'manages'. Even the most junior employee has decisions to make, tools or materials to organise and tasks to co-ordinate. Nevertheless it would appear that some people 'manage' more than others. (Watson, 1986, p. 24)

> Many of the managers are in turn managed from above, and many of the managed, in turn manage someone below. Few are those who only manage and many are those who are only managed; but there is a hierarchy of managerial relations far too complex to compress into simple class relations. Instead a society develops of the semi-managers and semi-managed. (Kerr *et al.*, 1973, p. 259)

This suggests that neither technical expertise nor authority to command are exclusive to management, and that being a manager or defining an operation as part of management is bound up with the amount of such activity or the seniority of its level. Management is, therefore, a process or a social relation among people rather than a person or thing in itself. It can be an aspect of someone's role within an organization rather than a complete role in itself. It also suggests that there is an interesting parallel between the relation which exists between the owners and the managers of an enterprise and the relation between these managers and the workers they employ. In each case the senior party has the formal right to control the junior party by virtue of being the employer, but in practice faces the problem of converting that formal right into a real achievement. If we put aside our reservations about how we can define management, we can proceed to examine some of the important traditional theories of what management is and the reasons for its development.

THE DEVELOPMENT OF MANAGEMENT SCIENCE

Management science developed as a means of codifying the distinct skills involved in management as well as providing the useful function (for managers) of reasserting the expert character of the business of management itself. The classical conception of managers as the authors of business strategy, and the organizers and monitors of the tactics necessary to achieve it, lies behind two main schools of thought which have developed on management.

The first concerns the development of management science in the sense of developing techniques and methods which allow management to be more effective in devising strategy and carrying it out. Such approaches have tended to take the role and social position of management as given, and concentrated on investigating how management objectives can be better fulfilled. They have usually concentrated on two aspects: the *structure* of management organization and the *strategy* to be pursued by managers.

One of the earliest and most important of these approaches was scientific management, developed in the United States by F. W. Taylor, and often known as Taylorism. Taylor was concerned with how managers organized workers to perform work rather than with the technology they used or other aspects of the management process. He portrayed the existing state of affairs in industry as 'ordinary management' where managers relied on the knowledge and experience of the workforce to determine in detail how work was to be done and on piecework incentive payments to induce the workforce to work speedily. Taylor argued that under this system workers need not use the most efficient ways of working, and management would have little or no idea of how effectively they were really working because of its limited knowledge (compared with the workers it employed) of the details of production. Piecework was of only limited effectiveness in encouraging workers to work efficiently because they could easily 'soldier': arrange among themselves a restricted level of work effort which they perceived to be 'fair' and then present this to management as the fastest way of working compatible with decent quality of work or avoiding costly machine breakdowns or extra wear and tear.

Taylor argued instead that management should study work 'scientifically', without recourse to the knowledge or experience of the workers, in order to calculate the most efficient way of organizing work and then direct the precise manner and speed of its execution. This would remove control of the work process from the workers and put it into the hands of management leaving the workers only the task of executing management's orders. This has sometimes been termed the divorce of *conception* from *execution*, the idea of which fits well with the model of management's role outlined so far. Taylor was arguing that the role of management in the modern corporation was to use its own expertise to plan and control the detail of what work was to be done and how it was to be done. This would enable management to fulfil its primary aim (which Taylor took quite for granted): the maximization of profit. Taylor emphasized that there would be a straightforward opposition of interests between management and the workforce in attempting to introduce scientific management techniques into the workplace, since workers would stand to lose not only their ability to restrict the pace of work but also their bargaining power (through their superior knowledge of the details of production) to attempt to do so in the future. But he also tended to argue that scientific management, by increasing productivity and paying higher wages, was ultimately in everyone's interests: it was simply the best way of organizing work.

There were other developments of the scientific management principle. As well as the formidable opposition it aroused from workers who had a much faster pace of work, the total workload under a scientific management regime also caused problems. It was in principle determined by the maximum physiologically possible by a worker with the appropriate mental and physical abilities. In practice this was so severe as to cause high levels of labour turnover: unable to resist the demands of management by 'soldiering', workers took the only form of protest left to them by leaving their jobs to look for less exhausting and oppressive work. Henry Ford encountered this problem at his automobile plant in Detroit where by 1913 over fifty thousand workers left in a year from a workforce of fourteen thousand. He countered it with a move to the '$5 day'. Male workers could more than double their earnings if they were over 21, had been with the company for more than six months and were, in the company's judgement, of good moral character. This combination of the Taylorist organization of work, often using assembly lines, together with paternalistic control over a highly paid workforce became known as Fordism.

Another seminal American experiment took management technique in a rather different direction. In its crudest form scientific management considered the shopfloor employee as a human industrial robot, trained to repeat a simplified and predesigned task with ever-increasing speed and dexterity. By contrast, Elton Mayo and the researchers in General Electric's Hawthorne plant in Chicago conducted a variety of experiments to try to determine the organizational, sociological or psychological factors influencing labour productivity. They argued that the pattern of their results showed that labour productivity could not be explained only by the 'formal' factors such as how work was organized, the conditions in the workshop and the payment system. What was also important was the 'informal' state of the attitudes and feelings of the workforce as human beings, and in particular their need to belong to a social group with which they could identify. The impersonal and bureaucratic organization of work implied by scientific management left no opportunity for groups and group sentiments to develop, and so these developed informally instead, often in ways which cut across the interests of management in maximizing productivity. The solution, according to the 'human relations' school of theorists, was for management to design formal groups into its organization of work and encourage the development of the loyalty of the group to management's objectives. This would satisfy both the psychological needs of the workforce to belong to a group and marry it to the management's aim of boosting productivity.

Human relations theory can be seen as complementary to the ideas of scientific management rather than as a challenge to them, particularly in the way in which the ideas were popularized and taken up, which tended to be reduced to the idea that as human beings rather than machines, workers needed to be kept happy to keep productivity high. As such the ideas of the human relations theorists came under much criticism for being 'cow sociology': supplying techniques to management to enable it to milk workers more effectively. Mayo and his followers were concerned about the alienating and bureaucratic tendencies in modern industrial life, but they did not consider carefully enough the relationship between these issues and the potential conflicts of economic interest between manager and worker. Managers adopting the insights of the human relations school were likely to be more interested in increasing management control over the workforce than tackling alienation as such. Where these two principles came into conflict, or where reducing alienation and promoting a sense of community conflicted rather than coincided with profitability, then there was little reason for managers to continue to pursue the former goal.

A further criticism and development of the scientific management principle came from the work of Woodward in Britain. She studied the management structures that a variety of firms had adopted, and found that they varied considerably. There was no clear relationship between using a particular sort of structure and enjoying superior economic performance. However, the variation could be accounted for in the sort of technology and organization of production the firms were using. Woodward distinguished between firms making specialist products on a one-off or small batch basis, mass production technologies where large numbers of similar items were produced, and continuous flow processes. These technologies were seen as being increasingly technologically complex in the sense of the predictability and controllability of the production process. As technology became more complex, so the number of levels in the managerial hierarchy increased. There were other differences which seemed to set up a contrast between the mass production plants on the one hand and the batch production and flow process plants on the other: for example, the former had more rigidly defined management responsibilities, more formal written lines of communication and a much wider span of control for first line supervisors.

Woodward found that once differences in technology were allowed for, the most successful firms 'approximated to the medians of the group [of technology type] in which they had been placed. This indicates that the medians for each group represent a pattern of organisation appropriate to the technology of that group.' (Woodward, 1969, p. 228).

The details of Woodward's findings need not concern us here (indeed Woodward herself was to re-examine the data she had collected and argue that her classification of technological complexity was an explanation inferior to that produced by looking at the worker tasks in the companies concerned). What was important about Woodward's work was that it challenged the idea that there was such a thing as one 'scientific' best way for management to organize itself or the workforce. Instead there were a number of different principles which successful 'organizationally conscious' firms could adopt, relating to the types of work they did.

A number of other theorists were meanwhile arriving at similar conclusions in a number of different contexts. In the United States, Stinchcombe distinguished between 'bureaucratic' and 'craft' administration of production, the first approximating to scientific management, whilst the second described situations where the production tasks were sufficiently non-routine to require the more direct involvement of the workforce in decisions about how work was to be done, in co-operation with management experts rather than simply receiving orders from them. Researching in the Scottish electronics industry, Burns contrasted 'mechanistic' and 'organic' styles of management. The former were appropriate to work which was regular and stable in its character and resembled the sort of division of labour envisaged by scientific management: a hierarchy of command with 'experts' at the top issuing orders to subordinate workers or specialists. Organic management was appropriate to work which was liable to change rapidly, or was varied or unpredictable, such as that in the high technology, innovative electronics sector.

> [Organic management comes about] when new and unfamiliar problems and requirements continually arise which cannot be broken down and distributed among specialist roles within a hierarchy. Jobs lose much of their formal definition. The definitive and enduring definition of functions becomes impossible. Responsibilities and functions, and even methods and powers have to be constantly redefined through interaction with others participating in common tasks or in the solution of common problems. Each individual has to do his job with knowledge of the overall purpose and situation of the company as a whole. Interaction runs laterally as much as vertically, and communication between people of different ranks tends to resemble 'lateral' consultation rather than 'vertical' command. Omniscience can no longer be attributed to the boss at the top. (Burns, 1971, p. 48)

The ideas of theorists such as Woodward, Stinchcombe and Burns offered a considerable challenge to scientific management orthodoxy because they suggested that only under fairly specific technological and economic conditions was management likely to be in a position where it could decide accurately in advance what work needed to be done, anticipate what problems would be faced and issue commands to subordinates which were not open to debate or improvement. It was more likely, particularly as the technological complexity and variability of production processes increased, that management would find itself developing more collaborative and co-operative relationships with those who were formally its subordinates. This would have to be reflected both in the structure of management organization – as Woodward's work emphasized – and in managerial thinking and behaviour: autocracy would have to mellow into more participative approaches (at least in part). In turn such approaches would be much more likely to stress the importance of managerial expertise in its claim for the legitimacy of its authority, and pursue less hierarchical ways of communicating and consulting with colleagues who were formally subordinate in the organizational hierarchy. Yet the social basis of management's power in the last instance would still be its role as employer: its right to hire and fire. It is the contrast between these two elements that underlies many of the contradictions and conflicts in modern management's position.

The wider role of management

Hitherto we have concentrated on the impact of management on the nature and organization of the production process, but it is important to remember that the organization of production (and of an efficient labour force) is only one part of management's role in directing a modern corporation. Under the overall goal of maximizing the short- or long-term profitability of the corporation, the process of management encompasses such matters as raising finance and finding profitable applications for cash surpluses, research and development of new market areas, products and technologies, the marketing of existing products and services, and the development of some form of strategy or direction for the development of the enterprise as a whole in the medium to long term. Some aspects of these issues concern the administration of activities within the corporation, others concern the relationship between the enterprise and other enterprises, as customer or as potential competitor or owner.

Prais (1976) examined the evolution of 'giant firms' in the UK this century and concluded that simple economies of scale in production were not the main reason for the rise of the modern large, perhaps multinational, corporation with many operating plants and often several different divisions. He found that reasons such as diversifying horizontally to spread risk and make savings on central functions such as finance or marketing, or vertical integration to control sources of supply and access to markets were important. In the United States, Chandler charted the rise of the modern 'M-form' corporation. He was concerned to explain the way in which modern large corporations had developed a multi-divisional structure, with a number of different levels of management. Chandler again takes the argument back to the development of increasing technical complexity and growing markets. These encouraged the development of more and more specialist activities whilst increasing the scale of operations. Eventually firms found themselves reorganizing their activities to use their specialists in more effective ways whilst the overall direction of the corporation split off as a distinct activity – what Chandler refers to as 'administration':

> Executives responsible for the fortunes of the enterprise . . . coordinate, appraise and plan. They may at the same time do the actual buying, selling, advertising, accounting, manufacturing, engineering or research, but in the modern enterprise

the execution or carrying out of these functions is usually left to such employees as salesmen, buyers, production supervisors and foremen, technicians, and designers. In many cases the executive does not even personally supervise the working force but rather administers the duties of other executives ... administration is an identifiable activity ... it differs from the actual buying, selling, processing, or transporting of goods, in that in the large industrial enterprise the concern of executives is more with administration than with the performance of functional work. (Chandler, 1962, pp. 8–9)

The development of administration gives rise to a four-tier structure in many modern corporations. A general office at the apex of the corporation plans its overall goals and strategies and allocates resources between fairly autonomous divisions. Divisional offices in turn control functional departments (manufacturing, engineering, marketing, purchasing, etc.) whilst the departmental head offices themselves administer operating field units: sales offices, factories, laboratories, etc.   .

Chandler traces this structure back to developments in firm's strategies as their products become more complex, their range of products and services more broad, and their activities more geographically dispersed with the growth of larger markets and modern forms of communication. For example, whilst Taylorist forms of management could survive in industries with technologically straightforward and undifferentiated products (such as steel), more technologically complex industries needed salespeople who are engineers, say.

The marketing of electric lighting, power machinery, and traction equipment was so complicated technologically that it demanded highly trained salesmen who understood the power and transportation needs of the customer more thoroughly than the customers themselves did. (Chandler, 1962, p. 28)

Chandler's ideas are important for showing that the structure of the modern corporation is more complex than a simple hierarchy of offices or command reaching from the board of directors or owner down to the most menial employee, all concerned simply with the organization of production and the division of labour. They also highlight the connection between the sorts of structure that have evolved and the strategies that senior management have pursued to build up their enterprises.

Whilst Chandler argued that the structure of the entire enterprise related to the strategy pursued by its top management, Child argued that this strategy itself was not nearly as tightly defined by external pressures like market forces as approaches such as economics often conventionally assumed (Child, 1972). Whilst it was true that management might well be constrained to act in one way or another, there was usually a good deal of real choice about what direction to follow. Indeed, it was often the case that enterprises took an active part in shaping their environment rather than passively reacting to it.

A theme running through much of the management literature we have reviewed is that developments in technology have prompted a parallel shift in the behaviour and policies of management. Whilst early managers might be dictators who could simply demand obedience, technological progress, together with rising standards of education and skills in the general workforce, have required management to develop a more co-operative and 'constitutional' role.

Management and the labour process debate

In contrast to the management theorists we have discussed so far, a quite different approach to the role of management has been developed by Marxist theorists who have taken as their starting point not the fact of management authority within the enterprise and the evolution of its character, but capitalist social relations of production in the enterprise and the role that this imposes on management as an agent of capital. Marx argued that in a capitalist free market economy, the pressure of market forces compelled the owners of means of production and employers of labour to maximize the 'valorization' of capital and thereby accumulate more capital in order to produce on an ever larger scale and so continue to compete in the market. By this Marx meant that attention had to be focused on organizing labour and production in such a way as to minimize the cost of labour to the employer whilst maximizing the value produced by that labour in the production process. Marx argued that it was important to distinguish between *labour power* and *labour* itself. Labour power referred to someone's ability or potential to work, whilst labour referred to the actual process of work itself. The significance of the distinction lay in the fact that in a market system where people worked for wages, what workers sold and employers bought was labour power, whilst what determined whether the capitalist was successful in producing profitably and thereby accumulating value and larger amounts of capital in the future was the labour which could be extracted from this labour power. To be successful, employers had to minimize the value of labour power whilst maximizing the value of labour. This was the nub of management's role: the transformation of labour power into the maximum possible amount of labour.

Maximizing the value of labour meant ensuring that the maximum possible amount of labour's efforts was devoted to the work that the employer wanted done, in the most effective way, so that as much value as possible would be created and realized in higher profits and the further accumulation of capital. Minimizing the cost of labour power meant using labour that was no more skilled than was absolutely necessary, since the more skills labour possessed the higher its value would be. This had two implications: control over the organization of the production process should be by employers to ensure that labour was not 'wasted', and the division of labour should be extended to ensure that tasks were broken down into the simplest components which could be done by cheap, unskilled labour. This would maximize the exploitation of labour, in the sense of maximizing the difference in the value of the labour power the employer bought, and the value of the labour which this labour power would deliver in the production process.

Following Marx's arguments, the theorists Marglin and Braverman in the United States argued that in a capitalist system employers were driven to take control of the labour process itself. They argued that the essence of human labour could be understood by the twin process of conception and execution. Conception was the way in which people work out mentally what needs to be done physically to achieve an end result. Execution was the actual doing. It might be a simple result like screwing together a nut and bolt, or it might be complex like designing and building an aeroplane. Braverman argued that employers could best exploit labour by divorcing conception from execution, and ensuring that they retained control over the process of conception. The result was the development of a process of production in which employers conceived exactly what it was most profitable to do, down to the finest detail, whilst the execution of this plan was to be left to the worker. Since the workers' tasks were preplanned and controlled by the employer, the workforce need not be skilled, and would be left with little alternative but to carry out the employer's plans. Ultimately this state of affairs would become embodied in the technology of production itself. Meanwhile the workforce would become deskilled – rather than taking any part in the understanding or design of the work they carried out, they would simply obey the orders of a superior, or the demands made by machinery – for example on an assembly line.

Braverman argued that Taylorism/scientific management was in fact the process of divorcing conception from execution in order to make the employer omnipotent in the workplace through the complete control of the design of work and production while deskilling the workforce. Managers were in the same position as employers for they could only obey the same market forces that drove the owners of capital themselves. Their role came directly from the social relations of production and the need to maximize capital accumulation and the exploitation of labour rather than from any technical requirements of production itself. The need for hierarchy in production relations could be seen to lie in the need to divorce conception from execution, deskill the workforce and take control over the design of work. Thus for Marglin the apparent indispensability of 'bosses' had no technical foundation – as the writers about technocracy or meritocratic management might suppose – but arose from the social relations of production. It was an artificial hierarchy imposed by capitalist production relations and the system of wage labour. For Braverman and the analysis based on his ideas which grew up around the labour process debate, the concepts of the divorce of conception from execution, of deskilling and subordination of labour, allowed the manner in which management developed and controlled the process of production and organization of work to be seen in a new way. Management did not have a neutral technical role but controlled the labour process in order to enforce the accumulation of capital and exploit labour.

Just as traditional management theory came to contrast situations where management exercised strict control over subordinates with those where there was a more 'organic' set-up or more autonomy, writers in the labour process tradition started to make this distinction too. Friedman (1977) argued that managers could choose between strategies of 'responsible autonomy' and 'direct control'. The latter referred to Taylorist systems of management, whilst the former were approaches where managers saw the need to utilize the skills and experience of groups within the workforce to make decisions themselves about some aspects of work organization, subject to the overall supervision of management: they had a degree of autonomy, but management was still responsible for ensuring that their work served the overall goal of valorizing capital. Edwards (1980) argued that the process of deskilling we have described was but one of the strategies open to management: it could be seen as technological control. An alternative was 'bureaucratic control' through systems of rules and regulations rather than either personal control by the capitalist or domination by machinery. The use of a particular strategy indicated the perceived strength of worker opposition to management plans and the economic strength of capital itself. Thus it was possible to identify different phases of capital accumulation associated with the dominance of different management control strategies in the workplace.

MANAGEMENT IN PRACTICE

The inner logic and value of these different theories of management can all be debated, but before we turn to that it is useful still to bear them in mind while we look at some of the empirical research on management behaviour and attitudes.

If we consider both the radical and traditional theories of management which we have briefly reviewed, a number of common themes emerge. First is the idea of management as a hierarchical system of decision-making and authority. It is a pyramidal power structure with either the owner or chief executive at the top, depending on whether or not we see the divorce of ownership and control as significant. Second is the idea that management is concerned with long-term strategy which is made in a fairly conscious manner in response to clear pressures. Thus in the radical scenario the pressure from market forces to maximize the accumulation of capital leads to the development of the divorce of conception from execution. In traditional management theory a range of longer-term objectives has been suggested such as long-term growth of the organization, profit maximization and so on. Third is the idea of management as professional or technocratic expert: either as the focus of the increasing complexity of modern economic life, or as the monopolizer of knowledge and control of the production process. Thus the pyramid of power is seen as resting in large part on the superior knowledge of those in higher positions. Lastly, there is an implicit assumption that although there are different levels or types of manager, what binds managers together as a class or as occupiers of a role is more important than divergences of interests or position between managers themselves. Taken with our first idea, this usually means that the fortunes and future of management are frequently seen as identical to those of the organization for which they work. What is remarkable about each of those propositions, plausible as they might appear, is the lack of empirical support for them.

Whilst there is certainly a formal chain of command and lines of authority within management, it is far from clear that boards or their chief executives are the apex of a decision-making pyramid. Pahl and Winkler (1974) in a rare study of boards of directors emphasized the difference between 'office' and 'control'. Some of the boards they examined were 'pro forma' bodies. They existed for legal reasons without actually doing anything. Functioning boards, on the other hand, were often the apparent apex of decision-making activity with other meetings structured round them and papers directed towards them. But neither did proposals emanate from these boards nor did they seriously choose between real alternatives. Senior management could ensure the 'right' decision by manipulating information reaching the board and ensuring that proposals were as vague as possible: 'pre-board meeting activity is not a preparation for a testing occasion, but a screening operation' (p. 109). In fact, any argument or disagreement at board level was seen as a *failure* of management and the board to work properly. This emphasis on avoiding dissent is more general throughout the management structure:

> At every level individual managers attempt to manipulate the meeting in advance so that their particular projects are given a clear passage. . . . The art of pre-emption is that the inevitability should never be obvious. . . . Skillful managers we observed regularly presented suggestions to their director as if they were really his idea. (Pahl and Winkler, 1974, pp. 110–11).

Thus rather than there being a simple pyramid of power with superiors exercising control downwards over subordinates and subordinates reporting upwards, subordinates 'controlled' their superiors by exploiting the fact that they had a greater range of information which they could manipulate.

Traditional conceptions of decision-making hierarchies were reversed in other ways too. Whilst we might assume that the most senior managers took the most important decisions, or concentrated on long-term issues, Pahl and Winkler found that they were often too busy to do so; it was the more junior managers who had the time to prepare more forward-looking projects and plans. Nor were such plans always sanctioned and reviewed by superiors, since properly prepared plans would usually demonstrate the 'obvious' choice, and as we have seen the emphasis on discussion, especially at board level, was on consensus rather than debate.

Other research has shown how important informal information is to managers, and how misleading it can be to assume that lines of communication and control are as they appear in an official organization chart. Managers need such information so that they can appreciate 'what is really happening' as opposed to the official information available to them which may have been reported with a particular end in view. It is not surprising to find, therefore, that managers spend most of their time on the telephone or in conversation rather than reading papers or attending formal meetings. The informal contacts which dominate much of a manager's day are vital for gathering information which the formal system cannot provide and also to build up a network of allies. In his early work Sayles (1964) showed how important it was for managers to have others within the organization that they could rely on to help, provide inside information, respond to problems and give support. They needed to build up a network of friends and trust through exchanging 'favours' and obligations. Indeed, as Stewart points out in her review of empirical research on what managers do, their day is characterized by performing short, episodic, fragmented tasks which often arise in response to immediate events. Rather than spending their time evaluating future developments and planning accordingly, most managers are most of the time reacting opportunistically to the detail of events. They are keeping things going – they are managing.

> An individual who for much of the day is switching his or her attention every few minutes from one person and subject to another has little opportunity, while that is happening, to reflect on what should be done or to plan what ought to be done. The pattern of the day is one reason for questioning the model of the reflective planner. (Stewart, 1983, p. 85)

Another outcome of this informality and fragmentation is the tremendous amount of discretion which managers have in how they actually do their jobs: research by Stewart (1983, 1980) showed tremendous variation among individuals in how they performed essentially the same function. This suggests that we should be wary of trying to prescribe too rigorously what it is that managers in different positions or under different conditions *must* do: managers seem to have a great deal of flexibility and choice over how they work.

The points made by these authors about the importance of the manipulation and filtering of information show that management is a political activity: different managers usually have different conflicting ends and priorities and will manipulate information to maximize the attractiveness of their own particular agenda. Moreover, these ends need not be synonymous with those of the organization as a whole. Indeed, it would be unlikely that they were. At most they might be what the manager thinks the ends of the organization ought to be, but they could concern the future and interests of their part of the organization, or significantly their own career in the organization. Burns has eloquently emphasized how important and elementary this distinction is, yet it is frequently overlooked:

> Organisations are co-operative instrumental systems assembled out of the usable attributes of people. They are also places in which people compete for advancement. Similarly, members of a business concern are at one and the same time co-operators in a common enterprise and rivals for the material rewards of successful competition and with each other. The hierarchical order of rank and power, realised in the organisation chart that prevails in all organisations is both a control system and a career ladder. (Burns and Stalker, 1961, p. xii)

This means, for example, that managers' behaviour will never be only about dealing with the problems that confront the firm, but about addressing them in a way which enhances rather than lessens their own career prospects compared with those around them. Thus Burns and Stalker describe a weekly management meeting:

> The Monday morning meeting was not only part of the machinery of the working organisation at management level: it was also a rink in which people displayed their suitability for promotion in front of the managing director. (1961, p. 151)

This distinction is important in any organization, but Burns and Stalker point out that it becomes more important as organizations become less 'mechanistic'. The looser the definition of job and role, the more flexible, changeable and uncertain the job of management becomes, the more so as technology becomes more complex and the rate of innovation speeds up, as then it becomes less feasible to identify the contribution of a particular individual or department. At the same time the space which individuals have to take different decisions increases, precisely because the environment is less strictly determined than before. A useful concept which brings together these ideas is that of 'organizational pluralism' which expresses the twin ideas that organizations are inevitably composed of groups which have both overlapping and divergent interests, and that there is usually considerable scope for those with decision-making power to make real choices in the decisions they take. This has the paradoxical effect of encouraging decision-makers to emphasize the unitarism of organizations and the constraints on their choice, in order to assert to groups disappointed with the outcome that it was both inevitable and in the interests of all.

An early work by Dalton (1959) emphasized what management as a political activity meant in practice, in contrast to the formal theories of organization structure or management behaviour. In a study of a number of different workplaces he sought to show the impossibility of developing objective and accurate measures of ability and performance, the considerable scope to manipulate information and thus distort what measures were available, and the depth of conflicts between individuals' career aspirations and the requirements of the enterprise or department as a whole. These three factors all added up to management being an essentially political, 'dog eat dog' activity, often far removed from the official accounts of what ought to be happening: 'The rubbery gauge of "ability" as a measure of fitness can mean anything powerful figures want it to mean' (p. 5). It was vital for managers to accumulate allies who could help them portray the performance of their particular contribution as good and vital, collude in evading awkward higher-level orders, or help punish unco-operative colleagues or departments.

Dalton emphasizes that whilst people's careers in organizations depend on their performance and co-operativeness as perceived by their superiors, there will always be an incentive to act in such a way as to demonstrate the vitality of their own contribution in contrast to those of others and their functions and departments. He takes as one example the model of a staff and line management structure. This is an organizational model in which management responsibilities are divided into a straight hierarchical line of managers responsible for production itself and issuing the orders necessary to keep it running, and advisory staff managers who provide the line with expertise in all the detailed areas of operation – personnel, maintenance, engineering, materials management or product development, for example. At first sight this seems an effective arrangement since it provides a simple, clear and identifiable line of command but obviates the need for line management to be an expert in everything. Dalton outlines some of the rather unlikely assumptions which have to be made in order to expect such an arrangement to work smoothly. Staff managers must be happy to offer advice without having any formal authority over whether their advice is taken up. The line has to welcome their ideas, which in turn always have to be feasible. Alternatively, if the staff management is to be given some authority it leaves the line manager without real decision-making control over the line. There is a further assumption that the two groups do not have other, less formal roles, such as reporting to more senior management on the performance of the other. There are likely differences in the career paths and educational or training backgrounds of the two groups, which may lead to a view that one or other group has an easier route to the top or has better access to senior management. In practice, relations between the two groups are likely to involve mutual informal deals to keep things going, in defiance of the letter and, if necessary, of the spirit of their own formal rules.

All the factors discussed above could be taken to suggest that management has a remarkable degree of autonomy and what might be seen as space to exercise strategic choice. In turn this could be taken to imply that the divorce of ownership from control is far-reaching: that management has the capacity to take on board a range of different priorities and policies in deciding how enterprises are managed – including, for example, adopting some ideas of the trade unions which represent the workforce they employ. It might imply that 'organizational pluralism' means that within the context of a market economy there is still substantial room for independent enterprises to run themselves in a variety of different ways and for this to be reflected in how they are managed. In contrast to the logic of deskilling and increasingly detailed managerial control of the labour process predicted by Braverman, capitalism could comprise a variety of forms of social relations at the point of production – including collective, non-hierarchical or democratic forms of management.

The theorists of the divorce of ownership from control and those emphasizing the meritocracy of modern professional management (such as Crosland and Galbraith) have in effect argued that modern managers use this space, this ability to exercise strategic choice, to run modern capitalist enterprises in new ways which are essentially different from those of the older owner employers. However, empirical research on how managers actually behave again suggests a different conclusion. What stands out is how managers tend to behave as if they owned the enterprises that employed them; as if they were themselves owner-capitalists. The first reason for this is that most managers do in fact own substantial amounts of the enterprises for which they work. Their shareholdings may be small in terms of the total value of the enterprise, but they are often large in terms of their potential contribution to the wealth and income of the individual manager. This gives him or her a direct material identity of interest and outlook with the shareholders of the enterprise. In addition, many managers are given share options – the right to purchase shares in the future at their current price – or other financial remuneration packages which link their income to the profit performance of the enterprise. Again this gives the manager a material stake in identifying with the aims of the owners.

Another pressure comes from the capital markets. Any managerial policy which prioritizes other objectives over short- to medium-term returns to shareholders runs the risk of a takeover battle from shareholder interests or another enterprise which could offer a higher share price and dividends by realizing larger short-term returns from the assets being managed. This pressure is particularly strong in Britain, where contested takeovers – cases where the current directors or senior management of a company oppose the takeover bid – are much easier to carry out and occur more frequently than in other industrial capitalist countries. However, even here there are counter tendencies. Just as junior managers can screen and select the information reaching senior management, it is possible for enterprise management to influence the picture of an enterprise that potential owners or finance houses, merchant banks, pension funds or other institutional investors have. Secondly, there has been an increasing number of cases in the last decade of managers collectively buying from the owners the enterprises for which they work. Usually this has been a case of purchasing the subsidiary of a large diversified enterprise. Such cases pose a direct reversal of the divorce of ownership from control, and have sometimes included new patterns of ownership and management. An almost unique but interesting example was provided by the privatized National Freight Corporation in Britain. The shares were sold by the government to its management and employees. The performance of the enterprise under its new self-management structure was far better than it had been previously, protecting employment and substantially increasing the value of the employee-owners' shares.

Lastly, empirical surveys of how managers actually think and behave show that although they may have the space to pursue a variety of different strategies, they remain firmly wedded to an ideology of the importance of profits and the 'bottom line' above all else. Pahl and Winkler (1974) concluded that managers might control and manipulate information, but they did so not to subvert or supplant profit-making, growth or returns on investment, but to pursue those goals just as tenaciously as owner-managers would. Professional management was defined in terms of how good a return to shareholders was achieved. Nichols (1969) has cogently argued that in many ways the 'space' for managers to pursue other strategies is no more than that enjoyed by owner-managers who may have adopted a more paternalistic outlook or sought to build up the size of their business rather than seek shorter-term returns. Moreover, as accounting techniques become more sophisticated and new technology enables the cost and profit performance of the detailed aspects of an enterprise's various operations to be monitored more closely, it becomes more possible to relate managers' performance to the 'bottom line' in the short term.

The peculiarities of British management, and its recent evolution

This question of what managers actually do, as opposed to what theoretical models suggest about how they might behave, leads on to the question of whether managers in Britain do things differently from their counterparts elsewhere, and whether their behaviour has changed as the crisis in the economy and industry has developed. We can point to a number of relevant debates, but as we consider them we should bear in mind the implications of Stewart's arguments about variations in managerial behaviour and approach. It is unlikely that we could describe British management in terms that could be applied to all managers, all of the time.

One of the most important determinants of the nature of management is that Britain was the pioneer of what came to be seen as the Industrial Revolution. The development of capitalist industry in Britain, therefore, proceeded with little state intervention: it grew up locally and independently. This genesis had an impact upon the traditions of management and in particular upon relations between employers and workers. (We consider these too in the context of class in Chapter 7.) One result was that the management of enterprises was a fairly empirical affair. Employers in the early nineteenth century found their own solutions to the problems they faced, in accordance with their own mores or religious beliefs, rather than following any established ideology or doctrines of management practice. These mores might be strict and harsh, or violently anti-union. Pollard (1965) cites many gruesome examples of the way in which early employers sought to deal with the problem of getting enough supplies of reliable labour or the problem of disciplining what workforce they already had in a context where people with any viable alternative shunned the loss of independence implied by reliance on waged work that might prove insecure. Alternatively, many employers whose entire project was fired by religious conviction pursued more paternalistic approaches towards their labour force. But there was little systematic reflection or theorizing of what good management practice was or ought to be, or how employers as a class ought to deal with the union question, for example. It is only towards the end of the nineteenth century that we find the concept of management appearing as opposed to ownership or employment. Child (1969) notes how it could be contrasted with an outright *laissez faire* ideology, since it sometimes embraced new attitudes to labour such as profit-sharing schemes or less hostile attitudes towards unionism, and stressed the importance of the welfare of the workforce in achieving productivity, but he points out that non *laissez faire* approaches were often liable to be dismissed as bringing 'sentiment' into business. But this empiricism was not just hostile to welfarism. The ideas of Taylor and scientific management never achieved the popularity and application in Britain that they did in the United States. Cadbury, for example, criticized Taylor's approach as inhuman and likely to foster conflict between employer and worker. As we argue in Chapter 7, one outcome of this was the specific form that industrial relations took in Britain. Another outcome was the informality of management organization and practice, both in terms of organizations which could represent and develop the interests of employers as a class and in terms of how work was organized within the individual enterprise.

Marginson *et al.* (1988) found that even where diversified British companies had developed a multi-divisional structure, their head offices usually still retained a powerful role in everyday operational issues – strategy and day-to-day operation were not clearly distinguished. Moreover, as diversification and decentralization proceeded, the chances of head office developing a strategy role receded. Thus it could be argued that 'short termism' is not just something imposed on British industry by the capital markets but is reflected in the way that British management organizes, or rather fails to organize, itself.

A third outcome was the relative neglect of management training and development. Management was seen as something that educated men applying common sense could do rather than as a profession that might be taught or learned. This was despite the fact that managers themselves sought a more professional status to bolster their contested legitimacy. Thus a range of surveys of managers and directors since the Second World War has found that only between one-fifth and one-third of managers have a university degree (Poole *et al.*, 1982, p. 286). Nichols (1969) also commented on both the lack of formal qualifications of directors and senior managers, and their lack of 'professionalism' in the sense of the absence of an identifiable set of norms and body of knowledge which they learned and applied in their everyday work. Instead, managers and directors in Britain stressed experience. These traditions are not ones which appear to have changed in the 1980s. One survey concluded that British firms continued to give training and development a low priority:

> They tend to see training as a cost and not an investment (Coopers and Lybrand, 1985), over half make no provision for systematic management training, and few are able to articulate clear training priorities or to identify abilities that managers should be able to possess . . . (Edwards and Sisson, 1989)

A second feature of business organization in Britain which has been widely discussed is the way in which the British economy has had a strong international orientation (Ingham, 1984). Imperial conquest was important in providing both the resources and the markets for the Industrial Revolution. Imperial trade was important for the growth of the British economy in the nineteenth and twentieth centuries. Through the City, Britain had a unique role in the organization and finance of world trade until after the Second World War. This has had two effects relevant to our study here. One has been an alleged concentration of attention on finance and 'making money out of money' at the expense of production and making money out of goods or services. This has involved not just the neglect of investment in production as opposed to commercial activities, but also questions of status and reward. Thus a career in the City is both more prestigious and better paid than one in industry. It has also been argued to mean too much emphasis on the short-term as opposed to longer-term returns. Secondly, the multinational character of British capital has meant that there have often been conflicts of interest or outlook between the needs of British enterprises as a whole, and their domestic activities located in Britain itself. Thus large British multinational enterprises with only a small proportion of their activities located in Britain may not have domestic British economic performance at the centre of their concerns. This has further hindered the development of any national organization which represents the views and interests of British capital and its senior management, since these views and interests are often contradictory.

These features can be seen in the way in which management in Britain has behaved in the crisis of the 1980s. The first aspect to consider is the way in which British management participated in, and allowed the crisis to develop in the way it did; for the most part it acquiesced in a government economic policy which in three years stripped away almost one-fifth of the country's industrial base, and as we saw in Chapter 2, ultimately did away with one-quarter of manufacturing jobs. It is difficult to imagine either the owners or managers of industry allowing this to happen without much resistance. There is evidence of managers opposing the government's approach in the critical early years of the decade: the Aldington Report from the House of Lords on Britain's trading position which criticized the effects of the government's policies on the country's industrial base comprised evidence from a range of senior industrialists alarmed at the effects of the government's policies. But there is also evidence of considerable division and conflicts of interest. In November 1980 the then director general of the CBI, Sir Terence Beckett, called for a 'bare knuckle fight' with the government over its policy of high interest rates, soaring exchange rate for sterling and drastic domestic deflation. At that point the rate of redundancies had reached ½ million per annum, and factory closures were running at record levels. Yet his speech was seen as extremely controversial. Many companies whose chairmen were close to the Conservative Party left the CBI, others threatened to go (Leys, 1985). Many CBI members from the finance sector or the City stood to do very well from the policy of high interest rates. The abolition of exchange controls was attractive to companies with substantial overseas interests, or those seeking to expand them. Thus there was a difference between the material interests of managers of companies with their production activities rooted in the domestic national economy, and others whose activity concerned the circulation rather than the accumulation of capital, or whose activities had a primarily international orientation: those whose fate was not intimately tied to the fate of the domestic economy. The former had no specific organization or means of representation in Britain – certainly the CBI did not play this role.

A second factor was that many managers were sympathetic to the government's ideology and its generally *laissez faire* approach. A survey by Poole and his colleagues of one thousand British Institute of Management members in manufacturing, commerce and the public sector gives us a valuable snapshot of management opinion in July 1980 (Poole *et al.*, 1982). About 80 per cent thought that trade unions had too much power and that the government should legislate about strikes, ballots, secondary picketing and the closed shop; that public expenditure should be cut and parts of nationalized industries hived off. Lower but still substantial majorities favoured public economic management through control of the money supply, and abolition of prices and incomes policies. The only area where managers took a less free-market approach was in other aspects of macroeconomic management and international trade. They were roughly evenly divided over government control of foreign enterprises in Britain, and management of trade, and government 'co-ordination' of investment, industrial development and restructuring. These attitudes certainly suggest strong support at the level of ideas for the sorts of policy the government advocated, even if many managers were coming to have misgivings about the short-term results.

Another topic on which Poole and his colleagues canvassed opinion was industrial democracy and participation. Whilst managers were evenly divided about whether more 'employee participation' was desirable in their organization, and generally approved of consultation and giving more information to employees, they were extremely hostile to trade-union-based board level participation: only one in ten thought that this was 'an appropriate form of participation'. Yet just such participation had been a keystone of the previous Labour government's draft legislation on the issue. Leys argues that Labour's ideas on boardroom participation focused managers' fears about the corporatist direction that the British economy was taking so that some came to express such views as:

> Mrs Thatcher's government is all that stands between [us] and a rapid slide into a down-market version of the German Democratic Republic. (Leys, 1985, p. 17)

Managers accepted the different economic policies of the new Conservative government, including their harsh effects on the economic environment they faced, and the much increased prospect of redundancy for individual managers as corporations restructured their operations or firms simply closed down. But what did managers make of this new environment? Commentators have often assumed that the new economic conditions forced British management to make basic changes in the way it ran businesses, and in particular to change industrial relations and the way it treated labour in the workplace. These changes were seen by some as amounting to an 'employers' offensive' in the workplace against the established position of unionism, including rolling back collective bargaining, developing new forms of participation which emphasized managerial leadership in the workplace and new 'flexible' ways of working which took advantage of a slack labour market and undermined the bargaining position of labour for the future. In fact the evidence for all these propositions is, to say the least, patchy.

It is not at all clear that a savage recession forcing unprecedented levels of job losses and plant closures is the context most likely to make managers rethink their approach to employee relations or to the process of management as a whole. Rather than focus on a long-term revision of their strategy (if indeed they have one) they are far more likely to search for an immediate, short-term solution to their urgent problems. As we saw in Chapter 2, in the period up to the spring of 1981, sterling was allowed to appreciate by one-fifth whilst the domestic cost of raw materials and fuel for industry rose by almost

one-third. This pincer movement made producers who faced foreign competition either in the domestic market or abroad dramatically less competitive:
it is fanciful to think that a solution to their crisis lay in a new approach to
labour relations. The government, true to its monetarist rhetoric at the time,
argued that wage reductions ought to have taken the strain, but this was simply
wishful thinking: reductions of the order needed to restore competitiveness in
the face of these cost pressures and sterling appreciation would have been
quite impossible.

The class background to industrial relations which we consider in Chapter
7 also suggests that any strategic reaction in this area was unlikely. Put simply,
after two centuries of avoiding taking a strategic approach to dealing with the
question of worker organization, and preferring to deal at arm's length with
trade union organization, focusing on substantive issues rather than procedural relations, British management was unlikely to reverse this policy in the
middle of a slump. On one side there was no qualitatively new approach to
labour, on the other there was no anti-union offensive. Instead, true to the
short-term focus of British industrial relations traditions, it was employment
which took the strain. Companies cut costs fast by reducing workforces in an
attempt to avoid bankruptcy. It is likely that there was increased pressure to
reform some working practices and intensify labour during the height of the
recession, whilst workers were being made redundant in large numbers.
Significantly Wadwhani *et al.* (1989) found relative increases in labour
productivity in unionized workplaces between 1980 and 1984, but not after,
which suggests that it was the immediate pressure of the recession that
brought changes rather than longer-term changes in working relationships.

Flexibility and flexible specialization

After the immediate crisis of 1979–82 passed, some observers reported
change in management in two main areas: flexibility and employee participation. There are two aspects to the flexibility theory. One is the argument that
the overall character of production in modern industrial capitalism is changing
and that a new phase is emerging in the world economy. According to this
analysis, mass production, with its emphasis on long production runs of
standard products and reducing costs by increasing volume, is being replaced
as the major form of production by 'flexible specialization' where the emphasis
is on developing markets by creating 'niche' products tailored to more specific
and diversified tastes. This requires much more varied production runs
of diversified products and puts an emphasis both on using technology to
make production more flexible and adaptable and on expanding markets for
products by expanding the range of products available (Piore and Sabel,
1984). If we recall our earlier discussion about the relationship between the
nature of the organization of work and the nature of how it is managed, and the
contrast between 'mechanistic' and 'organic' structures, then it is clear that

any such change would have a substantial impact on the way that management was organized and behaved.

The second theme has been that of flexibility in the use of labour. Some observers have argued that the much slacker labour markets of the 1980s have enabled employers to look for new, less rigid, relationships with their employees. Rather than relying on a permanent, full-time workforce, employers have been able to use more temporary or part-time workers, new shift or hours arrangements, or use more self-employed workers or subcontractors. In addition, employers have looked for more 'functional' flexibility from their workers, so that individual workers can be used to perform a greater range of jobs. Some have argued that such developments have been important in making labour markets more fluid and reducing high levels of unemployment by reducing the cost of labour to the employer. Atkinson and Meager (1986), in particular, have argued that these trends have produced a new form of organization – the flexible firm – which combines these elements by creating a core and peripheral workforce. In the core workers are permanently employed and are trained and rewarded to work flexibly. The periphery of temps, part-timers, subcontractors, self-employed and trainees is used only to cope with peak periods, allowing the firm to minimize its fixed costs and respond rapidly to fluctuations in demand. Atkinson and Meager's model suggests that in some ways the role of management becomes less important in comparison with the market: rather than managing a more stable workforce over time it hires and fires different parts of the peripheral workforce. But it also suggests a more thought-out and strategic approach to the overall use of labour, including the identification of core labour groups and the adoption of appropriate recruitment, training and bargaining policies.

There has been much discussion of flexibility and 'post-Fordism', not just in the specialist academic and management journals, but in the general media too. When surveyed, senior managers in Britain report that flexibility is one of their main priorities. The government argues that promoting flexibility has been central to its approach to the labour market and industrial relations, and that it has created an environment that enables management to work more flexibly because of fewer legal restrictions on what it can do and because trade unions have been encouraged to behave more 'reasonably'. At times, the government has been positively gushing in its view of developments:

> Recent flexibility agreements often . . . involve a general commitment to flexibility in whatever form it may prove to be necessary, rather than a commitment to remove specific rigidities named in the agreement and no others. Examples of this very broad flexibility commitment are the British Shipbuilders National Enabling Agreement to Revised Working Practices, the agreement between Nissan and the Amalgamated Union of Engineering Workers for the new car plant at Washington, and agreements at Findus, Toshiba and Continental Can. Agreements of this sort signal a complete change in labour practices from the attempt to defend traditional

positions against encroachment by market forces (which is likely ultimately to drive the firm out of business) to the attempt to develop the potential of the firm and its employees fully, thus giving the firm the maximum scope to reward its employees and safeguard their jobs. . . . The evidence is that flexibility agreements are now quite widespread. (Treasury, 1986, p. 3, quoted in MacInnes, 1987, p. 119)

However, the adequacy of the theory and empirical evidence for both 'flexible specialization' and 'flexibility' are weak. Karel Williams and his colleagues (1987) have suggested a number of flaws in Piore and Sabel's ideas. The first concerns the ability to define flexible specialization. Three aspects of production are identified: whether capital equipment is dedicated to a specific product or not; how much product differentiation there is, and how long production runs are. But the empirical evidence suggests that most producers do not lie at one or other end of each of these three dimensions and that the three rarely coincide. There are few examples of producers with only dedicated equipment, low product differentiation and long production runs. Nor have flexible specialization theorists been able to define how 'long' is 'long' or how 'differentiated' is 'differentiated'. Do the 132 possible specifications of one model of a mass produced car constitute flexible specialization? The second concerns the characterization of the twentieth century as hitherto the era of 'mass production' or 'Fordism'; some industries such as textiles or capital intensive process industries have never been organized in this way, whilst even mass production assembly industries have usually relied heavily on subcontracting rather than integrated production, and have been capable of producing high volumes of a range of different products. Thirdly, Williams *et al.* argue that there is, in fact, little evidence that mass markets are breaking up: there is such a volume of replacement demand in the world market for consumer durables that most producers can continue to produce on a mass basis so long as they continue to develop new products. Fourthly, they challenge Piore and Sabel's assumption that new microelectronic technology is always more flexible than the electro-mechanical equipment it replaces. They argue that in practice the costs of adjusting and reprogramming make this illusory. 'Flexible manufacturing systems' use computer control to co-ordinate a number of machine tools, offering the possibility of greater product variety; however, their capital cost is so high that they need very large volumes to pay their way. One case that bears out much of this argument was the experience of a steel foundry studied by Cressey and his colleagues. A new computer-controlled line was introduced which replaced what had previously been highly skilled craft work. However, problems emerged with finding enough volume to run the line effectively: as one craft worker commented: 'It's like having a Rolls-Royce to do shopping trips' (Cressey, *et al.*, 1985, p. 86). Lastly, they argue that there are many areas of industry where mass production remains the only viable way to organize work because it is manifestly more efficient in the amount of labour it uses and other costs over craft-based types of work, whether labelled 'flexible specialization' or not:

> 'New generations of computer controlled equipment may deliver a more varied output but they do not restore an economic system based on redeployable productive resources and low fixed costs. That is a world which we have lost.'
> (Williams *et al.* 1987, p. 433)

Thus whilst there might be particular market sectors, or geographical areas where craft-based production remains important, such industries and areas are interdependent with more mass forms of production. There is no empirical evidence of craft type industries becoming comparatively more important over time, nor can they be taken as a prototypical model for the future of industry and its management. To the extent that we might seem to be in the era of post-Fordism, that is only because large sections of industry have never been 'Fordized' in the first place, particularly in Britain where the smaller domestic market, combined with poor competitiveness internationally has often meant a smaller scale of operation by British firms.

The model of the flexible firm is logically separate from that of flexible specialization. It would be quite possible for managers in a variety of production or service environments to seek to reorganize labour in the way the model indicates. The question again is one of whether the model fits with the empirical evidence. A variety of research, covering labour market trends and employer behaviour, suggests that it does not, and that here too the continuities in management organization and behaviour are more apparent than change. Although the proportion of workers in the economy who are full-time, permanent employees has fallen in the 1980s, this is mostly due to the growth of self-employment. Some of this self-employment could be associated with changes in firms' employment practices, but as we argue below, this does not seem to be because of any flexible-firm type approach. There has also been a growth of part-time employment, but no more than we would expect from the increase in the level of activity in the economy and the shift in employment towards the service sector which has always used more part-timers. The proportion of temporary workers in the economy has hardly changed at all once allowance is made for people on special government training schemes. We should have seen more change in the figures if the flexible firm approach was becoming more widespread.

More detailed information has been provided by a research project organized by the Department of Employment. This surveyed around eight hundred workplaces, then followed this up with forty case studies of those which looked as if they might be following new 'flexible' practices in their staffing policies (McGregor and Sproull, 1990; Hunter and MacInnes, 1990). The study concentrated on 'numerical flexibility'. Both stages found that employers' reasons for using non-full-time, non-permanent employees were almost always 'traditional' ones. Temporary employees and agency temps were used for short-term cover for absences by permanent employees, or to do one-off jobs that would not be permanent. Part-timers were used to do tasks which only lasted for a limited number of hours, or to cover peaks in the working day or week. Self-employed workers and subcontractors were used for a variety of reasons, but it was unusual for them to be used simply to avoid a long-term employment commitment by the employer. Much more common were mundane occurrences such as using a self-employed window cleaner. Rather than developing radically new ways of staffing, most employers had an approach which was based on fairly conventional ideas about the relative merits and drawbacks of each type of worker, together with a clear preference for 'standard', full-time, permanent employees when there were not important reasons for preferring another type. Part-timers and temps were often seen as more difficult to manage and problems of continuity were seen as ruling them out of promoted positions. Temps were seen as less reliable and less loyal and unsuitable for jobs which required training or skills which the worker did not already possess. Employers did not expect to find men who preferred a part-time or temporary job. Indeed, the way they bundled up tasks into jobs suggested that they expected to be easily able to find female part-time labour but to need to provide full-time jobs for men. Conversely, employers attributed a substantial amount of female part-time work to worker preference. For some employers, particularly those who did not pay very attractive wages, it was easier to recruit part-time women workers rather than full-time ones, because the latter had fewer employment opportunities. Similarly, it seemed that much of the expansion of self-employment was worker-led. Employees with specialist skills in short supply found that they could make more money and stick to more interesting tasks by going self-employed or working through an agency.

The case study stage revealed that few employers had a thought-out strategy for using different types of labour, and that most thinking about staffing levels and recruitment was *ad hoc*. They did not analyse or treat their staff in terms of a 'core' and 'peripheral' workforce, nor was it realistic to divide the workforce into two such segments. Labour legislation was hardly ever cited by employers as a reason for using one or other type of worker, suggesting that the government's emphasis on the adverse effects of employment protection legislation on levels of recruitment is empirically unfounded. In the public sector there had been more moves towards numerical flexibility, but this was usually directly in response to legislation which required managers to undertake such exercises as competitive tendering for services. In practice such developments often represented little more than wage-cutting exercises for unskilled staff in a weak labour market position.

Ferner (1985), in his account of policies of management in British Rail, suggests that as the public sector came under increasing political pressure from the government, managers at BR changed their stance to a much greater degree than those in the private sector. Managers could see that, for example, taking a tough stance towards unions would be popular with their political masters. But even in the public sector managers who saw brighter career prospects flowing from a more hawkish approach had to reckon with the less tangible costs of forgoing the goodwill from workforces built up through a tradition of co-operation with their unions.

Functional flexibility is a more difficult subject to evaluate, since changes in what workers do is a permanent feature of any market economy. The question is whether there has been any qualitative shift in the extent of change and in the scope of activities that different sorts of workers are expected to take on. MacInnes (1987) has argued that any such change has probably been slight, and Cross (1988), studying over two hundred manufacturing plants, concluded that substantial changes in working practices were rare whereas marginal developments were common.

Human resource management and participation

Some observers have claimed that British management has taken the opportunity, afforded by the greater manoeuvrability it has enjoyed in the 1980s, to develop more participative approaches, enhance its leadership skills and develop a more integrated approach to the managing of people (usually referred to in this context as an enterprise's 'greatest asset'). The buzz term for these fashionable ideas came to be 'human resource management'. However, it is far from clear that such approaches represented anything like a new, integrated approach to employment policy on the part of firms as opposed to a passing fad having only a marginal impact. Guest (1987) found that most changes were pretty opportunistic rather than strategic, and Marginson and his colleagues (1988) found a dearth of any formal strategy and policy towards the deployment of labour in the large enterprises they studied. Given what we have already discussed about the neglect of training, including management training, this is hardly surprising. Storey commented:

> Management development is as prone to fads and fashions as any other realm of managerial theory and practice. The 'latest innovation' (no matter how peripheral to the vast bulk of the people in the organization in question) is inevitably the story which tends to make the headlines. Inside the companies the main impression is usually how little an impact in practice these nine day wonders make. (Storey, 1990, p. 6)

Whilst there has been evidence according to some surveys of an increase in management communication and consultation with employees, the interpretation of the significance of this has been controversial. Whilst Millward and Stevens (1986) argued that the evidence could be interpreted as an increase in participation, MacInnes and colleagues (MacInnes *et al.*, 1985; Cressey *et al.*, 1985) concluded that no underlying change had actually occurred and that most participation initiatives tended to be marginal.

One aspect of British employers' approach to personnel management which does not seem to have changed is the emphasis on money as a motivator of the workforce. As well as granting substantial real pay increases to their employees under the regime of free collective bargaining in the 1980s, there has been some increase in experimenting with more individually-based remuneration, with profit-sharing schemes and, to a lesser extent, with profit-related pay. Profit-sharing has also been seen as an aspect of employee participation and therefore a significant part of human resource management, but the actual empirical evidence contrasts strongly with the claims made for financial participation by its advocates.

Baddon and colleagues (1989) reported a survey of 350 companies and five case studies. They found that until the end of June 1988 over two-thirds of schemes approved by the Inland Revenue were executive share option schemes. The amounts of money involved as a percentage of wages were almost always very low, as was the proportion of capital transferred to employee ownership. Management objectives in introducing the schemes were vague, and little evidence emerged of management trying to match the properties of different available schemes to their priorities. Nor was there any management evaluation of the schemes. Few specific results were reported, as opposed to more general 'attitudinal' changes which respondents saw as 'unmeasurable': more company loyalty or 'corporate identification'. Employees were rarely, if ever, involved in the design or decision to introduce schemes. If financial participation is to have a motivational element, then it needs to relate effort to result; but as we have already argued this is desperately difficult to achieve, and almost inevitably contentious: who can produce an authoritative assessment of the relative contribution of different workers in different departments and of the relationship between that contribution and the profits for the year or the share price? In turn, such considerations of motivation bring one dangerously close to instrumental orientations, when the spirit of financial participation is supposed to emphasize common and collective purpose. But such commonality may be achieved at the cost of indifference: it's just a bonus, a small token of goodwill. As one worker put it:

> To me it's a gift, however small – something they give me . . . it's something they needn't give you. . . . I don't know why they do it really. (Baddon *et al.*, 1989, p. 158)

The study concluded:

> Our evidence suggests that there is no strong link between the adoption of financial participation schemes and an acknowledgement by a majority of employees that

they have become more aware of management problems or are able to engage in fuller participation. (p. 285)

CONCLUSIONS

This chapter has emphasized the way in which the process of management and the identity and behaviour of managers is more confused and contradictory than we might expect. There are no 'golden rules' about how to manage successfully, nor obvious social forces which determine what managers must do or reveal the logic of their behaviour to us. Yet this is not to go as far as to suggest that managers can do anything. We have also suggested, for example, the ways in which the character of British management might be understood.

The ambiguity of managers' situation contributes to the importance of legitimacy in management. Is the manager primarily the representative of property or expertise; or again, a disinterested arbiter of other competing parties? In practice, most managers must play all these cards, but they are, to say the least, hardly compatible.

Writing at the end of the 1960s, Fox addressed the problem of legitimacy in the following terms:

Those managements who are aware of the problem have tended to seek ways of strengthening their legitimacy through devices which did not compromise a prerogative which was in fact vanishing but which they felt unable formally to relinquish. It is no accident that the past few decades have witnessed a succession of personnel panaceas, most of which, on examination, show themselves to be attempts to convince employees that they have the substance of participation and influence while in fact giving them only the shadow. Only comparatively rarely has management grasped that the only sure and stable way of maintaining its control was to share it. (Fox, 1971, pp. 158–9)

The last two decades do not suggest that management have taken Fox's advice to heart, and for good reason. They have felt that to share control risks losing it, since there are other goals that people in organizations could pursue. Opening up new areas for debate could embroil management in discussions on all sorts of issues over which it currently exercises prerogative, either personally or collectively. To the extent that management and decision-making remain political exercises, bringing a new party into the game makes the calculation of tactics and strategy a more risky and difficult exercise. However, during the 1980s management has not been able simply to forget the issue of legitimacy because of higher unemployment, the return to *laissez faire* economic strategies or the new emphasis on the role of profits and market forces. It has not gone on the offensive to obliterate any challenge to its rule. Indeed, the distinction we have drawn between the individual career aspirations of managers and the less obvious 'interests' of the organizations for which they work make any global analysis or description of management 'approaches' of limited value.

Instead, most managers and managements have continued to find ways, under ever-changing banners, of convincing employees that they are offering the 'substance' of involvement, whilst giving only the 'shadow'.

4

WHAT ARE TRADE UNIONS FOR?

The post-war period in Britain has been a chequered one for trade unions. When one assesses their strengths in terms of membership growth, density of coverage, influence and morale one can identify periods of sustained achievement particularly in the 1960s and early 1970s. However, the recent decade has reversed that trend. Trade unions are suffering from falling membership, in some areas there have been drastic reductions in density figures coupled with low morale resulting in unions having to devote their energies to warding off threats to their own survival.

This chapter looks at the dimensions and causes of the 'crisis' facing trade unions. It does so by looking initially at the statistics of decline but more importantly, perhaps, it looks at the wider debate that has taken place about the primary aims and objectives of trade unionism; for one cannot assess success, or designate crisis without examining the contending views relating to the purpose of trade unions. Even in the periods of relative strength there has been a constant conflict over the strategies, values and fundamental orientation that unions should adopt; this ambiguity is historically embedded and becomes particularly acute in periods of recession.

THE CURRENT CRISIS

Crisis is an overused term, especially in industrial relations, and many of the previous uses of the term have been related to one-dimensional problems or challenges, e.g. productivity, strikes or market downturn (Cressey *et al.*, 1985). What distinguishes the recent period is the identification that a number of critical issues have combined to create what Hobsbawm has called a 'period of crisis' not simply for trade unions in Britain but for the wider labour movement, culminating in successive industrial and political defeats.

> Nobody can seriously deny that the British labour movement today is in a considerable mess. It is in a state of deeper crisis and confusion than was earlier foreseeable . . . we find a confused and divided labour movement, torn by splits

and internal squabbles, and isolated from many of its old supporters. (Hobsbawm, 1981, pp. 167–8)

Hobsbawm, in looking for the causes of this 'mess', identifies a number of contributory stands. Among the structural features leading to a weakened union movement he includes the long-term decline in manual occupations: these have fallen from 64 per cent of the working population in 1951 down to 46 per cent in 1985 (p. 3). For Hobsbawm, this growing dominance of white collar workers has a number of consequences, one being a change in the pattern of union organization away from a strong craft/industrial unionism that underwrote a particular collectivist style of proletarian life towards a more atomistic and sectional union movement. Ancillary features of this movement are the breaking of the ties between unions and the Labour Party, a declining Labour vote among unionists and an increasing 'economistic' tendency within unions that eschews social and political purposes and seeks instead short-term financial gains from union activity. Structural changes in British capitalism are in this view leading to a drastically recomposed labour market characterized by a growing preponderance of white collar and female workers, smaller establishments and consequently new forms of workforce differentiation. Hobsbawm sees sectionalism, narrow union interests and new 'business' style unions emerging out of the 'transformation' of the class base upon which labour has historically rested. Thus the structural changes have in their working through, profound material and ideological effects which express themselves in practices that have alienated both the voting public and many union members from the trade unions and the Labour Party. It is these long-term changes that have, in Hobsbawm's mind, allowed the Thatcher government to gain and retain power.

This analysis has been taken up and extended by Lane. He focuses on the waning influence of trade unions in the 1980s and contrasts the 'new realism' and the defensiveness of the present day with that of the 1960s. For him the economic boom of the earlier period allowed one form of unionism to flourish particularly in the form of shop steward activity at the plant level. Now, however, there has to be:

[An] appreciation of the possibility that certain conditions external to the workplace might have changed so dramatically as to affect future activity within the workplace. (Lane, 1982, p. 13)

Lane uses similar arguments to Hobsbawm, claiming that trade unions have forfeited legitimacy among their own members through their narrow pursuit of economic militancy. However, he too locates the more important long-term problems for trade unionism in the structural shifts taking place in the British economy. Hence the central part of Lane's thesis is the analysis of these changes and their likely effects on union strength. He cites four main features contributing to the 'ebb tide' of unions' influence:

1. A movement of industry away from cities to rural areas. The concomitant dispersal of the labour force into rural plants with little union tradition and few links with other unions or working class politics, has resulted in a lack of activity here and a declining city centre power base.
2. Plant sizes are falling relative to company size, hence the rise of the multi-plant, multi-product firm. In this context, solidarity is made difficult because of organizational limits and barriers, by the encouragement of plant-centred bargaining and by the lack of homogeneity across plant workforces.
3. Trade union practice as a result becomes isolated, contact becomes difficult and the industrial decline of the city also means the decline in the educational and cultural contact and provision that unions had provided.
4. The workforce is being recomposed, this does not simply resolve itself down to a reduction in manual jobs but results in different mixes of skills, sectors and work experiences. Growth still occurs, but it is achieved in limited areas, such as catering, retail and financial services. These are typically small establishments employing a majority of young and female workers with low unionization rates and again low workforce contact. The result of this trend taken with the others is a form of trade unionism imposed from above with a centralized format that engenders little work-force participation in union affairs.

Lane comes to similar conclusions to those of Hobsbawm regarding the 'legitimacy' of unions. He maintains that the growth in sectionalism has resulted in a slump in morale:

> Morale now is at such a low ebb that grave legal threats to the very existence of the unions are inadequately resisted. To some extent that lack of a will to fight in a period of exceptionally high unemployment is a simple product of fear. That is to be expected. What is much more worrying is rank and file uncertainty as to whether unions are worth fighting for. (Lane, 1982, p. 13)

For these two commentators the crisis affecting trade unions is the result of the interweaving of long-term structural change with current economic crisis and high and sustained levels of unemployment. Together these have exposed union practices that rested upon 'economism' as inadequate and ill-suited to retaining membership, morale and influence in a recessionary period. As union bargaining power and influence within companies declines, their basic legitimation and their ideological basis of support dwindles. The main criticism that Lane and Hobsbawm level is clearly about the political failings of the movement and its inability to demonstrate an alternative vision upon which unionism can be based: one that extends beyond the plant and the pay packet and into issues regarding the social purposes of work and a wider quest for a society founded on equity. This political failure is demonstrated in the activity of unions who pursue self-interest and 'subordinate equity to exigency' (Lane, 1982, p. 13). In essence, unions that adapt to this new industrial landscape were likely to end up as American-style business unions bereft of political aims and relegated to the role of opportunistic bargainers and recruiters of the 'new' workforce.

The debate started by Hobsbawm and Lane's intervention has highlighted some of the underlying preconditions that contributed to the Conservative victories of the 1980s and their carrying through of a series of legislative measures to reform and regulate union activity. To some extent the failure of unions to develop beyond 'free collective bargaining' was seen as contributing to union weakness when faced with a government which, in Roy Lewis's phrase, was set on a policy of 'ultra-restrictionism' (Lewis, 1984, p. 371). Lane, in searching for the grounds of the alternative perspective for the unions, returns to George Woodcock's question about trade union's purpose posed in the 1960s.

> It had to decide whether it wanted to be the collective entrepreneur of labour, adopt the jungle ethics of the market and practice business unionism, or whether it wanted to play a significant part in the creation of a new society constructed on a morality of equity instead of greed. (Lane, 1982, pp. 11–12)

For Lane the question, if it had been answered at all, affirmed the former rather than the latter.

The debate about a crisis for unionism has been addressed by others (Hyman, 1984; Bain and Price, 1984; Coates and Topham, 1986; Kelly, 1988) who, in addition to noting a certain political vacuity, also looked at other variables as measures of crisis. Most notably these have been based on unions,

Table 4.1 Trade unions – numbers and memberships, 1974–88

Year	Number of unions at end of year	Total membership at end of year (000)	Percentage change in membership since previous year
1974	507	11,764	+2.7
1975	501	12,193	+3.6
1976	473	12,386	+3.0
1977	481	12,846	+3.7
1978	462	13,112	+2.1
1979	453	13,289	+1.3
1980	438	12,947	−2.6
1981	414	12,106	−6.5
1982	408	11,593	−4.2
1983	394	11,236	−3.1
1984	375	10,994	−2.2
1985	370	10,821	−1.6
1986	335	10,539	−2.6
1987	330	10,475	−0.6
1988	314	10,238	−2.3

Source: Department of Employment Gazette, May 1990.

organizational strength and membership. Price and Bain, in particular, concentrate on such figures and the redistributive effects on the sectoral balance of union membership. The measure of the crisis in membership terms is seen in the loss of over 3 million members in the period of 1979–88. Table 4.1 indicates both the measure and the chronology of the 23 per cent fall in overall union membership.

Along with this fall in membership we see a continuing decline in the number of unions. However, the twenty-four largest unions, i.e. those with over 100,000 members, accounted for just over 80 per cent of the membership. On the basis of comparisons over time, certain sectors show a marked decrease in membership. These are found predominantly in the manual and manufacturing areas, as Table 4.2 shows.

Table 4.2 Trade unions – analysis by industry, 1982–6

Industry in which most members were deemed to be employed, 1982–6	Standard industrial classification	Membership (000)		Percentage change 1982–6
		(1980)	(Division)	
Agriculture, forestry and fishing	0	0.5	0.7	+40.0%
Energy and water supply	1	413	311	−24.6%
Extraction of minerals/ ores (not fuels); metals, mineral products and chemicals	2	144	87	−39.6%
Metal, engineering and vehicles	3	447	392	−12.5%
Other manufacturing industries	4	686	635	−0.7%
Construction	5	267	254	−4.8%
Distribution, hotels and catering; repairs	6	460	420	−5.6%
Transport and communication	7	742	686	−7.4%
Banking, finance, insurance, business services and leasing	8	337	352	+4.4%
National government	9	552	488	−11.6%
Local government	9	1,521	1,499	−1.4%
Education	9	745	779	+4.6%
Medical/health	9	658	694	+5.5%
Other	9	151	172	+13.9%
Membership of unions covering several industries	—	4,048	3,769	−7.0%*

Source: Department of Employment Gazette, January 1985 and 1986, May 1988.
* Due to a change in classification these figures refer only to the period 1984–6.

Large falls in areas such as extraction, mining, steel, energy supply, engineering and latterly in national government have been matched by only modest growth elsewhere, particularly in financial services, medical provision, education and other services. This has meant a growing numerical significance for white collar workers and a sustained shift in the social basis of unionization. In density terms, i.e. how many of the employed population are unionized, the fall is now approximately 14 per cent. This drop indicates the waning popularity of unions *per se* whereas the structural factors may be seen in the remaining fall in membership which is due to those jobs no longer existing or the previous members being unemployed.

The figures in Table 4.3 show aggregate union membership and density figures in their historical context. The fall in density in the 1980s is significant but not comparable to the recession of the 1920s and 1930s when density fell by as much as half. This may indicate that union organization as such

Table 4.3 Aggregate trade union membership and density

United Kingdom union membership (000)		Potential union membership	Density
1917	5,499	18,234	30.2
1920*	8,348	18,469	45.2
1926*	5,219	18,446	28.3
1933*	4,392	19,422	22.6
1938*	6,063	19,829	30.5
1950*	9,289	21,055	44.1
1955*	9,741	21,913	44.5
1960*	9,835	22,229	44.2
1965*	10,325	23,385	44.2
1970*	11,187	23,050	48.5
1975†	12,026	25,587	51.0
1977†	12,846	24,848	51.7
1978†	13,112	25,092	52.2
1979†	13,289	25,031	53.0
1980†	12,947	23,989	54.0
1981†	12,106	24,077	50.6
1982†	11,593	23,765	48.8
1983†	11,236	23,867	47.0
1984†	10,994	24,259	45.3
1985†	10,821		
1986†	10,539		
1988	10,238	25,524‡	40.0

Sources: * Price & Bain.
    † *Department of Employment Gazette.*
    ‡ Employed labour force minus H.M. Forces.

is not yet into terminal crisis. As Kelly points out, the rate of membership loss in the previous recessions was far higher:

> In just three years (1920–3) trade unions lost almost 35 per cent of their membership. In the earlier recession of the 1890s, trade unions fared even worse, losing almost 40 per cent of their membership in the years 1890–3. (Kelly, 1988, p. 270)

Internationally, the British experience is somewhat worse than that of northern Europe which still shows some growth in membership, but it is comparable to that of Italy and the Netherlands and better than in the United States (Kelly, 1988, p. 269).

Whilst such membership statistics do have a powerful influence on union finances and perceptions they may not adequately reflect trade union strength, as Coates and Topham point out:

> The rise in the number of unionists in the seventies despite mounting unemployment, reflects not a sudden expansion of trade union consciousness, but the artificial accretion of paper membership. That so many of these paper unionists do not feel themselves to be 'part of the union' constitutes a genuine problem of union democracy – a problem that the Tories have effectively exploited. (Coates and Topham, 1986, p. 12)

This introduces another perspective on union crisis that looks not at numbers but at the activity rate of the membership: at whether the union as an organization is internally vital. This debate has often centred around an opposition between membership activity at the branch/company level and the bureaucratic hierarchy of officials that tends to exert central control. Within British unions one can see trends towards both patterns with each reflecting union needs to adapt to external pressures (see Hyman, 1984). For an assessment of crisis, however, one might look at the extent of democratic structures, but possibly more telling would be an analysis of the membership rate of activity within whatever structures are extant. In this way one might contrast that 'paper membership' with what is only implicitly stated as its opposition: an active and involved membership. Most material on this tends to refer to formal practices with unions, for instance attendance at branch meetings, the rate of turnover of shop stewards, the number of unopposed elections and turnout figures for elections. Analysis of this from 1967 onwards does reveal for many observers evidence of low involvement and activity bordering on apathy. The fact that less than 20 per cent regularly attend branches, that turnover of representatives is a long standing problem and that officials are elected on small turnouts illustrates a further dimension of crisis, one that indicates a highly stratified membership in terms of preparedness to act in defence of 'their' organizations, to engage in campaigns, to strike or to act in solidarity with others. (See HMSO, 1967, *Workplace Industrial Relations Survey*, and Coates and Topham, 1986 for evidence of such union activity rates.)

THE THATCHER ATTACK

The dimension of union activity/preparedness to act in defence of their interests is crucial when we consider another main source of crisis that is commonly put forward. This is the political and legal attack launched upon the collective rights and functions of unions. Since 1979 there has been a catalogue of measures imposed on unions as actors by the Conservative government. The attack has been mounted on two levels: one being the willingness to confront union power through macho-management holding out against strikes; the other has been the systematic removal of collective and individual employment rights and the imposition of restrictions on various forms of unionized collective activity. The practice of the government in its actions, especially those relating to the public sector, bear witness to the first of these ploys and the display of hard-line tactics on pay, workforce reductions and the imposition of government-inspired cuts, creating in its wake a climate for industrial relations restructuring for management in private industry. Evidence that this attack was not merely a pragmatic response to market pressure was revealed prior to the election of the 1979 government. Indeed, most of the strategy of confrontation had been agreed to in 1978, as *The Economist* revealed in an article on a final report of the Conservative Party's policy group on the nationalized industry drafted by Nicholas Ridley ('Appamattox or civil war', *The Economist*, May 1978). Here a number of economic, management and industrial relations policies were agreed. Among these was the grading of the public sector into three categories of vulnerability to industrial action:

(a) Sewerage, water, electricity, gas and the health service in the most vulnerable group; (b) railways, docks, coal and dustmen in an intermediate group; and (c) other public transport, education, ports and telephones, air transport and steel is the least vulnerable group. (p. 21)

In the annexe to the report the party was urged to consider ways of pre-empting the inevitable challenge that would be mounted by 'enemies of the next Tory government'. It suggested that in order to avoid confrontation with unions in the 'vulnerable' industries, return on capital figures should be 'rigged' so that above-average wage claims could be met, and confrontation avoided. In this way the eventual battleground with the unions could be chosen by government who could then fight prepared battles. In a startlingly predictive passage the group agreed that:

The eventual battle should be on ground chosen by the Tories, in a field they think could be won (railways, British Leyland, the civil service or steel). Every precaution should be taken against a challenge in electricity or gas. . . . The group believes that the most likely battleground will be the coal industry. They would like a Thatcher government to: (a) build up maximum coal stocks, particularly at the power station; (b) make contingency plans for the import of coal; (c) encourage the recruitment of non-union lorry-drivers by haulage companies to help move coal where necessary; (d) introduce dual coal/oil firing in all power stations as quickly as possible.

There should be a large, mobile squad of police equipped and prepared to uphold the law against violent picketing. (p. 22)

When one then looks at the record of strikes in the initial years of the Conservative government one finds that this 1978 report accurately pinpoints both the conflicts that occurred and those that were avoided:

1979	British Leyland, 'Red Robbo' dispute.
1980	Steel strike lasted sixteen weeks ending in defeat for steel unions.
1981	Civil service strike.
	Miners appeased by quick settlement.
1982	Health service dispute.
1983	GCHQ, Cheltenham.
1984/85	Miners' strike.
1986	Teacher's strike.
1987	Printers' strike.
1989	Nurses' dispute.
1990	Ambulance drivers' strike.

The early period of Thatcherism saw a number of long, drawn out disputes chosen for the express purpose of teaching labour a lesson. The results of these disputes have been signal failures for the unions and members concerned. Taken on top of the doubts expressed about 'paper membership' and activity rates, this soon led to clear falls in both the number of stoppages and the number of days lost (see Table 4.4).

With the exception of 1984/5 – the year of the miners' dispute and the high

Table 4.4 Number of days lost through strikes

	Days lost (000)	Stoppages
1978	9,405	2,471
1979	29,474	2,080
1980	11,964	1,334
1981	4,266	1,338
1982	5,313	1,538
1983	3,754	1,364
1984	27,135	1,221
1985	6,402	903
1986	1,920	1,074
1987	3,546	1,016
1988	3,702	781
1989	4,128	701

Source: Department of Employment Gazette. 1984/5.
Figures show the distortion due to the effects of the miners' strike.

watermark of government confrontation – these figures support the government's contention of its success in confronting and defeating trade unions
through the strike weapon. There is a propaganda and ideological level to this
claim which ignores the possibility that those strikes that did take place
were more effective and occurred against a background of increasing legal
difficulty. Whatever the complexion one puts on to the statistics they are
difficult to interpret as a positive step forward for labour.

The other and connected line of attack has been the use of legislation to
curb union functions and rights. This has proceeded piecemeal since 1979
and has comprehensively undercut trade union rights on a collective basis,
whilst at the same time taking away previously granted individual union
members' rights. The primary attack has been mounted on trade unions as
collective bodies able to act and make agreements. This has been enacted
through the Employment and Trade Union Acts, 1980, 1982 and 1984 that
have, among other provisions, sought to bring about the following:

1. Restrict the ability of unions to enter into industrial action. A number of
   trade union immunities were removed, laying the unions open to court
   action if they were engaged in sympathy or solidarity strikes, if they went on
   strike without balloting or if they infringed the new definition of a trade
   dispute. Strikers have been open to dismissal for breach of contract, a
   feature seized upon by a number of employers, notably Rupert Murdoch
   and Eddie Shah in their newspaper disputes.
2. Restrict union action during strikes, with picketing now subject to a new
   code of practice enforced by the police.
3. Restrict the closed shop provisions, conferring rights not to belong to a
   trade union; also to enforce ballots on union membership agreements.
4. Balloting for elections of union officials, dispute activity and in relation to
   union political funds.

The upshot of this series of legal measures has been the steady erosion of the
previously voluntaristic system of industrial relations towards one where it is
now not uncommon for injunctions to be used in union–management disputes, where substantial financial penalties are imposed by courts, and, as in
the NGA–Messenger dispute, the miners' strike and the NUS/P&O disputes, the whole of the organization's finances are sequestered. Such powers
are new and largely alien to the previously established system. The TUC has
commented that:

> The presentation of much of the present government's trade union legislation has
> been consciously designed to foster and exploit anti-union prejudice. The aim of
> the government has been to bring about a permanent weakening of trade union
> strength, and to increase the power of employers to introduce change without
> consent. (TUC Consultative Document, 1988, p. 4)

This legislation has been supplemented by the simultaneous attack on many individual rights that workers as employees, irrespective of trade union membership, previously enjoyed. This body of rights was codified and strengthened by the previous Labour government's Employment Protection Act. Among the areas affected by legislation has been: the weakening of grounds for unfair dismissal, the eroding of maternity and sickness benefits, the abolition of provisions for employees in small companies, the extension of qualifying periods and the curtailment of rights for part-time or temporary workers.

Rather than 'reform' the industrial relations system the Conservative government has instead chosen to recast it on different foundations. In terms of the perceived crisis facing trade unions, this feature has to be considered of great importance, particularly when combined with economic recession and structural changes which render the market power aspect of unionism relatively ineffective.

A NEW UNIONISM?

The previous section has unravelled various strands of the proclaimed crisis facing the union movement: those strands have been identified respectively as having structural foundations leading to a political loss of direction; a growth in sectionalism and economism that alienates many of the trade unions' traditional supporters; an organizational crisis brought about by falling membership; a crisis of activity with a lack of commitment and vitality allied to the loss of market power, and a sustained political and legal attack by the Conservative governments of 1979, 1983 and 1987. It is this combination of factors that underpins a form of 'new unionism' which many see as both a cause and an expression of the crisis facing British trade unionism.

In such circumstances a rupture with 'old unionism' appears to become inevitable and the activities of unions such as EEPTU, AUEW and USDAW, which adopt programmes and policies suited to the 'new realism', become identifiable as a 'coherent' union response to the current climate. The form that such coherence takes is an emphasis upon policies that are accommodating, flexible, that adapt to and take note of the developments in the wider economy. Therefore, in a period of falling union membership and changes in the labour market, unions engage in increasingly bitter contests for membership with other unions whilst at the same time promoting 'union packages' that they can sell to employers in order to secure a growing membership. (This may not be limited to the 'new unions', as increasingly the other major unions get drawn into membership battles.) The recent period has seen an upsurge in single union agreements, especially in Japanese plants in Britain. The unseemly bidding to attract Nissan brought out the kinds of policy that might be offered in such 'sunrise' packages. Typically, one union would represent all staffs with an aim to ending inter-union disputes, often there would be agreement on a no-strike clause or the institution of pendulum arbitration, which effectively rules out disputes surrounding pay deals. (See Wood, 1985, for an account of the principles of pendulum, or last offer, arbitration.) The EETPU, according to Lloyd, developed such a 'market-based' unionism and has 'sought to present itself as the most saleable union commodity around', promising:

> Strike-free environments, a co-operative and enthusiastic workforce and union officials who will understand and co-operate with management's point of view. To its members it offers an end to class war rhetoric and practice, greater say over their workplaces through the extension of industrial democracy it seeks in those companies where the 'no strike' agreements operate, and – also in these companies – a single status, all-mucking-in-together working culture deliberately copied from the Japanese. (Lloyd, 1988)

The unions have also sweetened the packages by offering both private medicine provisions and embracing share ownership and profit-sharing schemes.

Such programmes are firmly enterprise-based and do not seek to challenge the corporate philosophy/culture of the company; rather they are willing to promote 'company consciousness' by connecting rewards packages to company success. One example of such a deal is the single union agreement signed by Komatsu with the Amalgamated Engineering Union. Among its main provisions was the inauguration of complete flexibility and an end to demarcation throughout the plant, a plant-based consultative union–management forum, an exhaustive negotiation and disputes procedure, and the possible acceptance of Japanese-style 'company councils' (*The Guardian*, 1986). Evident also is an attempt to secure agreements of three to six years' duration which offer management longer-term control over costs and some expectation of peaceful industrial relations during the period. One rather extreme instance of the new accommodation was offered by the EETPU's highly publicized enquiry regarding CBI membership. In the event, they were refused, but they did attend and speak at the 1985 conference. The recent expulsion of the union for its failure to comply with the Bridlington rules on membership poaching is the highwater mark of this policy and the recognition that, for the EETPU at least, this is not an issue which is marginal to them but one that can bring them security and growth. This is based on an estimation by the union of its recruitment chances; as Eric Hammond said: 'If we made a cold calculation we would have more members if we were outside the TUC than inside' (Hammond, 1985).

There is, in the analysis of the causes of the change in union attitudes, another feature that is cited which has resonances with many of the foregoing points. This is the effect of recession and technological restructuring upon labour markets. The argument runs that the older forms of job territory and job ownership are now being broken open by such influences. Hence the movements towards flexibility, work task integration, the separation of task from payment systems and the segmentation of the labour market into various tiers dependent not on skill but on flexibility, are breaking with old union boundaries and their union practices (Altmann and Dull, 1988, pp. 21–2). For instance, Cross cites the rise of the multi-skilled/multi-role engineer who is capable of providing polyvalent skills (Cross, 1985). Such flexibility is a challenge to existing craft-based union structures and the existing forms of workgroup representation who lose their distinct identities and clear interests. The Institute for Manpower Studies work undertaken by Atkinson (1984, also Atkinson and Meager, 1986) also show how the introduction of new technology and changing labour market conditions are leading to this growing segmentation of the workforce. Atkinson's model detects varying levels of workers who offer different kinds of flexibility: hence management can rely on strata of the workforce that are functionally flexible – in the case of the craftsmen, numerically flexible – and who have contracts that are loose or 'soft', and those who are financially flexible, responding to market forces on pay. The 'flexible firm' illustrates the varied ways in which the labour market within a firm can be adapted to both short-term and longer-term structural changes, be they technological or otherwise. Problems for trade unions arise from the difficulty of adapting to these new strata with old representational structures and in organizing the peripheral and temporary workforce who, according to ACAS (1985) and a report for GMBATU, are increasing in importance. The growing opportunism within the union movement is based on organizing such groups and offering a more 'progressive' face given the new circumstances of the 1980s.

Once more the notion of crisis is revealed as a complex one which cannot be merely associated with any single influence or with straightforward market recession arguments. There is no single unifying crisis that is hitting each union; instead there is a differentiated 'cocktail' of pressures bearing on the unions and with it a broad range of responses. The industrial unions in the declining 'smokestack' industries are facing quite different problems from unions in the retail, service or even light engineering sectors. Again the pressures may be leading to merger discussions, a growing hybridization and openness of union character, or again a move towards opportunistic recruiting and 'market unionism'. The movement towards single union deals is not exclusive to the EETPU; indeed, until July 1988 the EETPU had signed twenty-six agreements covering five thousand workers, whereas the T&GWU had agreed seventy-six deals and GUMBATU twenty-five (Smith, 1988). What is different in these cases is that the single union agreements do not come with the trappings of no-strike clauses, single status, flexibility provisions and enterprise participation programmes.

Although the thesis of a crisis is strongly put and difficult to ignore, one must be cautious in embracing it fully without consideration of the broader philosophic debate about trade unionism and its aims that has been a feature of the movement since its inception. We now want to consider the main points of the argument that states that this crisis is more than the structural shifts in the composition of the workforce and more than the immediate political attack on unions. At the heart of the Lane/Hobsbawm thesis is the idea that unions have lost their way politically and that this is the primary source of the pervading crisis. To address this question means looking at the accepted and historical division between 'politics' and 'economics' that trade unions in Britain have operated on, and to ask if there has been a real and significant shift in this. One might also ask if the new situation, with its particular combination of issues, has forced 'Labourism' into crisis. Is the division between the wings of the union movement a new one, or is the debate about the function, direction and political role of unions part of a continuing duality that has always been present?

The early debate

There is a large body of work on the issue of the appropriate political role of trade unions. Every major socialist theorist from Marx onwards has expressed a view regarding the contradictory position of trade unions in a capitalist society. This duality is based on the primary oppositional role that trade unions are forced to adopt given a capitalist mode of production. Hence to Marx, trade unionism is an explicit response to the exploitative capitalist wage relationship. In their trade unions, the workers

> continue to achieve equality of a sort with the capitalist in their contract regarding the sale of their labour. This is the rationale of the trade unions. (Marx, 1959, p. 1070)

But the very act of combination in opposition to the unjust sale of their labour power has profound political consequences. From such initial or immediate aims the trade unions become the focal point for the organization of a general working class offensive against the 'very system of wage labour itself' (Marx, in Lozovsky, 1972, p. 48).

Marx sees in trade unions a dual and interconnecting function. The first primarily economic, dealing with the day-to-day struggle with the owners of capital; the second political, as schools of socialism, as harbingers of class consciousness, with a 'historic mission' to end wage slavery. Marx's analysis is an optimistic one which sees no theoretical problem in holding to both functions. However, in actual trade union practice it is the function of improving wages and mitigating working conditions that tends to take precedence. He warns at one point that:

> The working class ought not to exaggerate to themselves the ultimate working of these day-to-day struggles. They ought not to forget that they are fighting with effects, but not with the causes of the effects; that they are retarding the downward movement, but not changing its direction; that they are applying palliatives not curing the malady. (Marx, 1977, p. 54)

Later theorists, Lenin in particular, take up this issue, asking whether trade unions can ever be an adequate vehicle for political change. His answer is firmly no, for trade unions are rooted within capitalist society: they are based in economism and spontaneity and being so promote a partial view of exploitation best characterized as a 'trade union' consciousness. For Lenin and later Gramsci, both theorists of the need for a revolutionary political party, trade unions do not produce a sufficient class consciousness. Rather, they represent:

> nothing but consciousness in an embryonic form . . . the class struggle in embryo. . . . A kopek added to the rouble is nearer and dearer to them than any socialism and any politics. (Lenin, 1921, pp. 62–3).

Gramsci's notion of 'industrial legality' also expresses succinctly the contradictory function that mature unionism spawns: as Kelly indicates, the creation of collective bargaining, its legislation and the cadres that operate within it lead to the acceptance of that compromise form of industrial legality as the 'permanent, normal and desirable state of affairs' (Gramsci, 1971, pp. 158–69); Kelly, 1988, pp. 56–7). These arguments regarding the limitations of trade unions as direct political actors have been summarized by Anderson. He too refers to unions as a necessary form that occurs within capital, capable only of expressing rather than transcending the capital–labour struggle. They are an institutional reflection of their capitalist environment, adopting to the 'natural hue of the closed capital dominated environment of the factory itself' (Anderson, 1967). They are essentially defensive organizations whose main weapon is an 'absence'; hence they are limited in their capability. Furthermore, their sociological base is not universal as is a party, it excludes intellectuals who are able to widen the cultural–political basis and consciousness. Lastly, for him, the unions' effectiveness is limited to one sphere of society, namely industry and commerce and cannot by that token present a structured and total challenge to the state. Syndicalism (the use of trade unions to achieve socialism) had its heyday in the period prior to 1926, in Britain the main protagonists against such a politization of trade unions were the Webbs. Their criticisms echoed much of the foregoing analysis. In their study of the practice of unionism they saw three main functions: unions were primarily collective bargainers; they provided mutual insurance, and they sought legal enactment to forward their interests. Prior to working people gaining suffrage the pressure that could be exerted politically in the latter function was limited and fitful. By means of petition, demonstration, lobbies and appeals, trade unions acquired legal stature and could mount campaigns around substantive issues. However, with the advent of the Labour Party as the 'political arm of labour', this set of functions became detached from the unions. In effect, by the 1920s, syndicalism, trade unions as agents of revolutionary political change, had been put down and new boundaries of legitimate activity were in force that separated unions from a 'political' role as defined within the reformist parliamentary arena.

This separation of the political from the economic is what Miliband (1973) denotes as 'Labourism', Britain's particular adaptation to the problems of trade union politics. Hyman puts it thus:

> The very existence of the Labour Party stems from the belief that 'politics' is external to unions' central functions and interests. 'Labourism' entails a definition of workers' interests within the framework of the existing social order and an identification of 'politics' (as a sphere of social and economic aims and aspirations transcending the immediate agenda of collective bargaining) with the institutional arena of parliamentary government. (Hyman, 1984, p. 58)

When, then, in the late 1960s the New Left Review began to reassert the importance of trade unions' implicit and oppositional class role, they were in effect taking up and reopening that old debate, the difference being that now the attack was also launched on the failings of the Labour Party as the political wing of the movement. It also attributed the source of political vitality to the workers, whether in or out of the union movement. However, once again this 'political vitality' is spontaneous and undirected and in need of a revolutionary body of theory to direct it: one which the rising New Left was willing to supply. (See Thompson, 1965, and Panitch, 1977.)

The pluralist debate

One school of industrial relations theory has achieved prominence in Britain and has had an influence in determining much of the state's approach both to trade unions and to the reform of industrial relations. This has become known as the Oxford School, which numbered among its ranks such people as Alan Flanders, Alan Fox and Hugh Clegg. Its importance can be seen in its writings, in the shaping of industrial relations practices, and in its work for the Donovan Commission of the 1960s. Its view of trade unions' function was nurtured specifically within the ambit of the post-war settlement and founded on a period of economic growth and relative political stability. In many respects, Labourism (the division of trade unions' political and economic function) was a given: trade unions were essentially economic agents and a necessary part of a pluralist society in that they balanced the power of management. As Fox puts it:

> Through collective organisation in trade unions . . . employees mobilise themselves to meet management on equal terms to negotiate the terms of their collaboration. The pluralist does not claim anything approaching perfection for this system. . . . Imbalances in strength . . . may be such that for one side or the other justice is distinctly rough. They are not seen as so numerous or severe, however, as generally to discredit the system either from the union's point of view or from management's. (Fox, 1974, p. 10)

As Flanders pointed out, the nature of the bargain that the unions and management strike is not a simple process. It may indeed forward the substantive economic interests of its members but it does more than this:

> It is also a rule-making process. The rules it makes can be seen in the contents of collective agreements. In other words, one of the principal purposes of trade unions in collective bargaining is regulation or control. (Flanders, 1970, p. 42)

Unions have then a 'political' role but it is a micro-political one, aiming at the equalization of power within organizations, regulating and controlling the unfettered rule of management. This ability to enforce substantive and procedural rules results in tangible gains for the membership and this school of thought represents the true *raison d'être* of trade unionism. Flanders is scathing about Anderson's contempt for 'pure and simple' trade unionism:

> Trade unions, by doggedly sticking to their immediate end, and refusing to be captured and exploited by any political party, have gradually transformed society. (Flanders, 1970, p. 39)

By stating with clarity the purpose of trade unions, i.e. as agents of regulation, Flanders is also reaffirming the boundaries of their action and simultaneously defining the constituents of 'order' in as much as the proper rules of the game are being observed.

This kind of analysis animated the Donovan Report (Donovan Commission, 1968), centred as it was on the growing problem of 'disorder' in the British industrial relations system. The main expressions of that disorder could be detected in three main areas: a growing strike problem, a series of restrictive practices and a wage drift that outstripped productivity increases. These three problems were not directly attributable to trade unions, rather it was the institutions of industrial relations that were in need of reform. Order needed to be restored, but within the traditions of voluntarism where legal enactments would be minimized and the state assigned a neutral role.

Goldthorpe identified a number of telling points regarding the orientation of this period. Primarily, he sees in the triumph of that particular branch of reformism, a management definition of order. To him the problems identified as disorderly were the result of trade unions pursuing and protecting their interests. He makes the point that if order had been pursued from a trade union/workforce perspective then we would have specified different problem areas and additionally have cogent arguments at hand for these apparently disorderly patterns of behaviour.

The narrowness of the function of trade unions defined by the Oxford School, where trade unions act as regulators, as balancing agents within a pluralist society, was attacked by Goldthorpe on a wider basis. He saw their analysis as being rigidly determined by the period in which it was set, promulgating an ideology appropriate to it, i.e. one of consensus, founded on limited state involvement, voluntary regulation of industrial relations and shared economic prosperity. Hence:

> [The] liberal commitment to voluntary reform is one which would be appropriate to a society in which there already existed some broad consensus on the principles governing the organization of production and the distribution of the product: that is to say, a society in which any disorder in industrial relations could correctly be attributed to institutional malfunctioning, and in which a general interest could then be assumed to exist in devising and implementing those institutional forms which would maintain order by, as it were, providing the channels through which the underlying consensus could best emerge. Given, however, an actual society which falls far short of this consensual model, and in which economic life is a matter of individuals and groups exploiting as best they can their positions within a generally unprincipled structure of power and advantage, the divergence of interest and value among the parties to industrial relations will tend always to militate against the possibility of their concerted action towards 'reform'. (Goldthorpe, 1977, p. 214)

The essence of the argument for Goldthorpe is that this form of liberal pluralism depends on a pre-existing consensus that renders areas of conflict both manageable and non-challenging. Thus although trade unions and management may come into conflict from time to time, there is underlying agreement about how the game is played and will be adhered to. In the context of 'Butskellism' this may have been appropriate and industrial relations could appear as a game whose regulation was essentially voluntaristic, two-sided and self-regulatory. However, as the post-war situation changes in its economic, political and social dimensions, so does the settlement upon which such liberal pluralism rested.

As the earlier parts of this chapter illustrated, some of these changes were easily documented in terms of recession and political oscillations, but others are woven deeper into the fabric of Britain's post-war circumstances. So the three truths upon which the pluralist analysis rested – the minimal state and voluntarism, trade unions as 'micro-political' regulators (collective individualism), and an 'environment of consensus' which contains conflict – are increasingly undermined. Different authors have stressed how at the same time as this analysis was being given credence there was evidence of contradictory tendencies. Whilst trying to avoid simplification of these stand-points, the main components of this change appear to be: the politicization of industrial relations, the rise of the strong state, and the breakdown of consensus.

Many of the arguments are interconnected, as Fox (1985) so ably shows. For him the process of change finds its root in the clear failure of British capital to develop the economy given the opportunities of the 1950s. Invest-ment in British industry was forsaken and instead there was a massive flight of capital out of the country, a virtual investment strike which held consequences for later internal relationships. So whilst the short term saw an increase in trade union ability to wrest pay increases, the underlying weakness, the growing productivity gap and inflationary cycle were establishing a political language, a repertoire of explanations regarding instability:

> Given its reluctance to submit to the implications of policies decided elsewhere, it was organised labour which was publicly identified as the 'cause' of the instability. (Fox 1985, p. 378)

So whilst the 1950s may have been labelled the 'age of affluence' these subterranean economic weaknesses 'were not to emerge as salient until the 1960s, nor become major problems until the 1970s' (pp. 378–9).

The Donovan Commission in its attribution of cause and effect was itself taking part in this elaboration of trade union culpability but against a back-ground where its recommendations could not directly address the roots of the 'disorder'. These longer-term changes were instead being expressed in a growing politicization of industrial relations that, having defined its language and agents of disorder, then expressed itself in active intervention through a range and battery of measures that were to culminate in the Thatcher onslaught. This movement can also be seen in the growing use of incomes policies, the involvement of governments and their agencies in productivity issues, health and safety, and a host of other substantive areas, trade union involvement in tripartite groups deciding economics or policy issues, the growth of legislation on collective and individual employment matters and the later Social Contract. As Fox points out, the growth of this intervention meant that for many trade union members their incomes and working conditions came to depend on government policy. The growing interdependence of decisions at a national level with the expectations of members was a direct politicizing agent: no longer could the state be seen to adopt a minimalist stance:

> The ideology of state 'even-handedness' between the classes had rested, for such plausibility as it had, upon the minimal state and the separation between economics and politics. So long as the state could manage to display some conviction in effecting to hold aloof from substantive policy intervention, it was possible to invoke as one of the legitimations of the system the myth of state impartiality. When,

however, the state was manifestly no longer holding the ring but moving, however reluctantly, into it, each contestant was bound to become alive to the issue of whether state participation in the arena was on balance benefiting itself or its opponent. (p. 406)

Industrial relations and a trade union's role and function were not simply the result of voluntary activity agreed between the parties to independent collective agreements. Whilst the period was nominally one of a growing use of collective agreements at plant and company level, subsequent changes have highlighted not the entrenched strength of that form of regulation but to a large extent its weakness, its fragmentation and tendency to sectionalism. The focus on the 'growth' in shop steward organization in surveys of workplace industrial relations (Brown, 1981) is important, but this should not be separated from the context, the overall environment that made those formats/institutions powerful or significant.

Fox's thesis suggests that the longer-running tendencies of structural economic weakness, the growing politicization of industrial relations and the change in the role of the state were more important factors in determining unions' abilities to withstand the ensuing political change represented by Thatcherism. For here, under the guise of the 'free market' or the *laissez faire* state was the most sustained state-led onslaught against trade unions. The attempt was made to end the political importance of organized labour, to re-inaugurate on a changed basis the tenets of Labourism, i.e. the separation of economics and politics. Gamble, in 1974, recognized this feature of Conservatism as a recurring motif, as an ingrained response to industrial pressure by unions:

> Conservative dealings with the unions have one overriding aim: it is to separate unionism as a political and as an economic force, and to squeeze the life out of the former. (Gamble, cited in Fox, 1985, p. 403)

What was different about the period post-1979 was the ability of the government to enact that separation in the context of low support for and wide-ranging disillusionment with Labour Party policies. The withdrawal of legitimacy from trade unionists, the dismantling of tripartitism and the hostility towards any form of trade union influence on policy-making were first steps. These were followed by a series of legal measures (see pp. 90–2) including the naked attempts to disassociate them from the Labour Party through the political funds ballots. It has resulted too in the use of police and troops on an unprecedented scale with the bending and adoption of measures in support of them (Hain, 1986).

Fox's analysis of the factors influencing trade union activity in the 1980s is multi-faceted and does not mechanically separate out any given one. In as much as we look for a thesis regarding trade unions in crisis we see instead a 'crisis of voluntarism', a distinct shift in the state's view of industrial relations and because of this a crisis of Labourism. For him the unions have been contributory factors in this process, supporting at one and the same time an ambiguous form of political corporatism which gave unions legal protections and some influence in industrial and political decision-making. They also sought an economic liberalism, a 'freedom' to pursue their own interests via 'free' collective bargaining. This has consequences for the unions when the political agenda changes and market principles are applied across the board, given their support for 'freedom' from incomes policies and for being part of the 'free for all' then their rationales for opposing that set of principles reified in monetarism becomes increasingly strained:

> Trade unionists in creating machinery for a certain measure for their own emancipation, were also to some extent spinning a web for their own entrapment. (Fox, 1985, p. 436)

Hyman (1984, p. 47) takes up this theme. He too depicts the growing politicization of industrial relations and the strains on that form of Labourism that held up to the 1970s. He points out that although the growth of unions in the white collar sector may well have tended to break the link between them and the Labour Party, the state has intensified the political issues bearing on such unions. This has strained severely the balance of action that unions have to respond to; it shows how far the analysis has moved from the Oxford School's two agent, voluntaristic bargainers set within a self-regulatory system. The current situation shows the influence of 'significant others' in that process of regulation – primarily the state; it also shows how changes external to enterprise bear upon the context and the ability of the parties to conclude those bargains. Not only has the state become active, but the parties within the system can gain or lose power: the premise that trade unions automatically or in essence provide 'countervailing power' or ensure an equality of power has been shown to be suspect. During the 1980s the ideological basis of trade union activity has shifted, the rise of the New Right has influenced managerial pronouncements regarding trade union legitimacy to the extent that some are calling for revenge for the period when they were 'held to ransom'.

What Hyman rightly asks for, is a rejection of pre-given models of unions' political or economic role but instead to see them as:

> secondary or intermediate institutions . . . already 'organised' by those to whom they sell their labour power and whose actions they are designed to influence; and unions' policies are shaped by this pragmatic mediation between the members they represent and the external agencies with which they deal. (Hyman, 1984, p. 61)

Hence trade unions' functions and aims are determined by three main areas of pressure: from external influences – those 'significant others' of the state, employers and other agencies; from their members' own aims, and by the particular method of policy formulation and internal processes that they adopt. Most analyses of trade unions have tended to operate on a distinction between the organizational strength of the unions and to the more subjective or conceptual strengths represented by notions of solidarity, fundamental aims, etc. Hyman instead looks to other interconnections:

> Any adequate interpretation of trade union development must therefore link theoretically the active initiative of members and representatives, the purposes and ideologies which inform their actions, and the external material forces which influence and constrain them. (p. 61)

In such a way we can begin to understand not the slipping of the trade union movement into crisis, but instead tease out the particular features bearing on unions with varied membership potential in different sectors. This kind of analysis is, unfortunately, not available at present. In all the foregoing we have explanations of crisis attributed to trade unions in general but, as with all real world experience, this is not universally applicable: there are still unions in growth, there are unions adapting easily to the new situation, there is diversity of strategy and aim. Hence, broad arguments employed by Hobsbawm, Lane and Fox are a starting point – the contexts within which to situate the crisis facing unionism as a whole. The next important step is to take Hyman's injunction and begin to differentiate the crisis as it affects those individual unions.

TRADE UNIONS' RESPONSE TO CRISIS

This is not the place to attempt to detail the effects of those substantial changes on individual unions. Hyman has attempted to do this to a limited extent (Hyman, 1984), but restricts himself to major unions and general responses to critical policy issues. What can be said is that each union has distinct internal constitutions and policy machines that mediate pressures, that memberships are different in skill, gender and expectations, and they do have varying mixes of public and private, manufacturing and service sector membership. If we consider such variables against the background of the multi-stranded indicators of crisis previously stated (see pp. 77–87) we can see that a general model of crisis would be difficult to apply with conviction. Hyman and Fryer (1975) look at the effects of changes in external material forces on the policy-making bodies and organization features of unions, from this they gain indications about why some trade unions move towards the 'business-unionism' model in periods of organizational challenge. However, as this chapter has tried to suggest, the notion of a simple set of responses to crisis is difficult to sustain. It is not simply an opposition of a radicalized political vision versus opportunistic right wing movement towards American-style unionism (a style which in trade union terms has been singularly un-successful in mobilizing a mass membership in the United States (Milton,

1986), with membership dropping below 18 per cent of the workforce and all but wiped out in some states).

In the British situation there are contradictory trends in the context of recession, for as Batstone has pointed out:

> The range of bargaining is still significant, although it has declined somewhat over the last five years, largely due to the adoption of 'macho' tactics by a minority of managers. (1984, p. 294)

Batstone contends that shop steward influence remains high and suggests that shop stewards can still constrain management freedom of action. This is in line with evidence on membership that Kelly also uses which indicates no serious threat to basic unions' structures. Furthermore, an analysis of those in work suggests that 'real wages have kept pace with inflation during the recession'.

> One of the most intriguing features of the recession has been the capacity of trade unions through collective bargaining to achieve rates of pay rise equal to or greater than the rate of price increase. (Kelly, 1988, p. 273)

This tends once more to underline the diverse situations encapsulated in the phrases regarding 'trade unions' and 'crisis'. There always have been contending arguments about strategy, function and structures of unions in crisis. This debate has intensified and with the post-war pressures of change pushing unions to adopt different structural responses, with no common pattern:

> [They are not] developing in any easily discernible direction according to a common pattern or trend. Indeed if anything, the government and structure of British unions appear to be more diverse, contradictory and conflicting at the end of our period of study than they were in 1961. (Undy *et al.*, 1981, p. 23)

However one classifies unions, be it industrial, craft, general and white collar, or along open and closed lines, or between democratic and autocratic, this does not take on board the deeper differences in approach of aim and function expressed in the debate about unions' proper oppositional role. Figure 4.1 sets

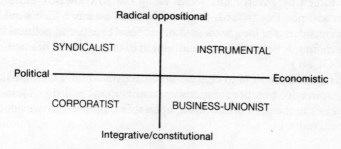

Figure 4.1 Matrix showing union functions (horizontal axis) in relation to oppositional role (vertical axis).

out the relationship between these two dimensions and shows how Scargill and Hammond can be part of the same movement but take very different paths. One axis takes the continuum of economic versus political activity as a base whilst the other points at the strategies used in terms of oppositional or integrative approaches. This is a somewhat crude division but is heuristically useful when considering union positions and directions of travel.

Broadly, we can see four main trade union orientations to strategy and activity laid out in the figure. Whilst the syndicalist category may seem somewhat historical in the UK, much of the Institute for Workers Control literature in the 1960s and 1970s was steeped in this tradition as were many of the shop steward activists. If one looks at the arguments put forward by Fox, Hyman, Hobsbawm and Lane in this light, then the pattern of movement is seen by them as consistently from left to right. The politicization of industrial relations has not necessarily resulted in an overtly politicized union movement, for the corporatist strategy has in effect been denied them: for the politicization of industrial relations in the absence of a Labour government in power causes Labourism to become a self-defeating strategy especially when one takes Fox's argument about the death of consensus and the minimal state into account. In general terms, then, union strategy has had to be founded on the strengths in the membership and in the membership's ability to act. This has meant the rise of radical instrumentalism on the one side – exemplified in the actions and rhetoric of Scargill – and integrative instrumentalism on the other, as with the EETPU. In the aftermath of the Wapping dispute, the options for trade unionism were seen clearly following this dichotomy, when faced with 'Hammondism', the only 'coherent alternative presently on offer is Scargillism' (Lloyd, 1988, p. 17). With the defeat of the miners the latter is in abeyance and the trend appears to lie in the acceptance of the new realism and accommodative strategies. It is also possible to show with the boxes of the matrix how pressures on individual unions have forced them to move in a certain direction. If one took the CPSA, for example, then from what was likely to be judged an integrative and fairly corporatist union in strategic terms, has been forced by government action along the axis towards more overt opposition and possibly towards forms of political activity which would not have been considered before, witness their proposal to ballot on political funds which has definitely been taken as a movement in their political orientation as a result of GCHQ.

The crisis has done little to concert union activity. The TUC remains as weak in its directive functions: unions are autonomous and do choose their own responses to the pressures bearing upon them. In this they are adhering to traditional traits, i.e.:

[Britain's] most persistent dispositions are individualism, both atomistic and collectivist, and the tradition of the minimal state. (Fox, 1985, p. 439)

It is this tendency that Fox sees as an obstacle to an easy designation of answers to the question of trends in industrial relations. Unions are party to society's influence and have in their responses to these institutions, customs and significant others fashioned their own responses and disconnected strategies.

CONCLUSION

This chapter has looked at the kinds of arguments offered that underpin the claims about crisis in the trade unions. The recurring theme is that of the duality of the aims that underlies trade union activity, and how in problem periods such duality become manifest. What is said to be distinctive about this designated crisis is the loss of political direction and the inability to designate a vision of equity to which unions might subscribe. This is witnessed by the movement towards a radical instrumentalism and to a form of business unionism exemplified by 'Hammondism'. The question that remains is whether the 1980s 'crisis' represents a decisive break with those older debates and if the current oscillation of strategy is one that counterposes what are essentially two different kinds of instrumentalism.

The arguments about recomposition can be overstated but it does appear to be the most important long-run factor affecting the unions, especially in terms of recruitment and policy arguments, and it underlies many of the flashpoints of the recent past. The direction that this indicates is difficult to predict, for whilst we might agree on the underlying influences pressing for change there is still an effort of interpretation needed to pin them down. For the changes occurring are varied, with at least three identifiable. There is a long-term declining unionism that is sectorally specific, mainly affecting unions with an industrial character, i.e. NUM, NUR, printing and steel unions. There are, at the same time, direct challenges to unionization. We might call these anti-unionism encased not only in state attacks such as GCHQ but also in the 'union-busting' activities of some consultants. We also see how imported models of non-unionism have gained ground (Beaumont, 1987; Cressey, 1986).

As a response to such changes and the needs to ward off organizational crisis there is a hybridization of unionism taking place in which the old characteristics of craft, industrial and general unions are becoming difficult to sustain or use meaningfully in the face of conglomerate unionism such as that of the Manufacturing, Science and Finance Union. This hybridization, together with the wave of amalgamations in the late 1980s, culminating in the NUPE/NALGO/COHSE talks, is profoundly reshaping the union landscape.

In this sense we might be witnessing a segmentation that is qualitatively different from before, which shifts away from the old aristocracy/craft and unskilled/general union dichotomy into a more finely-grained situation where the problems that those unions and union structures confronted become simply redundant and unhelpful in analysing current practice. Such a segmentation will pose severe problems for the unions in terms of a general appeal to solidarity or class identity and similarly for the Labour Party in its relationship with the broad swathe of unions and through them working people.

The second element of the 'crisis' appears to be a crisis of Labourism. What distinguishes the 1980s from the 1930s is that there has been the experience of Labour holding political power for thirteen years. There is a sense in which the future does not hold either the promise or the capacity for experimentation that it did then. Furthermore, the ability to reconstruct a socialist/Labour movement programme in which trade unions have a leading role as popular articulators of progressive policies seems, as of now, to be somewhat distant. As unions adapt to market and political changes so the political strategies and relationships that have been held need to be rethought. Kelly in his conclusion asks if the British labour movement can now be seen as an adequate base on which to build a class consciousness:

> Some labour movements, such as those in Sweden or Italy, may be able to construct class-conscious majorities, but the fragmented nature of trade unions and industrial relations makes this an extremely difficult task in Britain. (Kelly, 1988, p. 303)

This means a relative downgrading of the union voice in the movement unless the unions can rediscover and adapt the impulse towards equity into popular policies for the 1990s. The question posed by Lane in his *Marxism Today* article about future union strategies still holds: will they simply wait for a market upturn hoping that they remain structurally intact so that they can then pull on their kicking boots? Or will the unions recognize that they have an opportunity to reform and reassess the kinds of political relations that they might forge, based on a changing industrial profile with new possibilities in terms of membership relations?

The other factor unmentioned so far but becoming increasingly important is the role of unions in relation to Europe. The 'social Europe' package – the opportunities for enhanced worker participation, enhanced protections and benefits currently being discussed in the Commission and Strasbourg Parliament – adds a dimension to the potential rethink that should not be underestimated. The social charter, the European Company Statute and the calls for enhanced social dialogue might reawaken the confidence of British labour, for the lessons of the 1980s and the monetarist onslaught may induce unions to seek forms of institutional influence in the enterprise represented by workers' councils and co-determination. This together with a European-level package of protections and the upgrading of the floors of basic rights in areas such as working environment, health and safety, training and redundancy arrangements might provide one basis for renewal.

5

INDUSTRIAL CONFLICT – A MEASURE
OF CRISIS?

A great deal of attention has been given to one form of industrial conflict, the strike. It is only one of a number of forms of industrial action which may express worker discontent. However, although there are boundary problems as to what to include in the category, it is clear, as Edwards points out, that: 'the strike is a fairly distinct type of event which can be studied separately from other forms of job action' (Edwards, 1981, pp. 297–8). But does the fact that they are readily identifiable justify the attention? According to Edwards they are, because they break the usual pattern of 'order' in industry: 'If conflict is central to processes of social change, the strike, as an extreme form of industrial conflict, is an important subject for study' (p. 298). If this is so then we would be justified in looking at strike trends in a particular country. We could then ask whether this provides any basis for comparing one country with another. There are a number of studies which have this as their aim; we take some examples for expository purposes and see how fruitful this is. Such a project is not as straightforward as we might wish, but in exploring the problems we hope to show how attempts are made to construct explanations about the nature of industrial conflict in particular societies.

FRANCE

A good place to start is with Shorter and Tilly (1974). This is not only because of its intrinsic interest but also because it provides a point of continuing reference and comparison. There is a clear sociological dimension to the work. Whilst the authors focus on the strike as a distinctive form of collective action, they want to relate strike activity to other forms of conflict and collective action, where possible, such as the growth of unionization.

How are strikes to be explained? Shorter and Tilly suggest that three distinct emphases may be located. There are those which point to strikes as a product of deprivation; those which reference breakdown, discontinuities in social arrangements that lead to anomie; and those which focus on interests – groups of people organizing around a collective definition of interests and discovering or developing their power position in the process. Shorter and Tilly take three well-known contributions to illustrate these emphases. Kerr offers a version of the deprivation thesis, with the leading idea that although dissatisfactions at work persist, the nature of the response changes. We are offered a broadly evolutionary picture of the institutionalization of conflict in industry (Kerr, 1960). Hence there is postulated a natural history of labour commitment, which over the long run has this kind of sequence:

> The form of protest also shifts from the individual's protest expressed through turnover and absenteeism, to the guerilla warfare of the quickie strike or boycott over immediate dissatisfactions, to permanently organised economic or political action or both, and finally to the petty and covert sabotage of the trained bureaucrat whose chains can be rattled a bit but never lost. (Kerr, 1960, pp. 335–6)

The thesis embraced by Kerr was further developed in *Industrialism and Industrial Man* (Kerr *et al.*, 1960). One of the features of pluralistic industrialism towards which, they maintain, industrial societies are evolving, is a movement from class war to bureaucratic gamesmanship. Hence they point not only to a relationship between social structure and forms of protest, but also to changes in the incidence and intensity of them:

> Persuasion, pressure and manipulation will take the place of face to face combat of an earlier age. The conflict will also be, by and large, over narrower issues than in earlier times when there was real disagreement over the nature of and the arrangements within industrial society. It will be less between the broad programmes of capital and labour, and of agriculture and industry; and more over budgets, rates of compensation, work norms, job assignments. The great battles over conflicting manifestos will be replaced by a myriad of minor contests over comparative details. (Kerr *et al.*, 1960, pp. 292–3)

As Shorter and Tilly see it, whilst Kerr has a long view of the role of conflict in industrial societies, the deprivation argument applies to short-term considerations and most conspicuously in the early period of industrialization so far as strikes are concerned.

The notion of strikes as a consequence of social breakdown is illustrated by Smelser (1959). In general terms this is the argument that the process of structural differentiation which accompanies industrialization leads to disorientation and anomie in the lives of people. The strain thus generated leads to social protest, including strikes. Although drawing upon Parsonian systems theory, Smelser's work clearly has affinities with that of Durkheim. Shorter and Tilly describe this as a medium-run approach to the explanation of strikes, although they are not precise on what they understand by medium-run.

The argument which relates strikes to contending interests tends to focus on changes in the structure of power and communication in the process of industrialization. Here Thompson (1968) is the example proferred. The collective action of British workers is partly explained by Thompson in terms of traditional rights to land, work and bread under the 'moral economy' of the eighteenth century and which the expansion of markets and rise of the factory system and urbanization were threatening. In addition, as the nineteenth century progressed, working class interests were expressed in new forms of consciousness and action. This emerged in concrete historical circumstances in response to demands and pressures placed upon them by industrial capitalists. The articulation of interests leading to collective action is, in Shorter and Tilly's view, best treated as a medium to long-run explanation.

The thrust of Shorter and Tilly's review is therefore to identify deprivation, breakdown and interest as three kinds of explanation and cross-classify them against short, medium and long-run perspectives. It does not follow, nor do they imply, that the three types of explanation are mutually exclusive. Rather the suggestion is that they are each most plausible within different time frames. Nevertheless, their own stated position is different:

> We shall offer much argument and some evidence, to the effect that breakdown of social bonds and controls tends to reduce rather than to increase the capacity of the affected population for collective action. We will concede somewhat more to deprivation, especially in the short-run, but will generally insist that it only spurs collective action where organisation of the deprived population is already extensive and its interests well articulated. On the whole, our line of arguments runs along the interest row of the matrix: short-run interest, medium-run interest, long-run interest as well. (Shorter and Tilly, 1974, p. 89)

The basic position taken up by Shorter and Tilly is that economic, organizational and political interests operate at all time scales. Derived from this is the general proposition that prosperity favours strikes and economic hardship hinders them. But it is conceded, as a qualification, that well-organized workforces will promote defiant struggles for survival in economic recession and in this respect the deprivation thesis is given limited support. In addition, they contend that as a labour organization develops, the strike as a political weapon is fostered. This is essentially an 'interest' argument:

> Strikes have an important role in the struggle for power. We go beyond the vast majority of interest accounts as well, since they treat strikes as relatively direct expressions of changing economic interests. In our account, economic interests only find their expression in strike activity in so far as they are mediated and supported by organisation for collective action. The existence of that organisation, moreover, involves workers in the struggle for political power, and makes the strike available as a political weapon. How widely it is used for that purpose will vary from time to time and country to country, depending on the nature of the accommodation the leaders of organised labour have made with other wielders of power. But once labour has organised on a national scale, we expect the capacity to strike to be its most important weapon in the struggle for power. (p. 10)

Intertwined with the emphasis on organizational interests and the posited relationship between strike activity and economic prosperity is a concern with the significance of the organization of production in its effect on strike activity. The authors make use of Touraine's threefold developmental account of shifts in technology: the artisanal, mass production and science-sector phases (Touraine, 1965). Indeed, this categorization is used by Shorter and Tilly as a means of periodizing the historical experience of strike activity in France. It can be summarised as follows.

Period 1: 1800–1880, the artisanal phase. The empirical reference is to craftsmen and apprentices or groups like miners with a strong occupational identity, working in small enterprises, whose hierarchies are connected by formal and informal networks of relationships, which can promote local solidarity. The workers have immediate control over and contact with their materials. Industrial glassmaking is a good example.

Period 2: 1880–1945, the mass production phase. This is associated with the conveyor belt, repetitive, low-skilled tasks and a loss of job control in the wake of the technological imperatives of the assembly line. Textile mills and later car factories stand as central examples. The technology is combined with an administrative system which is most fully developed under the principles of Taylorism, which in France was evident from 1910.

Period 3: 1945 onwards, the science-sector phase. The empirical reference here is to automated, continuous process plants such as chemicals. As in the artisanal phase, the worker has an overview of the productive process and has some power and responsibility for what goes on. The basis of the organization is different, however. Craft consciousness is replaced by enterprise consciousness. This is fostered by liberal personnel policies – high wages, generous pensions and fringe benefits – all of which serve to integrate the employee into the plant. Touraine himself described this categorization as an evolutionary movement (clearly different from Kerr's scheme already mentioned on page 106). In his terms the movement is from a 'professional' system of work to a 'technical' one, with the intervening mass production phase seen as an alienating, dehumanizing production system, with its fragmenting detailed division of labour, with little opportunity for the worker to exercise control and responsibility over the nature and quality of the product.

We can see, therefore, that Shorter and Tilly, in reviewing approaches for the explanation of strikes are actually wanting to replace them with another framework within which they seek to interpret raw empirical data on strikes, so far as they can discover it. In this way the attempt is made to give social significance to the strike statistics:

> The single most compelling fact of French strike history is the enormous increase in the sheer number of strikes during the last century and a half. The incidence of strikes, both in absolute numbers and relative to the labour force available for

participation in conflict, rose almost steadily from the 1880s, when concentrated working class organisational efforts began, until after the Second World War. (Shorter and Tilly, 1974, p. 47)

But to bring even more purchase on the matter, Shorter and Tilly cross-classify the threefold organization of production (with its periodization) against the type of labour organization (see Figure 5.1).

The arrow in the figure indicates the co-existence of industrial unionism in large enterprises (accompanied by a growing concentration of ownership) with the decentralized enterprise unionism, associated in France with the CFDT (Confederation française democratique du travail). The figure summarizes and underpins a crucial part of Shorter and Tilly's argument that 'the configuration of industrial technology, shopfloor relations and working-class institutions one finds for each of these phases produces substantially different styles of strike activity' (p. 17).

That is why it is not only the number of strikes which has to be considered but also their duration and the numbers of strikers involved. Shorter and Tilly point out that the 'shape' of strikes as affected by these dimensions has tended to change over the total time period in France.

The early period tended to involve few workers in small plants. The strikes could last for quite a long time but were not frequent. In contrast, by the 1960s strikes involved on average over five hundred workers but usually did not last longer than a day. The change was from small-scale, intense but relatively unusual events to large-scale, calculated everyday activities. This leads Shorter and Tilly to the general conclusion that strikes do not necessarily decline as industrialism proceeds. Instead they suggest an association between large, short duration strikes and politically active unions. More particularly, in the case of France this is identified with the rise of

Organization of production	Craft union	Industrial union	Plant-level organizations
Artisanal	Decentralized narrowly occupational		
Mass production		Centralized bureaucracies	
Science-sector		↓	Enterprise unionism

Figure 5.1 Type of labour organization.

the Popular Front in 1936 when there was a wave of sit-down strikes and a generally turbulent period of industrial relations.

Shorter and Tilly's overarching theme is that politics and organization are inherent features of collective action. Hence to look at strike waves would be to look for variations in political life and organizational forms. They do in fact offer a succinct summary of their argument which seeks to encompass the 138 years covered in the book. It is a clear statement but complex in its ramifications:

> The timing of strike waves depends largely on the timing of political crises, but their form is the result of somewhat more complex combinations of circumstances. Some aspects of waves are determined by such variables as technological change, which operate in a rather *cyclical* fashion, going from artisanal to mechanical, then back again to the post Second World War period to a modern adaptation of the classic artisanal. Other aspects of waves are determined by changes in French society that seem to go in a *linear* way, becoming more and more pronounced with the passage of time instead of oscillating. We have in mind here: (1) the 'nationalisation' of working-class politics, a process which commenced with the mobilisation of the 1880s and 1890s; and (2) an increase in the scale of those institutions regulating working-class life which has been in progress since the days of Louis Napoleon. (p. 105)

Shorter and Tilly do provide us with a wealth of statistical detail and an illuminating commentary, together with illustrative accounts of particular strikes. For our purposes it suffices to emphasize certain points about their approach. Firstly, it contains a theoretically informed approach to the problem of analysing strikes. The study of strikes over an extended period is seen as a way into a more general problem, namely, how to account for the relationship between social change in an industrial society and the organizational and political concomitants of collective action in general and industrial conflict in particular.

Secondly, the attempt is made to use the study as a way of testing existing theories of industrial conflict. Take, for example, their discussion of regional variations in strike activity in France. They conclude:

> One clear message emerges from our analysis: the city helped to transform the nature of industrial conflict. As time passed, the bulk of the strikes became concentrated in the greatest city, Paris, the hub of French social and political life. At any given point in time the metropolis was more conducive to effective organisation and intense conflict than either the small town or the isolated cluster of industry. (p. 283)

This is contrary to the thesis found in the well-known article by Kerr and Siegel on inter-industry differences in strike proneness (Kerr and Siegel, 1954). According to them, strike-proneness is notably to be found among the 'isolated mass': homogeneous occupational groups of geographically and/or socially isolated workers. Yet Shorter and Tilly show that, at least in France, it is not the isolated but those workers who are integrated in the wider society that were the most strike-ridden. They reason that this is not so surprising since organization is easier to accomplish. Moreover, 'if the strike was, as we have claimed, a means of mobilising workers for political action, the most suitable locus for strike activity would be under the noses of politicians and administrators' (p. 283).

Thirdly, even more general theoretical issues in social theory are addressed. In particular, there is a coda on Marx. In effect Shorter and Tilly point out that it is not news to Marxists to emphasize the political dimensions of strikes since Marx saw industrial relations, class relations and relations of power as inextricably linked. But there is a caveat:

> What may more seriously upset Marxist arguments is our speculation that a fourth major phase in the interrelationship between economic change and political protest is now afoot, in the form of disputes among office-workers and science-sector professionals. These people are not exploited toilers at all, and attempts to explain away their militancy as that of a 'white-collar proletariat' are bound to miss an essential reality. (p. 350)

Lastly, Shorter and Tilly embark on an ambitious attempt to put French strike statistics into an international perspective. They take two periods for which they claim to have adequate data – 1900–29 and 1945–68 – and using the three criteria of frequency, duration and numbers involved compare thirteen western industrial countries (see Table 5.1). On the basis of this they seek to identify both the similarities and differences and to suggest why they are as they are. For the period 1900–29, whilst some differences between countries are acknowledged, Shorter and Tilly are far more impressed with the similarities. They explained them as follows:

> In the first half of the twentieth century the working classes in all western countries mobilised themselves for political action, with varying degrees of effectiveness and within disparate constellations of national politics; this mobilisation generated everywhere a great wave of strike activity, observing the essential similarity of patterns of conflict among workers with similar modes of representation in the central polity. (p. 306)

Given that, allowing for differences of detail, there is a family resemblance, this is used to further the view that explanations of industrial conflict which focus on national character or individual psychological traits – the 'disciplined' German or the 'volatile' Frenchman, for example – are not fruitful. Similarities or differences have to be sought in the social, political and industrial structures.

In the 1945–68 period, it is the differences between groups of countries that are noted. Broadly, they distinguish between a west European, north European and North American pattern. But even if we accept their view that

Table 5.1 Strike characteristics for 13 western industrial countries, 1900–29 and 1945–68

	Strike rate per 100,000 workers	Strikers per strike	Man-days lost per striker
Belgium			
1901–29	6.4	400	—
1945 (50)–68	2.6	1,100	7.6
Canada			
1901–29	5.3	280	27.5
1945–68	5.2	420	17.3
Denmark			
1900–29	11.5	140	33.8
1945–68	1.8	640	13.4
Finland			
1907–29	15.9	180	25.7
1945–68	6.0	780	13.4
France			
1900–29	7.8	300	15.1
1946–67	12.8	1,130	2.3
Germany			
1900–29	11.1	290	15.7
1951–68	—	—	5.4
Netherlands			
1901–29	13.0	100	32.0
1945–68	2.5	240	5.6
Italy			
1900–23	12.1	320	14.2
1950–68	18.1	1,030	3.3
Norway			
1903–29	—	—	33.9
1921–29	9.3	570	—
1945–68	2.2	310	15.3
Spain			
1910–29	6.0	420	23.2
Sweden			
1903–29	18.0	210	40.8
1945(46)–68	1.3	260	13.5
United Kingdom			
1900–29	3.8	—	—
1911–29	—	1,100	26.7
1945–68	9.9	400	3.4
United States			
1900–29	7.4	—	—
1916–29	—	530	—
1945–68	6.4	540	16.1

Source: Shorter and Tilly, 1974, p. 333.

the data are adequate for comparative purposes, it always needs to be borne in mind that the assumption is that the strike, measured on three dimensions, is a sufficient indicator of structural differences and similarities. Even within their own classification we can observe that not all the countries easily fit these clusters. The west European group, for example, in the post-1945 period contains France and Italy as central cases – with frequent strikes of great size and brevity – with the UK treated as marginal because the strikes tend to be brief, frequent and small. Then again, Belgian strikes were large, short but infrequent. In effect, what Shorter and Tilly do is to say that they represent different meanings in different political contexts. Thus France and Italy are seen as countries where the post-war strikes are mainly protest strikes aimed at gaining more working class participation in national politics, whereas strikes in Britain are forms of extra-parliamentary action but are essentially protests over the local distribution of power in the workplace. Germany is described as having moved from the west European group in the early period to the north European pattern. Oddly, the fact that we are dealing with a different geographical and political entity is scarcely registered. This group of West Germany, the Netherlands and the Scandinavian countries is seen as one where the working classes have entered the polity, but it remains unclear as to why the United Kingdom should not, on this reckoning, have similar strike trends. What this means is that 'special' cases demand special explanations but in doing so cast doubt on the adequacy of the original indicators. Moreover, if we take the North American example (Canada and the United States) we are told that whilst the shape of strike activity was similar in the early and later period, they actually meant different things. In Shorter and Tilly's judgement, the early period was a time when the North American working classes were not represented in the polity, whereas in the later period they were. It was the separation of politics from industry, however, that permitted the contained conflict of strikes within the industrial sphere. Hence 'admission to the polity need not automatically lead to the withering away of the strike' (Shorter and Tilly, 1974, p. 330). The indicators do not, therefore, tell their own story, which is both the challenge and problem of comparative studies.

SWEDEN

Here we take as our point of departure the work of Korpi and Shalev. They take Sweden as a test case to examine the general validity of theories of industrial conflict, taking as their stalking-horse the theoretical perspective of pluralistic industrialism, which they see as a dominant mode of thought in social science literature. We have already encountered this in the work of Kerr *et al.* (1960) but Korpi and Shalev spread their net quite widely including, for example, Ross and Hartman, Daniel Bell, Ralph Dahrendorf, J. K. Galbraith, John Dunlop, Wilbert Moore, Hugh Clegg and the Oxford School of industrial relations. What binds them together, in the view of Korpi and Shalev, is their tendency to give only a limited role to industrial conflict in advanced industrial societies. This is partly because of the role of collective bargaining and the institutionalization of conflict and partly because of the rise of political democracy. Moreover, political and industrial conflict have tended to become institutionally separated.

Korpi and Shalev see the pluralistic industrialism perspective as having its intellectual roots in Weber's approach to class and stratification. Against this they want to offer a Marxist perspective emphasizing the importance of production relations in explaining the nature of industrial conflict in capitalist societies. This approach 'implies that there are intimate ties between political and industrial conflict, something which clearly contrasts with the pluralist insistence on an increasing separation between them' (Korpi and Shalev, 1979, p. 169).

What does Sweden teach us? According to Korpi and Shalev, the country which since the Second World War has had a reputation for industrial peace, is not so consistent with the tenets of pluralistic industrialism as might have been supposed. They point out that the institutions for regulating industrial conflict in Sweden were already in place in the early twentieth century, yet at that time industrial conflict was at a high level. In their view, the decline in industrial conflict came close on the heels of the advent of a Social Democrat government in the early 1930s. Hence the availability of political options for the labour movement is more important than the institutionalization of industrial relations in affecting the character of industrial conflict. We can see that this is in general terms supportive of the Shorter and Tilly position which we have already discussed. There is an important implication for the way in which the explanation of industrial conflict is preferred:

> Rather than seeing the institutions of industrial rules as crucial and independent factors for the extent of industrial conflict, the present approach conceives of these institutions primarily as intervening variables, which are themselves independent of the power structure of society. (p. 170)

Korpi and Shalev argue that a crucial explanatory feature of trends in industrial conflict has to do with shifts in the distribution and changes in power resources between contending groups in capitalist democracies. One inference drawn from this is that where political parties based on working class support have strong and stable control over the executive branch of government, conflicts of interest between capital and labour can shift to the political arena. Indeed, it is in such soil that we are most likely to see the withering away of the strike. But things are not always so straightforward. In a later article Korpi discusses the increase in unofficial strikes in Sweden during the 1970s. He relates this to a period of high unemployment and high inflation rates (Korpi, 1981, pp. 66–86). The economic context has its own contribution to make, notwithstanding the political explanation concerning the role of the working class in the political arena. But he still holds onto the power resource argument: 'The unofficial strike can be seen as an attempt by the worker to redress the imbalance of power resources in the firm based on the management prerogatives and on the actual control by management within the firm' (p. 82).

Very ambitiously, Korpi and Shalev seek to examine the adequacy of their general thesis by looking at the experience of industrial conflict in eighteen capitalist democracies and take, as they say, the Second World War as a convenient dividing line for the 50–100 year period for which stoppage statistics are available. We can most readily see what kind of exercise this is by reproducing their complex tabulation, complete with accompanying notes (Table 5.2). On the basis of this exercise they conclude that there are five variants of industrial conflict in capitalist societies, which we may summarize as follows:

1. Sweden, Norway, Austria. Long-run decline in industrial conflict accompanied by social democratic rule allowing working class a share in political power.
2. Eire, United States, Canada. High rates of industrial conflict of long duration with no working class based parties in government.
3. France, Italy, Japan, Finland, Australia, New Zealand. High rates of industrial conflict of short duration where working class parties have significant electoral support but do not govern. The unions are divided and weak. The state plays a more active role in industrial relations than in (2). Lacking an 'inside track' to the state, the working class responds by activity in other forms of collective pressure, such as the strike.
4. Belgium, United Kingdom, Denmark. Fluctuating, unstable access to governmental power. Strikes maintain their significance quantitatively in the post-war period as much or more than pre-war.
5. West Germany, the Netherlands, Switzerland. Deviant cases which do not fit the general thesis. Low levels of industrial conflict but no governmental working class power. Mechanisms of extra-parliamentary consultation in policy-making may explain this, together with cultural and ethnic heterogeneity.

How is such an approach to be evaluated? Korpi and Shalev enter their own caveats. The study cannot be regarded as definitive; the table does not have anything to say about the conditions of working class organization in the countries listed; and all the indices used have considerable problems of reliability both over time and between countries and also raise questions of construct reliability (Korpi and Shalev, 1979, p. 180). These do seem to be formidable difficulties in their own right and the fact that they feel able to proceed perhaps tells us more about their commitment to the labour movement thesis than the adequacy of their evidence.

Table 5.2 Working class power and organization and industrial conflict in eighteen capitalist democracies

	Characteristics of industrial conflict			Power resources of Left parties				Working-class organization		
	Long-run change in involvement	Post-war involvement	Post-war duration	Role in post-war governments	Inter-war cabinet participation (%)	Post-war cabinet participation (%)	Post-war vote share (%)	Post-war density of unionization	Importance of union confederations in collective bargaining	Union and party organizational splits
Sweden	Decline	Low	*	Continuous control	46	94	52	Very high	High	—
Norway	Decline	Low	*	Almost continuous control	12	79	51	High	High	Party (minor)
Austria	Decline	Low	*	Shared control	5	51	48	Very high	High	—
Germany	Decline	Low	*	Exclusion until 1966	12	24	38	Medium	Low	Party (minor)
Netherlands	Decline	Low	*	Interrupted participation	—	24	34	Medium	High	Party (minor) Union (religious)
Switzerland	Decline	Low	*	Minority participation	—	19	29	Low	Medium	Union (religious)
Denmark	Stable	Low-medium	Low	Partially interrupted control/participation	48	60	45	High	Medium	Party (minor)
United Kingdom	Stable	Medium	Medium	Interrupted control	19	46	46	High	Low	—
Belgium	Stable	Medium	Medium	Interrupted participation	17	28	38	High	Medium	Party (minor) Union (political and religious)
United States	Stable	Medium	High	—	—	—	—	Low	Low	—
Canada	Stable	Medium	High	Exclusion	—	—	15	Low	Low	—
Ireland	Stable	Medium	High	Intermittent low participation	—	8	13	Medium	Low	—
Finland	Increase	Medium	Medium	Recurrent participation	9	39	47	Medium	Medium	Party (major) Union (political)
Japan	Increase	Medium	Low	Exclusion since 1949	—	3	37	Low	Low	Party (major) Union (political)
New Zealand	Increase	Medium	Low	Intermittent control	15	32	46	Medium	Low	—
Australia	Increase	High	Low	Intermittent control	10	22	48	High	Medium	Party (major)
France	Increase	High	Low	Exclusion since 1958	5	10	42	Low	Low-medium	Party (major) Union (political and religious)
Italy	Increase	High	Low	Intermittent low participation	—	12	38	Medium	Low-medium	Party (major) Union (political and religious)

Perhaps the most developed and incisive critique of Korpi and Shalev's explanatory framework is that of Batstone (1985, pp. 46–64). There are six main points:

1. Korpi and Shalev pay insufficient attention to institutional factors in industrial relations and of trade union organization. This is the more surprising since in their work on Sweden itself they do take this into account and one would expect to find it in work with a Marxist perspective.
2. Whilst they recognize the divisive features of religious, ethnic and linguistic differences for the working class, they do not explore the ways in which the labour process creates divisions of interest.
3. They do not seriously analyse the role of the state. Again this is surprising given their Marxist perspective.
4. They do not give much weight to the role of employers' organizations as a possible explanation of international variations in strike activity. Once employers' organizations are formed they may be expected to have an effect on the activity of trade unions and sometimes of political parties.
5. Having emphasized the importance of the production process as a source of industrial conflict they do not pursue the point. Batstone remarks:

> It would seem reasonable to expect that greater attention be paid to the way in which political action either reduces issues of conflict at the point of production or shapes the resolution of disputes so as to reduce resort to industrial action. (p. 52)

6. They have to resort to *ad hoc* explanations for their deviant cases of West Germany, the Netherlands and Switzerland.

These points, together with the authors' own caveats, lead us to doubt the adequacy of their comparative work.

In his book *The Democratic Class Struggle* (1983) Korpi formulates his position on the politics of industrial conflict. This usefully reminds us of the theoretical thrust which runs through the empirical and analytical material:

> In the democratic countries the conflicts of interest between the classes find expression not only in industrial relations but also in politics. A marked shift of the expressions of this conflicts from the labour market to the political arena can take place in countries where socialist parties gain a strong and stable hold over government power and can begin to employ political means to influence the distributive processes in society. Contrary to the Leninist interpretation of Marxism, I assume that it is then possible to advance the interests of the working class through the government and the parliament. In contrast to some writers on neo-corporatism, I assume that the institutional arrangements which are developed in this process need not be seen as means of social control over the workers, but can, under certain circumstances, be used to translate the organisational power of the wage-earners into the formation of economic and social policies favourable to working class interests. (p. 181)

We have already given reasons to doubt the adequacy of this theory as put forward in its comparative formulation. But what about the particular case of Sweden itself? It was, after all, the conviction that the theory worked there which stimulated Korpi and his colleagues to spread their net more widely. A thoughtful commentary and critique of Korpi's position is to be found in Fulcher's paper (1987). There are, of course, a number of variants of corporatist theory, both Marxist and non-Marxist, which merit exploration in their own right. In the present context, however, we can note Fulcher's contention that there are three main ideas associated with the corporatist interpretation of social democracy:

> Firstly, that Social Democratic governments abandoned socialist goals and accepted capitalism. Secondly, that the state, the unions and the employers have co-operated in managing the economy and dividing up the national product through central and extra-parliamentary bargains. Thirdly, that the labour movement has integrated and subordinated labour. (Fulcher, 1987, p. 231)

In the Swedish case, one issue under debate is the significance of the 'historical compromise' of the 1930s, when the labour movement obtained political power through the Social Democratic Party, whilst accepting the continued existence of private enterprise. Whereas the corporatists see this as a time when the Social Democrats abandoned their socialist goals and came to terms with capitalism, the labour movement theory emphasizes that through cumulative reforms and welfare policies Sweden became more socialist. In Fulcher's judgement, the corporatist account is the more convincing although he accepts that this perspective can underestimate the strength of radicalism within the labour movement. Basically, he contends, the Social Democratic governments from the 1930s to the 1960s accepted the principles of capitalist economic growth. Fulcher does accept that redistributive effects of government policies have taken place eventually and that during the 1970s substantial wage and income equalization took place. This gives some support to the labour movement theory, except that it does not really explain the incidence of industrial conflict. Fulcher points out:

> Firstly, labour had to wait a long time for redistribution, and by the time this was happening labour peace was breaking down. Secondly, the nature of the redistribution, which was within the ranks of labour, and the fact that it increased profits by holding back the demands of the higher paid, makes it difficult to understand why it should lead to labour peace. It is more plausible to argue that a redistribution of this sort increased than that it diminished industrial conflict. (p. 243)

The interpretation of industrial conflict in Sweden is, for Fulcher, one which emphasizes the corporatist theory as a better point of departure but which then recognizes that corporatism can carry within it its own contradictions. This is because there are inherent problems of conflict in a system which depends on the co-operation of power organizations. An interest group which gets too much of its own way can threaten future co-operation. A trade union which is too closely regulated in its demands by the state or the employers will alienate its members and generate discontent.

The arguments around the issues of corporatism and labour movement perspectives will no doubt continue. Clearly they need to be disciplined by and related to evidence. But the existence of such a debate is a sharp reminder that problems of explaining industrial conflict are empirical (what shall we count and how shall we count it?), and analytical (how shall we relate to other social phenomena?) and theoretical (what is the overall framework within which we construct our thesis?).

THE UNITED STATES

We have seen in the Shorter and Tilly study of strikes in France and the work of Korpi and his colleagues on Sweden that emphasis is placed on the importance of political integration of the working class in explaining variations and fluctuations in strike activity. When they turn to comparative work, although their analyses are differently structured, they both see the United States as a case where high strike rates are a result of relative exclusion from the political sphere of working class interests. Indeed, this suggests an inversion of the common view that high strike rates are an indicator of radicalism and class consciousness.

The adequacy of the 'political' interpretation of strike variations and its application to the United States has been forcefully challenged by Edwards (1981). Part of the problem may be in the use of the term political: there is a difference between strikes which are for political ends and strikes which have political implications. Moreover, if we take into account the range of participants in strike activity, different individuals and groups may give different emphases and definitions to the same strike. Indeed, the same actors may even change their definition of the same strike as it progresses. More generally, the 'political' and the 'economic' are not so mutually exclusive as those who make the distinction sometimes suppose.

Edwards accepts that the political environment in which industrial relations are located is relevant to the explanation of strike rates, but maintains that, since the system of collective bargaining is the mechanism for resolving disputes in all western countries, attention must be given to this as a critical intervening variable. For example, the scope of collective bargaining is wider in the United States than most countries, with its emphasis on the contract bargain. Consequently, with much at stake, when a dispute arises over the contract, the parties will be less likely to settle quickly.

While not ignoring other explanations, Edwards suggests that American strikes have been characterized by struggles for job control over an extended period, which has itself experienced changes in industrial structure and bargaining arrangements. It is the intensity of struggles for control which is treated as a key variable for explaining differences in strike patterns in Edwards' account. For example, in the pre-New-Deal period, there is general agreement that there was strong hostility among American employers to trade unions and extended battles for recognition and trade union rights. This led, in Edwards' view, not to political strikes (the Shorter and Tilly contention) but to fundamental battles over control of the workplace. Indeed, contract bargaining reflects this struggle for control. The subsequent post-war conflicts taking place within that framework were still about control and support an explanation for the long duration of strikes:

> Thus the strikes in the automobile industry in 1946 were seen by management as an attempt by the unions to gain controls over certain key issues, of which details of company profits assumed the greatest significance. The 1959 steel strike took on its intense form only after management sought to alter a contract clause concerned with manning arrangements . . . (Edwards, 1981, p. 237)

Thus strikes have co-existed with continuing struggles to establish collective agreements and bargaining rights. In other words, long and intense strikes can occur for two distinct reasons. In such a situation even strikes over ostensibly economic matters such as wages may also be seen as symbolizing something more than the immediate issue. And this is true for management and for labour. The picture that Edwards paints is of a country whose history was characterized by long, sometimes violent, struggles. Much of the violence has now been eliminated through the emergence of collective bargaining but the tradition of long strikes remains self-perpetuating: 'the system has been built on the premise that a long strike is the only way to ensure that one's interests are properly defended, a premise which has been strengthened by other aspects of the system' (p. 240).

The position, as Edwards sees it, is of a politically conservative, but militant and strike-prone workforce, hence the rise of business unionism. Referring back to Sombart's classic study *Why is there no socialism in the United States?*, Edwards points to such factors as a high standard of living and a rapid rate of economic growth:

> How far unions caused real wages to be higher than in Europe is an open question, but the fact of this relative prosperity enabled business unions to stress the solid material benefits to be gained from their own approach, compared with the less obvious and immediate gains from a more radical programme. Not surprisingly, business unions, when faced with the reforms of the New Deal, put their weight behind the establishment of collective bargaining and eschewed more overtly 'political' changes. (p. 249)

Moreover, the characteristics of the labour force tended to reduce more general class solidarity. It was geographically widely dispersed; consisted of native and immigrant workers, black and white; and could be further exacerbated by employers' policies, with their use of material and welfare incentives. All these contributed to the frequency and size of strikes, which were moderate compared with their long duration once they started. Edwards concludes that since the 1880s, despite changes in industrial organization and the emergence of collective bargaining, there has been no dramatic change in the amount of strike activity:

> This is because America's regulatory institutions have not challenged the way that strikes have been fought. Strikes have been direct clashes between workers and employers. They have not been mere demonstrations or indirect means of exerting political pressure. They have been battles over control of the workplace. Although industrial change has affected the nature of these battles, it has not altered their over-all importance. As a result, American strikes have retained a unique degree of intensity, which is likely to arouse the interests of analysts for many years to come. (p. 253)

THE UNITED KINGDOM

In discussing explanations of strike trends in the United Kingdom we focus on two studies: Cronin's *Industrial Conflict in Modern Britain* (1979) and Durcan et al.'s *Strikes in Post-War Britain* (1983). They are somewhat different in scope and style but both acknowledge their debt to the seminal work of Knowles (1952).

Knowles paid special attention to the British experience between 1911 and 1947. It was Knowles who showed that the propensity to strike, or strike-proneness, could be variously measured beyond considerations of length, frequency or numbers involved. He distinguished three main types of strike: basic (those over issues of wages and working conditions); frictional (those arising over the employment of certain classes of people, work arrangements, rules and discipline), and solidarity (those concerned with issues of trade union principle, including sympathy strikes). Whilst he produced a great deal of statistical analysis, derived from such considerations, his material, culled from a wide range of sources, made him sensitive to the dangers and difficulties of classification. As he observed:

> Any such classification must be somewhat subjective, since not only do most strikes break out on a multiplicity of issues, the relative importance of which may change in the course of the strike, but the main issue on which the strike is fought may turn out to be more or less relevant to the real cause of discontent. (Knowles, 1952, p. 11)

Cronin, in his study, gives himself an ambitious remit:

> Studying the evolution of strike activity as a whole should enable us to follow the complicated transitions that have occurred in the structure and location of the working class, its consciousness and collective organisation. It should also afford many glimpses of the general trajectory of industrial capitalism since the late nineteenth century. (Cronin, 1979, p. 11)

The two studies of Britain, which we have described, do not go into comparative work looking at other countries' experience. However, a Department of Employment study published in 1978 does seek to offer empirical evidence on strike trends in Britain and to relate this to international comparisons (Smith *et al.*, 1978). They had policy concerns in mind. Dixon points out in the foreword:

> In recent years, there has been a growing concern about the nature and extent of strike activity. There has been, within the United Kingdom, a feeling that strike action has contributed to our poor economic performance, while the reporting of strikes in Britain in the foreign press projects an adverse image which may have harmed our ability to attract international investment. (Smith *et al.*, 1978, p. 3)

The term 'British disease' was widely used to characterize the view that Britain was especially strike-prone and that this has dire effects on the British economy. Smith and colleagues look at this claim from both a historical and comparative perspective.

Smith *et al.* give a consolidated list of industrial stoppages in Great Britain and Northern Ireland from 1893–1976, using official statistics of numbers of strikes and number of working days lost. So far as the number of stoppages is concerned the figures show much unevenness through the annual series, with high numbers occurring immediately before and after the First World War, in the late 1950s and early 1960s and with particularly high figures for 1969 and 1970. There has also been an overall trend towards a larger number of strikes, with each peak higher than previous ones. This lends no support to the view that the strike is 'withering away', a view which might more understandably have been held in the 1940s and early 1950s, when Knowles did his seminal work. Moreover, if one took account of the different pattern of strikes in the coal mining industry then it was observed that in 1956 coal mining stoppages constituted 78 per cent of all stoppages but in 1970, a peak year for stoppages, they made up only 4 per cent. Indeed, it is argued that over the post-war period, until the early 1960s, there was a fairly stable level of stoppages, if the coal mining strikes are excluded.

When we turn to working days lost it can be shown that more than 10? million days were lost in 1893, 1897–8, 1908, 1911–12, 1919–23, 1926, 1970–2 and 1974. No long-term trend is apparent and, of course, the high figures for particular years are much affected by very large stoppages. These are typically long official disputes. For example, in 1972 over half the working days lost were attributed to two official strikes in mining and construction. We can see in the early 1970s the re-emergence of strikes in the coal mining industry after a long period of quiescence. If we go beyond the period studied by Smith *et al.* to the year-long dispute in the industry in 1984–5, then a large proportion of the 27 million days lost in 1984 and the 6 million days lost in 1985 will be accounted for in that way.

Smith *et al.* also have interesting things to say about inter-industry and intra-industry differences in strike activity. Taking the period 1970–5, which was one of high strike activity measured both by numbers of strikers and working days lost they conclude that:

> Despite a decline since the 1950s in numbers of stoppages in coal mining, five industries – coal mining, docks, car manufacture, shipbuilding, iron and steel – normally account for at least a quarter of stoppages and a third of days lost, although they account for little more than 6 per cent of employment. (p. 25)

They then looked closely at intra-industry variations for the period 1971–3, looking at manufacturing industry. They showed that for this period only 2 per cent of plants employing only 20 per cent of the manufacturing workforce were affected by stoppages in an average year. They concluded that, contrary to the image, Britain did not have a widespread strike problem. In practice it was concentrated in a few plants and in certain non-manufacturing sectors. As Smith *et al.* point out, the Donovan Commission, reporting on industrial relations, was well aware of the concentration of strikes in particular plants and industries but nevertheless initiated the drive towards procedural reforms because of its preoccupation with unofficial strikes. Their own gloss and comment on the appropriateness of this in policy terms is revealing in its scepticism:

> One rationale for this approach might be that, in so far as poor industrial relations can be held responsible for Britain's poor economic performance, the weakness must be far more widely pervasive than strikes themselves, and therefore require general remedies. But if that were so, the nature of the industrial relations' weakness needs to be much more clearly defined to formulate effective remedies. If the extent of industrial action and of strikes in particular is the major area of concern, a general reform policy may be justifiable on the grounds that the measures involved do not adversely affect the industrial relations' environment in hitherto strike-free establishments, or at least do not so badly affect the environment that such plants begin to experience strikes. However, it may also be argued that it is inappropriate to propound general remedies which must incidentally affect all plants in order to have an impact on the 2 per cent of plants which suffer strikes in an average year or – even more to the point – on the quarter of one per cent of plants which are seriously affected. (p. 90)

When it comes to international comparisons, Smith *et al.* are well aware of the pitfalls. There are variations in the methods of data collection, in definitions as to what is to count, and in particular as to whether to include political strikes. With all the qualifications, information is given about sixteen countries for the period 1966–75 and consciously extending the data which the Donovan Commission had collected for 1964–6. The overall conclusion reached was that the United Kingdom ranked seventh out of fifteen countries when the comparison was limited to the selected industry groups of mining, manufacturing, construction and transport industries, and sixth when all industries are included. Whatever theoretical mileage can be obtained from international comparisons, Smith *et al.* use them to demonstrate that the 'British disease' is not peculiar to Britain nor even is it at its most virulent there. This was in line with what the Donovan Report had shown for the shorter period.

Writing as a historian, Cronin suggests that just as the pattern of food riots provide an insight into the dynamics of eighteenth-century social order, so the analysis of strike patterns in Britain reveals something about the rhythm of the modern economy and its effects on those who live and work in it. But, he insists:

> Unlike other forms of collective action . . . the meaning of the strike is more liable to change over time, and the analysis of strikes is less likely to reveal a stable 'moral economy' of the poor underpinning militancy than a series of different mind-sets, or constellations of beliefs and expectations, fuelling strike activity at different times. (Cronin, 1979, p. 13)

This guiding orientation leads him to his working assumption that we should expect:

> the persistent, rapid and uneven character of social change since the industrial revolution to impact a noticeable discontinuity to patterns of belief and modes of collective action (p. 13).

Table 5.3 Stoppages of work due to industrial disputes in the
United Kingdom, summary for 1970–85

	Number of stoppages beginning in year (All industries and services)	Aggregate number of working days lost in stoppages in progress in year (All industries and services) (000's)
1970	3,906	10,980
1971	2,228	13,551
1972	2,497	23,909
1973	2,873	7,197
1974	2,922	14,750
1975	2,282	6,012
1976	2,016	3,284
1977	2,703	10,142
1978	2,471	9,405
1979	2,080	29,474
1980	1,330	11,964
1981	1,338	4,266
1982	1,528	5,313
1983	1,352	3,754
1984	1,206	27,135
1985	840	6,732

Source: Department of Employment Gazette.

Cronin develops an approach which emphasizes both the historical specificity of the experience of particular societies and the likelihood of discontinuities. Accordingly, he offers us a statistical portrayal of strikes in the
United Kingdom between 1888 and 1974, as measured by numbers of strikes
and numbers of strikers. The industries for which information was available
during this period covered textiles, clothing, building, transport, metals,
engineering and shipbuilding, mining and quarrying, motor vehicles and
miscellaneous. He draws the following conclusions.

Strikes have tended to come in waves. Whilst allowing elements of approx-
imation, Cronin identifies the high strike periods as 1889–92, 1910–13, 1918–
21, 1926, 1957–62 and 1968–72. These are situated against a trajectory
of long-term changes and are differentiated from short-term fluctuations.
The periodization offered by Cronin to identify long-term changes is:
1873–96 (the Great Depression); 1896–1920 (the Edwardian boom); 1920–
39 (the inter-war depression); 1940–67 (war and post-war economy), and
1968–74 (slow, halting growth). We cannot pursue all the detail of Cronin's
analysis but call attention to the relationship he seeks to establish between
a long-term trend of economic development with the medium-term period of
strike waves. He offers the following formulation on causal relationships in
this respect:

> Economic growth is a permanent problematic in history, a perpetually disrupt-
> ive force. In each period, it proceeds through an expansion or alteration of
> methods of production and distribution which transforms previous patterns, and,
> in the first instance, negatively affects certain aspects of workers' lives. Workers
> need time to adjust, to grasp what is happening to them, and to develop the ideas
> and tactics with which to cope with the new problems. The unequal division of
> power in industrial society probably guarantees that most often it is the employers
> who initiate and the workers who react. Usually changes in the character and quality
> of economic life make themselves felt first in employers' policy, but only gradually
> in workers' consciousness and attitudes, and still more slowly in their collective
> actions. There is, therefore, a time lag during which a new set of attitudes and
> expectations is developed; then, given a favourable economic or political conjunc-
> ture, workers translate this new consciousness into strike action. (pp. 57–8)

This issue of workers' consciousness, however, remains a problem as
Cronin has to recognize. There may be a gap between economic changes as
represented, say, by the trade cycle and workers' reactions. Consequently:

> Because of the time lag, it is both necessary and difficult to specify the mechanisms
> and paths by which economic trends make their way via economic policies and
> problems through workers' shifting attitudes and organisational responses to
> produce novel forms of strike behaviour. Theoretically, there may be detours and
> blockages at each stage, and a comprehensive analysis must be able to anticipate
> these as well as to discover the ultimate reflection of economics in strike waves.
> (pp. 64–5)

We can see from this extract that, even allowing for complexity, there is something of a base-superstructure argument here. It is economic factors which count 'in the last instance'. Whilst he argues that strike waves are correlated with a growth in unionisation, both of these are seen as:

> reflections of a broader learning process on the part of workers stimulated by the effects of different phases of economic development. A common dynamic rooted in economic change informs conflict and organisation, and affects both the desire and the ability of workers to execute collective action. (p. 40)

So what we have is a general perspective in which strike waves are based on the idea of uneven economic development. He is sharply critical of trade union historians who emphasize the evolutionary nature of change in Britain, both in trade union organization and in the wider polity. He has in mind both Pelling's *History of British Trade Unionism* (1972), whose evolutionary assumptions he is moved to dismiss as 'smug', and the general thrust of the Oxford School of industrial relations, with its emphasis on the gradual development of bargaining and conciliation machinery. Cronin finds himself more in sympathy with writers who in their different ways emphasize historical discontinuities. He refers, for example, to Kondratiev's theory of long waves of economic change, periods of 40–50 years, with 20–25 years of expansion followed by a similar period of contraction or slow growth (1935, pp. 105–15). But this he sees as a starting point, rather than a dogmatic assumption. Hence he maintains:

> Each stage of development seems to be characterised by different leading sectors, by distinctive technologies, by shifting entrepreneurial styles, by alterations in plant size and layout, by differences in the composition of the labour force, its precise occupational mix, and its conditions of life. In short we need a social history focusing upon qualitative aspects of economic growth. (p. 39)

Cronin cites two examples of the kinds of contribution which do give us a qualitative dimension to economic change, in the work of Dunlop (1948) and Hobsbawm (1964, pp. 120–57). His reservation is that both of them link strike waves to downswings in the Kondratiev cycles, so that in essence the explosion of conflict is related to an accumulation of grievances or a deterioration in workers' living standards. Cronin comments:

> In fact, explosions of strikes in Britain are as likely to have occurred during the upswings of long wages – e.g. the upheavals of 1910–13, 1919–20 and 1957–62 – as during prolonged slumps. Still, the connection between trend periods of economic development and strike waves may well hold whether the trend is up or down. (p. 57)

In other words, it is the disruption which may cause heightened industrial conflict, rather than necessarily the experience of increased deprivation. This clearly has something in common with Durkheim's view of structural change providing the potential for anomie and social disorder, which we discuss in Chapter 8.

In this instance, Cronin does less than justice to Hobsbawm. As a historian, Hobsbawm emphasizes that the specific combination of tensions that gives rise to explosions of industrial conflict demands individual analysis. But he points out also that:

> Not every trade cycle produces such general inflammability. In Britain, after 1850, it seems to occur roughly every other decade. Longer trends in our indices throw little light on this problem. The 'explosions' of the early 1870s and 1900s appear in secular boom periods, those of the 1830s and 1880–90s in secular depression phases. That of 1872 occurs at the end of a period of probably falling unemployment, rising money and real wages; that of 1889 during one of heavier unemployment, stable money and rising real wages; that of 1911 while unemployment falls, money wages remain stable and real wages fall. The troubles of the 1830s – if one is to hazard a guess about the period – may have coincided with rising unemployment, falling real and money wages. Continental 'explosions' occur against movements which are hardly more uniform. (Hobsbawm, 1964, pp. 138–9)

Indeed, Hobsbawm turns out to be much more agnostic about the relationship between economic periodization and 'explosions' of industrial conflict and states that no regular relationship between them can be ascertained, though admits that it is tempting to seek them at the end of each period. But he acknowledges that it fits for some but not for all. (See Hobsbawm, 1964, p. 153 for an extended footnote on this.)

Cronin eschews the comparative method which many of the writers we have reviewed tend to employ, even when they start with one particular society. This is because he sees strike waves as indicators of social change in a particular society and looks for explanations which are historically specific to that society. This informs his critique of Shorter and Tilly whose work we have already discussed. His evaluation of Shorter and Tilly recognizes that there is strength in their approach in the emphasis given to the role of political and organizational factors and their implications for industrial relations. But for Cronin their analysis is close to a form of technological determinism and this not only neglects the co-existence of industrial conflict across industries with different technologies in some explosive periods, but also tends to assume that the impact of technology on workers' attitudes and behaviour is direct and unmediated. He concludes:

> Their formulations lack any mechanism with which to explain the odd time pattern exhibited by both strikes and union growth, or any factor to mediate between structure and behaviour. By leaving out the subjective dimensions they telescope and oversimplify the complicated process by which the structural features of industrial society come to inform collective action. (p. 37)

It is instructive to compare Cronin's study with that of Durcan and colleagues (1983). *Strikes in Post-war Britain* covers the shorter period of 1946–73. Published some four years after Cronin's study it only once explicitly refers to it. Given that McCarthy is a well-known figure in the Oxford School of industrial relations, with which Cronin took issue, it is interesting that the authors express agreement with Cronin's conclusion:

> The basic point to emerge from this study is that social conflict is not the manifestation of some fixed and undifferentiated quantum of discontent that expresses itself in one form or another at different points in time. Rather, social and industrial conflict are the means used by ordinary working men and women to assert their changing needs and aspirations in the face of trends and problems that even their rulers and employers cannot control. (Cronin, 1979, p. 195)

There are, for all that, some differences in approach and substance to which we draw attention in the ensuing exposition.

Durcan *et al.* give a clear exposition of the nature of the available data, methods of measurement and classification, and problems associated with them. What about other forms of conflict in industry besides strikes? Here the authors offer a robust defence of their procedure. Clearly strike statistics, whatever their problems, are the most abundant form of conflict information and they claim that other forms of conflict are essentially to be seen as complementary activity so that any crucial explanation derived from the analysis of strikes may be treated as relevant to other non-strike sanctions that employees may use. They do not really demonstrate this, partly no doubt because of the intrinsic difficulty of getting widespread data for non-strike action. The possibility remains in some circumstances that non-strike indicators of industrial conflict such as output restriction, sabotage, high labour turnover and systematic absenteeism, may be alternatives to strike activity rather than co-existing with it.

The post-war period is divided into four phases: 1946–52, the post-war peace; 1953–9, the return of the strike; 1960–8, the shopfloor movement, and 1969–73, the formal challenge. A standard procedure is followed in each phase. A distinction is drawn between gross and net strike activity (the latter excluding coal, whose different trajectory of strike activity is well-established). The published aggregate data are then analysed by industrial distribution, reported cause, regional distribution, extent, size and their official or unofficial status. This is then extended by examining the statistics on major strikes involving the loss of five thousand or more working days and, in this context, including coal. These chapters and the overview which is offered are primarily descriptive in character and what comes through clearly is the rise in strike activity on a number of measures since the early 1950s. Whereas for Knowles, with whom they make explicit comparisons, the problem centred on explaining the reduction of strike activity between 1911 and 1947, for Durcan *et al.* it is the resurgence of the activity which poses the major problem.

What about the approach to explanation? Here differences with the Cronin approach can be discerned. This comes out notably in the significance attached to the economic environment in explaining trends. Durcan *et al.* draw attention to the difficulties of generalization in this area for methodological and theoretical reasons. They argue that studies of this kind have to come to terms with the fact that there are different measures of strike activity. The number of strikes, number of strikers and number of days lost do not all move in the same way at the same time. There is a tendency for studies in this area to give pre-eminence to the number of strikes measured. This is linked with a further tendency to assume that workers are the initiating agents in a strike, with employers merely taking a reactive role. Where explicit causal relationships are posited then wages or earnings defined in money, real or net terms are seen as the motivating factor. All of these assumptions are treated with scepticism by Durcan *et al.* If, in any case, the strike is extremely limited in its occurrence, then it may be inherently problematic to treat it as if it were a general activity. This is based on such findings as:

1. During the period 1946–73 only 4 per cent of employees were, on average, involved in stoppages each year.
2. Strike action never involved more than a small minority of the workforce for a small part of the year. Twenty of the thirty-four industries studied averaged less than 2 per cent of their workforce involved in strikes and only three averaged 20 per cent or more.
3. When time lost was measured against the size of the industry's workforce, nineteen industries averaged losses of less than an hour per employee per year and only two industries averaged losses of more than a day per employee per year.

The general stance and proposed strategy for analysis which Durcan *et al.* take is summarized well in the following statement:

> Those who explore the assumed relationships between strike statistics and other economic series usually fail to distinguish between the determinants of strike activity and the factors producing changes in the volume and form of collective bargaining: in effect the explanations they offer for strikes usually fail to take their role into account. This is partly because the separation and identification of bargaining influences cannot be adequately achieved at the macro-level which is the level of most studies and economic series. In consequence, although it can be shown that strike activity has some sensitivity to business cycle fluctuations, we conclude that the relationship between strikes and the economic environment is best studied at a less aggregated level than that of a national economy. (Durcan *et al.*, 1983, p. 215)

In pursuit of this approach Durcan *et al.* take three developed examples from coal mining, the docks and the motor vehicle industries. What they seek to establish is the importance of a more detailed analysis and therefore to warn against explanations of a mono-causal kind in terms of macroeconomic variables alone. This is well illustrated in their comment on the coal industry:

> The record indicates that although both product and labour market factors were an essential part of the story, they interacted with political, organisational and cultural influences which sometimes affected quite crucially the form and content of strike action. (p. 271)

Cronin was certainly aware of industrial differences in strike activity and spends a whole chapter of his book on the matter.

The basic difference in comparison with Durcan *et al.* is that Cronin wishes to emphasize the features which transcend the experience of particular industries 'because the normal focus on the distinctiveness of miners or dockers or pottery workers has so often led to a neglect of the broader changes that have made and remade the landscape of British society' (p. 188).

Yet for all that, it is Durcan *et al.* who actually lay more emphasis on the role of the state and its impact on industrial conflict. As they point out, governments can act in different ways in response to similar economic constraints. In post-war Britain during the period studied they see a growing role in government policy particularly in the attempt to impose wage restraint. By the end of the period that they studied, the early 1970s, there were attempts to regulate industrial conflict with the passage of the Industrial Relations Act, 1971. The authors point out that this was met with an unprecedented wave of protest stoppages and argue that, if anything, the effects of the law were counter-productive, so far as the control of industrial conflict was concerned. Of course, by the early 1980s, with another Conservative administration, more legislation was enacted, with still different consequences. This we return to later.

Since *Strikes in Britain*, the Department of Employment has published further data (DoE, 1986, pp. 266–99). The two relevant tables for the period 1975–84 are reproduced here (Tables 5.4 and 5.5). The notes on criteria employed by each country are in the appendix to this chapter, but it is especially noteworthy that the United States revised its series from 1981 so that only disputes involving more than one thousand workers were included. Before that the minimum number of workers was six. The *Employment Gazette* article calculated that this has reduced the recorded number of working days lost by between 30 and 40 per cent. It was further calculated that if the same procedure was applied to the UK average incident rate for the period, the figure of 500 would fall to 400. From the tables it can be seen that in 1984 the United Kingdom had a worse record on stoppages than any other country, mainly as a result of the coal mining strike. We can see that whether with reference to selected industries or to all industries and services, 1984 took the United Kingdom to the top of the league for strike activity as measured by

Table 5.4 Industrial disputes – working days lost per thousand employees* in all industries and services, 1975–84

	1975	1976	1977	1978	1979	1980	1981	1982	1983	1984	Average† 1975–79	1980–84	1975–84
United Kingdom	260	150	450	410	1,270	520	200	250	180	1,280	510	480	500
Australia	700	760	330	420	780	640	780	400	310	240	600	470	530
Austria	—	—	—	—	—	10	—	—	—	—	—	—	—
Belgium	200	290	220	330	200	70	n.a	n.a.	n.a.	n.a.	240	[70]	[220]
Canada	1,300	1,360	380	830	840	930	890	610	460	390	940	660	790
Denmark	50	110	120	70	80	90	320	50	40	60	90	110	100
Finland	150	680	1,310	70	130	840	340	100	360	750	470	480	470
France	230	290	210	120	210	90	80	130	80	80	210	90	150
Germany (FR)	—	20	—	200	20	10	—	—	—	260	50	50	50
Greece	460	520	810	630	1,040	1,740	480	840	n.a.	n.a.	700	[1,010]	[830]
Ireland	390	1,030	570	770	1,750	480	500	500	380	470	920	470	680
Italy	1,970	1,810	1,160	710	1,900	1,140	730	1,280	980	610	1,510	950	1,230
Japan	220	90	40	40	20	30	10	10	10	10	80	10	50
Netherlands	—	—	60	—	70	10	10	50	30	n.a.	30	[20]	[30]
New Zealand	220	490	430	380	370	360	380	310	360	400	380	360	370
Norway	10	90	20	40	—	60	20	170	—	60	30	60	50
Portugal	n.a.	n.a.	130	n.a.	200	200	330	170	230	100	[160]	200	[190]
Spain	200	1,470	1,940	1,380	2,310	790	680	370	590	890	1,440	660	1,080
Sweden	100	10	20	10	10	1,150	50	—	10	10	—	240	140
Switzerland	—	10	—	—	—	—	—	—	10	10	—	—	—
United States	230	300	260	270	230	230	190	100	190	90	260	160	210

Notes:

[] Averages based on incomplete data.   — Less than five days lost per thousand employees.   *Employees in employment: some figures have been estimated.

†Annual averages for those years within each period for which data are available, weighted for employment.

Sources: Working days lost: International Labour Office (ILO) Yearbook of Labour Statistics 1980 and 1985. Employees in employment: ILO, OECD and SOEC publications.

Department of Employment Gazette, July 1986.

Table 5.5 Industrial disputes – working days lost per thousand employees* in selected industries (mining and quarrying, manufacturing, construction, and transport and communication) 1975–84

	1975	1976	1977	1978	1979	1980	1981	1982	1983	1984	Average†		
											1975–79	1980–84	1975–84
United Kingdom	540	300	840	840	2,410	1,150	330	460	330	3,120	980	1,070	1,020
Australia	1,370	1,440	610	850	1,580	1,360	1,700	900	620	510	1,170	1,030	1,100
Austria	—	—	—	10	—	—	—	—	—	n.a.	—	—	—
Belgium	350	570	420	660	360	140	n.a.	n.a	n.a	n.a.	470	[140]	[420]
Canada	2,780	2,560	830	1,920	1,650	1,510	1,870	1,410	600	930	1,940	1,280	1,610
Denmark	130	240	260	100	150	210	720	100	80	150	180	250	210
Finland	300	1,270	2,220	150	260	1,250	560	220	390	690	840	620	730
France	390	420	260	200	350	170	160	260	160	170	320	180	260
Germany (FR)	10	40	—	360	40	10	—	—	—	510	90	100	100
Greece	n.a.	n.a.	n.a.	n.a.	850	1,280	720	920	n.a.	n.a.	[850]	[970]	[940]
Ireland	640	1,910	890	1,110	3,610	650	930	630	550	650	1,650	690	1,170
Italy	1,790	2,290	1,560	880	2,560	1,630	970	1,930	1,480	730	1,820	1,350	1,590
Japan	390	150	70	60	40	50	20	20	20	20	140	30	80
Netherlands	—	10	140	—	180	30	10	60	40	n.a.	70	[40]	[50]
New Zealand	n.a.	1,000	840	830	810	750	810	710	840	960	[870]	810	[840]
Norway	10	70	30	90	10	140	40	390	10	60	40	130	90
Portugal	n.a.	n.a.	n.a.	n.a.	290	350	490	290	440	180	[290]	350	[340]
Spain	450	3,140	4,100	2,220	3,940	2,240	n.a.	n.a.	n.a.	n.a.	2,730	n.a.	[2,730]
Sweden	20	10	20	10	20	—	60	—	10	20	20	480	240
Switzerland	—	20	—	—	—	—	—	—	—	—	—	—	—
United States	n.a.	n.a.	n.a.	n.a.	n.a.	540	470	300	590	160	n.a.	410	[410]

See notes to Table 5.4.
Source: Department of Employment Gazette, July 1986.

working days lost. The 1,280 figure was even higher than the 1,270 for 1979, the period which was labelled the 'winter of discontent'. However, in that year three other countries recorded higher figures. When we look at the averages for the period, we can see that there is not much change over the two five-year averages and that, in general, the United Kingdom remains in the middle of the bunch.

We can see, then, that strike statistics can be used to develop different kinds of argument: as indicators of social and industrial change, as an attempt to test theories – of corporatism, of the labour movement, of the role of the economic environment, of inter- and intra-industry differences and so on, and as part of a political debate about the state of a country's industrial relations compared with others. Whilst it is appropriate to consider such matters, if only to reflect the preoccupation which academic commentators and policy-makers give to them, it by no means exhausts ways of thinking about and analyzing industrial conflict, its forms and meanings.

INDUSTRIAL CONFLICT IN CONTEXT

To propose that industrial conflict must be contextualized in order to be properly explained and understood has the appearance of an unexceptional sociological axiom. Yet its accomplishment is far from easy. Consider firstly the range of activities which can constitute industrial conflict: strikes, boy-cotts, lock-outs, sabotage, individual bargaining, collective bargaining, labour turnover, absenteeism, output restriction, go-slows, work to rules, sit-ins, work-ins, riots. The variety is such that it has led Hyman to describe industrial conflict as a conceptual 'put-down' and to cast doubt on its adequacy as an analytical category (Hyman, 1982). Part of his objection is that the very term industrial conflict has managerial connotations in that the activities covered by it interfere with managerial objectives of control, production and profitability. By the same token, they are judged negatively. Yet they can sometimes be seen from another perspective as forms of positive and purposeful labour action. According to Hyman, therefore:

> Any adequate sociological analysis of such activity must locate its occurrence within the structure of opposing interests inherent in social relations of production in capitalist industry: between those who appropriate surplus value and those who sell their labour power, between those who are agents of the coercive priorities of capital and those who are subordinated to their control and surveillance. Within the context of antagonistic relations of production, industrial conflict cannot be fully understood except in terms of the opposing strategies of those whose interests, and hence whose underlying orientation and objectives, are themselves in opposition. (Hyman, 1982, p. 404)

Hyman makes clear that he is not making some simple identification that all industrial conflict is rational, but it should not be dismissed as 'mindless', or 'aimless' or 'meaningless'. The degree of understanding or information about a situation may vary considerably and some strategies and tactics may prove to be better calculated than others in terms of specific objectives. Some may backfire and prove counterproductive. This suggests not that the category of industrial conflict is inadequate but that it needs to be sensitively handled. The sociological problem is to identify particular forms and expressions of conflict and to tease out their significance for the social order in which they take place. We know that the kinds of activity listed under the category of industrial conflict can be located in all industrial societies – early and advanced, capitalist and socialist – even when some of these activities were defined as illegal or subject to harsh sanctions, including in some cases capital punishment. To try to contextualize these activities is to try to identify and characterize the dialectic of power and control in employment relations. In doing so we would argue that it is appropriate to look at the vocabulary of motives employed by the participants to the conflict as well as the structures within which the activity takes place.

The term vocabulary of motives is explicitly used by Mills, where it refers to the justifications which are given for past, present or future forms of conduct (Mills, 1963). Part of the purpose is to convince or persuade others of the appropriateness of particular forms of behaviour, or even to motivate them to behave in a similar way. So it is that the same outward act, say a strike, can mean different things to the participants in different times and places, and different actions, say output restriction and absenteeism can sometimes have roughly equivalent meanings attached to them. In particular situations where conflict develops and protests are articulated, the actors will be able to draw on a repertoire of activities and deploy a vocabulary of motives to justify in moral terms what they are doing.

We return to the question of strikes but, by way of an alternative illustration of the problems and possibilities of analysis let us consider briefly the issue of sabotage. Historical examples of machine-breaking by Luddites and arson by agricultural workers are well documented, and the activities of syndicalist and anarchist workers movements in Britain, France and the United States in the late nineteenth and early twentieth century provide relevant material. But when sabotage comes to be defined by its advocates or practitioners it covers a wide variety of activities such as output restriction, go-slows and work to rules, which in our list were categorized separately. In fact, Brown's useful source-book *Sabotage* begins with an account of a 'ca-canny' or go-slow in Glasgow docks, which was operated by the National Union of Dock Labourers in 1889 (Brown, 1977). This followed an unsuccessful strike when the men were encouraged to return to work to replace the 'scab' labour and then only work as effectively as the blacklegs. This proved to be successful in obtaining the halfpenny an hour rise that the strike had failed to achieve. The union executive in fact argued that this action taught the masters a few lessons in political economy. If the price for labour was too low then organized labour would control the amount and quality of goods produced or work done. So the action is organized in relation to a concept of the price for labour, which is treated as a commodity in the 'labour market'. We can see the vocabulary of motive here and how the action is justified in terms of what is right and effective. The action is pragmatically regarded as more effective than the strike in this particular situation where 'scab' labour can be otherwise used. Not only does this give meaning to the action but it also has a rational character in terms of defined means and ends.

The Glasgow incident was used as a telling success story by the French anarchist Emile Pouget (Pouget, 1910). The practice of sabotage was strongly advocated by revolutionary syndicalists in that country. Sabotage included go-slows, work to rules and 'la méthode de la bouche ouverte', that is making public the secrets of employers to embarrass or shame them. At the beginning of the twentieth century there was much discussion in the French union CGT as to whether sabotage was a central or incidental tactic for workers to use. It certainly became part of the rhetoric and theory of syndicalism and thus provided a context in which the practice of sabotage could be justified by its participants. What is generally noticeable, as Brown points out, is that, whether in France, or with British syndicalism, or again with the American IWW – all organizations with which sabotage was associated as a tactic – it was fairly mild in formulation. It was conceptualized not primarily in terms of the destruction of the means of production but about ways of reducing effort and impeding efficiency. Rhetoric, however, does not always accord with practice and both employers and unions could be worried about the destruction of machines. What can be noted is that sabotage was sometimes advocated and practised when other means of protest were blocked or ineffectual. This was the point of Giovanitti's comment on the activities of the IWW (Industrial Workers of the World) in the summer of 1913:

> Now that the bosses have succeeded in dealing an almost mortal blow to the boycott, now that picket duty is practically outlawed, free speech throttled, free assemblage prohibited, and injunctions against labour are becoming epidemic – Sabotage, this dark, invincible, terrible Damocles' sword that hangs over the heads of the master class, will replace all the confiscated weapons and ammunition of the army of toilers. And it will win, for it is the most redoubtable of all except the general strike. In vain may the bosses get an injunction against strikers' funds – Sabotage will get more powerful against their machinery . . . (Brown, 1977, pp. 45–6)

One instructive attempt to offer an analytical approach to the study of sabotage is to be found in Taylor and Walton's paper, (in Cohen, 1971). The authors argue, as we have done, that it is inadequate simply to classify actions, since the same actions may mean different things in different contexts and to different actors. An overview of their position is given in Table 5.6 which

Table 5.6 Meanings and purposes of action

	1 Attempts to reduce tension and frustration	2 Attempts to facilitate or ease work process	3 Attempts to assert control
1 Does it aim to restructure relationships and redistribute power?	No	No	Yes
2 Does it necessarily make work easier?	No	Yes	No
3 Does it directly challenge authority?	No	Yes	Yes
4 Is it spontaneous or planned?	Spontaneous	Planned	Planned
5 Is it an arbitrary or specific target?	Arbitrary	Specific	Specific

cross-classifies the ideal type categories of meanings and purposes of action against the questions that the authors raise.

The three ideal types point to situations where there are different experiences of power relations. The first is one of relative powerlessness. Sabotage, whether of an individual or collective kind, is a reaction to this. Taylor and Walton suggest that in situations where collective bargaining is not present, and industrial relations are primitive and not well organized, then examples of type 1 are more likely to be found. Needless to say, the actions can still have far-reaching consequences, as in the case of the carpet factory worker who set fire to the factory causing £2 million worth of damage. Or, the New York computer programmer who, 'worried about his job, took out some unofficial insurance by feeding the computer a secret subroutine around his pay roll number. The worst happened. He was fired and the computer digested his pay roll number in order to make his pay-off settlement. Instantly the subroutine clicked into action, and the machine solemnly erased its own memory bank' (Cohen, pp. 231–2).

The second type is still relatively defensive but it has the clear purpose of trying to make work activity more manageable. In Taylor and Walton's view this characteristically takes place in work situations involving payment by results and piece-rate schemes. It can involve the improper use of tools and machines to make things easier to reach production norms and output quotas. A graphic example of this is found in Haraszti's experience in a Hungarian engineering plant (Haraszti, 1977). There the workers described the activity of beating the management production norm on the milling machines as 'looting'. It involved ignoring the technical instructions and the safety regulations, stepping up the cutting speed and feeding the job through faster. His workmates told him that if he wanted to make a living there he could not let things run smoothly. He described his experiences as broken milling teeth shot past his head like bullets:

> Slowly and unobtrusively, my neighbour strolls over and examines the shattered head. 'There are plenty of these in the stores', he says. 'It's a disposable tool.' (Haraszti, 1977, p. 48)

Such activities, then, may affect the quality of the work or the safety of the worker, though sometimes the rule infringements may lead to more efficient organizational activity, as Roy's experience in an American engineering workshop suggested (Roy, 1954). Whilst such sabotage may be individual it is commonly based on shared understandings of what is necessary to get the expected take-home pay and is, therefore, grounded in a collaborative system. This may even involve managerial connivance. This was Haraszti's experience:

> Management knows all about looting. After all, it is not just the workers who practice it, and live off it, but the bosses as well. If they fix my pay for a hundred per cent performance at around 8 forints an hour, then, quite literally, they force me to loot. Just how could their production plan be implemented if this compulsion was not built into it in the first place? (Haraszti, 1977, p. 46)

The third type in the Taylor and Walton scheme is the most aggressive in that it is challenging the existing structure of power relations. In their view this will most likely take place in a context of militant trade union activity. They cite the example of the car workers in Turin who, in 1969, after a series of ineffective strikes, resorted to smashing buildings and equipment and attacking strike breakers. In fact there were widespread demonstrations outside the factory and an occupation within as well as the sabotage (Partridge, 1986). Another example from the car industry which can be cited is the events at the General Motors plant at Lordstown in 1970, which was a strong reaction against the attempt to implement rigid scientific management principles in a new plant. Dubois offers the following account:

> The intensification of work there was tremendous – the number of cars assembled there each day broke all records. For a time. The workers soon responded with strikes and acts of sabotage. What were their aims? First, they wanted to gain control over their own working hours and have more free time during the day . . . for this they planned to sabotage one workshop after another, to create the maximum disruption. Their second objective was to make their sabotage fun: with fire hoses they turned workshops into vast swimming pools; they had contests to see who was the best saboteur (seeing who could blow up his engine so as to send the bits furthest away). Games like this broke the monotony of fragmented work, and freed the workers from inhibitions and their fear of management (managers barely dared

to venture into the workshops involved). Finally, and this is interesting if only for its rarity, this sabotage was also a protest against a specific new process: a new six cylinder engine was being assembled, hastily designed and flimsy. The Lordstown workers, having vainly suggested ways of improving its quality, decided that they would themselves check each one produced. Their sabotage prevented the engine ever reaching the market: so many engines were rejected for various defects that there was soon nowhere in the workshops to keep them all. This particular outburst of sabotage produced results as soon as it was put into operation. (Dubois, 1979, pp. 67–8)

Edwards and Scullion (1982) take up the question of sabotage in relation to five companies in engineering, clothing and textiles, alongside other forms of industrial conflict. Although they are critical of the database from which Taylor and Walton derive their findings, they accept the point that the concept of sabotage remains important as a way of looking at certain kinds of action at the point of production. Most forms of sabotage which they discovered in their factories were of the utilitarian kind: that is, they were concerned with specific aspects of work and were not a self-conscious attempt to undermine or challenge managerial control (Edwards and Scullion, 1982, p. 154). Thus in a components factory the workers cut the cycle times on the moulding machines in order to increase their earnings. Foremen knew the practice went on, but looked the other way since production targets were still being met. Their own empirical work led them to two main conclusions. Firstly, that in practice, aspects of technology and the payment system encourage its use in some settings and not in others. Secondly, that most sabotage involved utilitarian struggles for relatively small shifts in the terms of the effort bargain, rather than activity with wider implications in terms of control. It certainly did not represent any developed form of syndicalism.

We have used the discussion of sabotage for illustrative purposes. There are problems of definition and classification, nevertheless the attempt to situate actions and to be aware of the vocabulary of motives through which the actions are justified is a fruitful way of putting industrial conflict into context. But definitions of the situation are also often contested, one vocabulary of motives may find itself in competition with another as a struggle unfolds and develops. If we return now to the phenomenon of the strike, when we think of it in terms of causes and processes it is surely right, as Hyman suggests, that methodologically and empirically this is often a complex matter:

> Paradoxically, the predominant purposes of collective action may become explicit only after a stoppage is already in progress, by articulation of a rationale that selects one or more salient complaints or demands from among the strikers' preexisting grievances and aspirations. Such a process of selective articulation is inevitably influenced to an important degree by opinion leaders among the participants, by influential outsiders, and by the more general industrial and social environment in which the dispute occurs. For example, union organisers may seek to develop a

stoppage by unorganised workers into a struggle for membership and recognition – a process familiar to the historian of British labour, and notable particularly in the rise of general unionism at the turn of the century. Political activists may seek to develop disputes into mass support for demands reflecting the perspectives of their own organisations (their success will reflect the extent to which they do encapsulate aspects of the strikers' own priorities). (Hyman, 1982, p. 415)

If we say then that industrial conflict has to be contextualized in order that meanings can be identified and explanations proferred, we now have to add that, not only are we dealing with social processes but also struggles over what is an appropriate context in which to interpret the events. Those struggles become part of the events themselves and play their own part in shaping outcomes. In the case of large, long-running disputes like the British miners' strike of 1984–5 this takes on the character of a drama, albeit with a range of texts and sub-texts purporting to describe what is going on (see, for example, Beynon, 1985; Adeney and Lloyd, 1986; MacGregor, 1986 and Samuel *et al.*, 1986). There was, for example, a political context, which related the strike to a more general government strategy, which had been outlined as early as 1978 in the Ridley report, a confidential document published by *The Economist* in May 1978. The report concerned the nationalized industries and attention was given as to how to counter any 'political threat' from 'enemies' of the next Conservative government. This included such advice as: choose the battleground for confrontation in an area that the government can win, such as British Rail, British Leyland, British Steel and the civil service. Plans were also indicated for the eventual battle in the coal industry including the idea of developing a large mobile squad of police 'equipped and prepared to uphold the law against violent picketing'. Ian MacGregor was one of the chief managerial actors in the higher-profile disputes of the 1980s and in his own account writes of his experiences with British Leyland and British Steel before he became chairman of the NCB. The chapter titles of his book mirror precisely the sense of battle with an enemy 'Coal: war is declared'; 'The first skirmishes'; Battle commences'; 'The second front'; Economic warfare'; 'Peace moves'; 'Where are reinforcements?'; 'NACODS enters the fray'; 'Battle for the media'; 'Desertions in Scargill's army'; 'Laying the final trap'. He describes how he called on the Prime Minister to provide more effective policing because 'all over the country men were being deprived of their freedoms and liberties, they were being threatened and intimidated – as were their families' (MacGregor, 1986, p. 192). This is how he defined the problem to her: ' "Well," I said, "you've got to do something, because you are dealing with a well-rehearsed and organised rebellion here. You know, from what Scargill has said, that he is out to topple the government. If it goes on, I fear it will succeed." ' (p. 193)

There was the economic context. What did or did not constitute an uneconomic pit? These were naturally in part technical questions yet their answer depended on wider considerations of energy policy and the time-span that was being considered. Big questions concerning the role of nuclear energy, the activities of the Central Electricity Generating Board and policies for privatization all enter into the picture. The question of what is or is not an uneconomic pit is accountancy-driven and not a matter of absolute definition (Beynon, 1985; Williams, 1989).

There was the community context. Many mining communities knew themselves to be threatened with extinction if their pits closed – as has subsequently happened. The account of the strike at this level cannot be explained simply in terms of union strategy and tactics, of the leadership of the NUM president, Arthur Scargill, or the divisions within the union, but of a struggle for survival. In this respect the strike was a defensive matter for particular communities. Hence issues of violence and rough behaviour were not defined in terms of miners' violence but of police violence experienced on the picket lines and in some villages. The privations and the hardships, the debts and difficulties that miners and their families found themselves in as the year-long strike progressed were defined in terms of a defence against alien economic forces. The strike thus becomes symbolic of a defence against those who in the name of economic realism would destroy whole communities – shipbuilding, steel, coal and so on.

Of course, commentators may go on and attempt to recontextualize the strike, linking political, economic and community questions together. Thus Williams viewed the government's policy as one which was prepared to let such rundowns and closures of communities occur. Not only will such people be politically marginalized but they will be controlled by centralized communications and new forms of policing. This then becomes the basis for a more general point:

> Capitalist policy, which is still one of buying in the cheapest market and selling in the dearest, has in recent decades been profoundly subversive of what is still the most freely chosen social order of our people: that is, existence as an independent and self-sustaining nation. The continued legitimacy of appeals to either *law* or *order* rests primarily in this identity. Thus when supposedly public corporations, in steel or electricity or now coal, openly subordinate the interests of this true national, to their own immediate market calculations – hauling coal, for example, across the seven seas to undercut, reduce or close down any supposedly national industry – a profound social crisis has begun. (Williams, 1989, p. 126)

In our discussion of industrial conflict the burden of our evidence has been to limit its significance as a measure of crisis. Certainly, in a society like the United Kingdom much conflict has been institutionalized and is regulated within defined structures. Even the advent of new right policies has not affected much of the day-to-day conduct of industrial relations. Most of the forms and expressions of industrial conflict can be effectively interpreted in terms of struggles over the effort bargain or the frontiers of control within the enterprise (Edwards, 1986). The outcomes of these struggles may vary according to the skills and resources of the participants and the specific situations in which they are located. Yet this should not prevent us from seeing that some events like the miners' strike raise much wider issues. When the government of the day define a large number of working people as 'the enemy within' it prompts questions about the relationship between government and civil society. When whole communities are destroyed by what are defined as economic necessities, then the relationship between economy and society is called into question. Such conflicts are not simply economistic but they may serve as a sign of social crisis and, ironically, a harbinger of a deeper economic crisis.

Appendix Industrial disputes: comparisons of coverage and methodology

	Minimum criteria for inclusion in statistics	Are political stoppages included?	Are indirectly affected workers included?	Sources and notes
Australia	10 or more days lost	Yes	Yes	Information gathered from arbitrators, employers and unions
Austria	No restrictions on size	Yes	No	Trade unions provide information
Belgium	More than one working day's duration	Yes	No	Local police reports sent to National Conciliation Service. Follow-up questionnaires sent from National Statistical Institute
Canada	10 or more days lost or of more than a half day's duration	Yes	No	Reports from Canada Manpower Centers also Press and Provincial Labor Depts
Denmark	100 or more days lost	Yes	Yes	Voluntary reports from employers' organizations sent annually to Statistical Office
Finland	More than 4 hours' duration unless 100 or more working days lost	Yes	Yes	Returns from mail questionnaires to employers and employees
France	No restrictions on size. However, public sector and agricultural employees are excluded from statistics	No	No	Labour inspectors' reports
Germany (FR)	More than 10 workers involved and more than 1 day's duration unless 100 or more working days lost	Yes	No	Compulsory notification by employers to Labour Offices
Ireland	10 or more days lost or of more than one day's duration	Yes	Yes	Reports from local employment offices
Italy	No restrictions on size	Yes since 1975	No	Local police reports sent to Central Institute of Statistics
Japan	More than half a day's duration	No	No	Interviews by Prefectorial Labour Policy section or local Labour Policy Office of employers and employees
Netherlands	No restrictions on size	Yes	Yes	District Employment Offices inform Central Bureau of Statistics. Public servants are forbidden to strike
New Zealand	More than 10 working days lost. Statistics exclude public sector strikes	No	Yes	Information gathered by district offices of Dept of Labour
Norway	More than one day's duration	Yes	No	Questions to employees' and employers' organizations
Portugal	No restrictions on size. However, statistics exclude disputes which involve more than one company	Not known	No	
Spain	No restrictions on size	Yes	Yes	Monthly returns made by local province delegates of Ministry of Labour Statistics. Figures exclude Catalonia
Sweden	More than one hour's duration	Yes	No	Press reports compiled by State Conciliation Service are checked by employers' organizations and sent to Central Statistical Office
Switzerland	More than one day's duration	Yes	Yes	Federal Office for Industry, crafts, occupations, and employment collects press reports, and checks with trade unions and employers
United Kingdom	More than 10 workers involved and of more than one day's duration unless 100 or more working days lost	No	Yes	Local unemployment benefit offices make reports to Department of Employment HQ, which also checks press, unions, and large employers
United States	More than one day's or shift's duration and more than 1,000 workers involved	No	Yes	Reports from press, employers, unions and agencies, followed up by questionnaires

Note: Details for Greece not available.
Source: Department of Employment Gazette, July 1986.

6

WHATEVER HAPPENED TO INDUSTRIAL DEMOCRACY?

Industrial democracy is a contested concept, born out of the continuing struggle within capitalism regarding the boundaries of the authority of property and the limits imposed on the rights of labour. Post-war Britain, as elsewhere, has seen dramatic shifts in the appreciation and the definition of the concept and the forms of its realization. The debate about the meaning of industrial democracy is important in shaping the whole industrial relations landscape especially in relation to the questions of power that it raises, in its probing of the legitimate roles of management, unions and workers within the state and enterprise, and in its potentiality for restructuring organizations. The differences of approach and the conflicts of interest upon which they are based lead to the confusion and diversity of definitions we find between and within management and the labour movement. The idea of a single agreed notion of what constitutes industrial democracy is the first casualty of this. This conflict over meaning has become an element of the crisis for the British Labour movement. As Cressey and MacInnes (1980) pointed out, the division between those holding incorporationist views and those seeing industrial democracy as progressive runs deep. Brannen found that whilst the issue of industrial democracy has been a major intellectual preoccupation for social theorists:

> One of the problems which confronts anyone writing in this area is the variety of meanings given to terms such as 'worker participation' and 'industrial democracy'. (Brannen, 1983, p. 13)

In its format, its aims and its philosophical underpinning the range of what is considered to be industrial democracy varies from overtly politically defined notions of workers' control through to existing internal forms of management–workforce regulation and on to ameliorative forms of participation in aspects of work organization and environment. Each post-war decade seems to have brought new models and approaches which tend to structure the thinking and the approach to industrial democracy. The models of industrial democracy or 'participation' which gained currency in the 1960s tended to be those based on 'socialized' economies with Yugoslavia being the prime example (see Blumberg, 1968, Singleton, 1970). Here industrial democracy meant a thoroughgoing change in the structure, aims and hierarchy of the enterprise. In Yugoslavian self-management, the enterprise became a political entity. Democracy was constituted in the workplace through the decision-making structure of the enterprise. Elected councils of workers replaced the boards of directors, provision was made for the election of management and open discussion about investment levels, the distribution of surpluses and forward planning. In the West this tended to be in competition with the other route to democracy encased in the West German model of co-determination, a statutory model operating in the context of a stable social democratic consensus. Here the state, industry and trade unions have authoritative roles to play. Thus, the umbrella of welfare provisions, progressive taxation systems and macro-democratic structures are in part matched by micro-structures at the enterprise level. The approach to participation under this model has tended to be relatively formal, deriving its legitimacy from legal provisions. Institutionally this has meant the creation of works councils, worker directors and representatives at the highest enterprise level, together with a corporatist or tripartite arrangement above it. Industrial democracy here is based on an *a priori* statutory division of rights and responsibilities and for this reason tends to be formalistic in character (see Fricke, 1986; Streeck, 1984). Recent years have seen the growth of participatory formats that proclaim an organic unity of interests within enterprises. Under this model the aim is the submersion of identity and other interests to a large corporate goal, with participation taking place through workgroups and structures that attempt to improve aspects of corporate performance. The quality circle, problem-solving group with high levels of workforce activity, the building of a corporate consciousness and cradle-to-grave security, are components of this model (Cressey, 1986; Ouchi, 1981). This is often found in non-union settings where the aim of management is primarily the individualization of employee relations, the isolation and minimization of conflict, and a collectivist consciousness.

Industrial democracy can also be based on the needs of various groups within the enterprise and be voluntary in character. The more important groups in terms of function who have claims to be heard, are accommodated in the decision-making process. This approach is increasingly followed in the United Kingdom, and to some extent in the United States, with systems based upon 'free' collective bargaining and internal power-broking. Industrial democracy here, if talked of at all in such direct terms, takes account of shifts in relative advantage of the parties, is voluntary and, therefore, is not guaranteed or institutionalized as in the previous model. The character of the participation here is power-based and responds to and accommodates the needs of new groups, be they needs for bargaining, consultation or other involvements in decision-making. Participation, in this sense, is not programmed and joint activity is valued only to the extent that it meets the needs of the enterprise, the plant or the various groups involved. These four developments are not exhaustive of the range of models which might be constructed nor of the elaborate typologies which might be developed. They are useful in as much as they indicate the particular options that have been debated in Britain and found appealing at given points in time. This chapter will look at the British post-war debate on industrial democracy to ask why and how it came to be defined the way it has. With those models in mind we can see that there have been significant shifts in both the debates and the possibilities seen for the inauguration of these differing types of industrial democracy. As late as 1979 the Bullock Commission reforms on enterprise and boardroom activity were still in play, with a White Paper suggesting that in all enterprises over five hundred employees action on improved representation via worker-directors had to be put in place. Against managerial hostility, a state-led and statutory concept of industrial democracy was being promulgated, building upon a host of collective and individual legal rights that had been won by trade unions and employees (Elliot, 1978). By the 1980s, however, the situation was very different. There was no state action proposed in this area, 'participation' has become a voluntaristic issue *par excellence*, an issue for the parties within enterprises to decide upon and inaugurate. The interim has seen no statutory reform, the state has largely opted out of its role as a 'best practice' employer, the trade unions are divided regarding the usefulness of industrial democracy and the Labour Party has only vague pronouncements about the content and direction of policy.

Voluntarism in this context does not deny the possibility of experimentation or the inauguration of participation schemes but what it does do is deny the state any role in that process. Furthermore, voluntarism appears to be supporting the re-establishment of single lines of authority within the enterprise rather than extending and sharing such authority. This has marked a significant reversal and a dismantling of the cumulative protections trade unions had and the previously held rights upon which such collective concepts as industrial democracy could be built. The result has been the shattering of the broad consensus regarding industrial reform characterized by 'Butskellism' and with it the 'Labour vision' of progress towards the equalization of authority within enterprises. In the process of the development of post-war thinking on industrial democracy certain explanations have been tendered to explain why, latterly, the concept has attracted such negative associations and why the drive for reform has been so dissipated.

The primary explanation is premised on the changed political landscape of the 1980s – the Conservative government's policies leave little room for statist or social democratic definitions of industrial democracy. The crisis of industrial democracy is essentially the result of a political oscillation which of itself does not necessarily indicate the need for a drastic rethink of the issue. This

approach is deficient as an analysis of whatever happened to industrial democracy as it looks at the end of the process rather than the beginning. It tells us
nothing fundamental about the material and ideological changes that have
been happening and therefore can offer no analysis or self-criticism regarding
the failure of that reform programme. For instance, some of the reasons for
the political success of Mrs Thatcher may be due to the Labour movement's
own failure to develop its thinking clearly and realistically in those areas such
as industrial democracy.

A second set of explanations about the demise of industrial democracy
centres on the fact that, in Britain, there are few tangible successes to point to,
with most of the notable experiments ending with little sustained institutional
or organizational change. There has been a signal failure to develop a
distinctive 'British way' or coherent tradition of industrial democracy. Consensus has been lacking, not only because the state, employers and unions
hold different views and draw conflicting lessons from the failure of those
experiments, but also because there are serious internal differences within
these groupings about what they want to see inaugurated. This is a viewpoint
that needs exploration indicating as it does the underlying weakness of the
Labour movement's own conception of industrial democracy and its lack of
vision and political will when in power. Continual arguments persist regarding
the content and role ascribed to industrial democracy, if a corporatist position
of full-blown state legislation and intervention is the answer or whether an
economistic position of a trade union defence of industrial interests was best
served by a reliance on the extension of some areas of collective bargaining
(Kelly, 1988; Flanders, 1970). Questions must also be raised about whether
there has ever been in place a coherent concept of industrial democracy that
overcame the problems of semantics that themselves prevent a broad basis of
support being laid. The different underlying philosophies and aims do emerge
in any cursory analysis of the arguments put forward for industrial democracy.
These include moral and ethical justifications on the grounds of equity and
fairness. It is also put forward as a means of increasing industrial efficiency,
the better use of creativity, commitment and human resources being the
result. Alternatively it is seen as a means of power equalization essentially
extending and completing the democratic rights of the citizen as worker.
Lastly, in terms of justifications, industrial democracy is seen as an agent
in the quest for self-realization. Participation schemes, job enlargement
measures and semi-autonomous workgroups are seen as contributory parts of
a movement to enhance the quality of working life and offer 'real' measures
of industrial democracy through the control and improvement of the work
role.

The existence of these and other competing aims shows on the one side the
wide and sustained basis for the calls for industrial democracy; however, it
can also result in serious fudging and oscillations in the conceptualization and

realization of industrial democracy. Some groups have tended to be fairly coherent on the issue, management for instance has tended to see 'participation' as useful only in its tendency to enhance efficiency, whereas the Labour movement has been caught in continually shifting grounds in relation to industrial democracy and the means by which the self-regulation of industry was to be achieved. In the British Labour movement we see contending streams that have periodically emphasized co-operatives, workers' guilds, syndicates, trade unions, nationalized industries, state bodies, as well as parliamentary and party action as the correct agents of advance. This constant shifting of emphasis is symptomatic of an indecisiveness over aim which has been highlighted in periods of potential advance. The dilemma concerns the way in which trade unions and workforces should take up industrial democracy, and the format and responsibilities they should adopt. Should they take on elements of management, with its responsibilities for running the company, or should it be no part of the trade union or workforce remit to take up such a pro-active orientation? For to do the former leaves them open to dangers of incorporation into management and their value system, to role confusion where they lose their historical position as an opposition to capital and to charges of neutralization in an economic and political sense. These arguments were succinctly set out by Clegg who took the view that unions cannot cross the divide and take on industrial management: they are the 'opposition that can never become a government'. He echoes the sentiments of the Webbs in seeing any compromise in their oppositional role as a weakening of trade union representation (Clegg, 1960).

This chapter explores the post-war debate and practice of industrial democracy and the grounds upon which such collaboration could take place, in particular it looks selectively at the various critical points of that experience using, where available, academic research findings to highlight the problems encountered. One of these 'critical points' occurred immediately after the war when the issue of the form and content of nationalization was being decided. This is followed by a look at studies by the Institute for Workers' Control in the late 1960s and early 1970s. The worker-director experiments are also discussed as are the recent re-evaluations of industrial democracy since the publication and agitation for an Alternative Economic Strategy. In all of these discussions a contrast has to be drawn between the 'Labour vision' of industrial democracy together with all the associated polemical baggage that goes with it and the much more ambiguous reality and sometimes indifferent constituency it was trying to reshape, a reality that academic research dwells upon. Much of this section highlights the changing dimensions of the gulf between polemics and reality and how industrial democracy is in a sense always caught in this gulf. It is part of a progressive political programme that looks forward to reforming industrial and organizational practice. In this sense it is a part of a socialist beyond, a sought-for rather than an achieved instance.

In the other sense, participation programmes and schemes are part of the fabric of our industrial experience, especially relevant to the micro-political struggles that are part and parcel of every organization's practice. In critical periods the differences between the aims of reform and empirical reality are rendered sharp and decisive. It is in such periods that decisions are made that have important and lasting effects.

NATIONALIZATION

The immediate aftermath of war saw a surge in socialist voting and sentiment. The 1945 Labour government was elected on a platform of socialization of the 'commanding heights' of the economy. Of the Labour MPs, 120 were trade union sponsored and 29 of them held cabinet posts in the new parliament. The major question that arose concerned how 'socialization' was to proceed. The pre-war debates (well documented in Coates and Topham, 1970; Coates, 1975) show evidence of the strong syndicalist strains born of the early shop steward movement which straightforwardly associated socialization with workers' control. Hence the question regarding nationalization is posed in a particular way, as here by the rail union:

> Will nationalisation make us free? And their answer has been that it will not unless with national ownership goes direct control of the railway services by the railways themselves. (National Guilds League, 1917, quoted in Coates and Topham, p. 265)

An element of syndicalism persists in trade union and Labour Party debates on nationalization up to and beyond the Second World War, re-emphasizing the notion that nationalization is primarily a means of installing industrial democracy marked by workforce control. However, after 1926, the debate is increasingly dominated by questions regarding the appropriate role of unions, of the state and of management in such socialized enterprises. More weight begins to be given to the state's use of economic planning, to the formation of efficient industries and to the rational application of state-dictated social priorities. The debate thus begins to centre upon a conflict between those who saw nationalization as necessary to the creation of plan, order and full employment and those who sought industrial democracy (Coates and Topham, 1970, pp. 273–4).

Ramsey MacDonald's period of power saw the inauguration by Herbert Morrison of the London Passenger Transport Board; this model henceforth becomes the dominant one for Labour. Rather than have as right a 'class-determined' place on the controlling committees of the industry or enterprise, the workers have now to earn that place in terms of the contribution they can make. Morrison held that it was no part of a socialist programme to install worker control or challenge the 'commodity status' of labour through nationalization. Instead, as Fox indicates, his model of socialization owed more to the 'independent public corporation':

> [An] ancient model whose modern form had been pioneered by a Conservative government of the 1920s. Management–worker relations were to remain of the conventional kind, though supplemented by 'joint consultation' which, it was hoped, would improve as well as humanise communications and raise efficiency. (Fox, 1985, p. 364)

This clash of philosophy regarding the role of nationalized industries was fundamental and represented a hinge upon which the Labour Party was to swing in the post-war years. The contrasting positions and definitions used in this period have been ably put together by Ramsay, whose arguments for and against worker representation in the socialized industries are set out in Table 6.1. This is represented by 'Morrisonianism' on one side and the views of the influential union leaders Dukes, Bevin and Clay on the other.

The points regarding role confusion and lack of workforce interest (2 and 5) are especially resonant with the post-war experience and can be applied with equal force to the arguments about later reforms. Following the 1945 election it was the Morrisonian view that took precedence. In subsequent analysis questions have been raised about the status and solidity of the party's plans for nationalization and the paucity of well-thought out plans. The way in which 'socialization' was to proceed was not precise, the formulations of the 1930s' debates tended to depict worker-directors as worker control given that a 50 per cent representation on the board was achieved. The lack of policy for the actual implementation of any schema is well described by the minister who had responsibility for the nationalization of the mines.

> For the whole of my political life I had listened to the party speakers advocating state ownership and control of coal mines, and I had myself spoken of it as a primary task once the Labour Party was in power. I had believed, as other members had, that in the party archives a blueprint was ready. Now, as Minister of Fuel and Power, I found nothing practical and tangible existed. There were some pamphlets, some memoranda produced for private circulation and nothing else. I had to start on a clear desk. (Emmanuel Shinwell, quoted in Coates and Topham, 1970, p. 311)

The Morrisonian model elevated a particular kind of state socialism, a concern for economic efficiency under central political direction. The public corporations rested on three principles: the *appointments* of experts to manage, the *accountability* of the industry and managers to ministers and that the industries be managed in the spirit of *business efficiency*. As Shell put it, 'each one of these principles reflected the complete rejection of decisions for some form of "workers' control"' (Shell, 1957, p. 516). Many commentators with hindsight now see the choice as simply part of a wider task that the Labour government, and to some extent the trade unions, had set:

Table 6.1 Arguments for and against worker representation on public sector boards

Against (Morrison view)	For (Bevin/Clay/Dukes)
1. A disinterested, neutral management elite, not a property-owning ruling class, should run the industry by right of expertise	1. Socialism must be more than just a change in legal ownership – to change one set of bosses with another would not change the subordinate role of the worker
2. Any worker representatives on the board would be seen as having 'gone over' to the bosses	2. If the Labour Party lost an election the running of the industry would fall into the hands of bosses' representatives with no defence through union representation
3. Unions would lose their independence and ability to bargain by being implicated in management decisions	3. Workers know production better than anyone, and can do most to raise efficiency if given the chance
4. Ministerial and parliamentary supremacy would be undermined by equal or majority union representation on the board	4. No other group had a serious claim to representation to compare with that of the producers of value
5. Lack of worker interest – they want cash and success before participation	5. Workers are interested in control, but only if it is genuine, not just participation on a nominal basis
6. Success and efficiency should take priority over democracy, especially at first. Experts must take decisions	6. Even if experts are required, they will advise not direct – final decisions can be taken by representative with the help of their advice
7. If workers get a say, all sorts of other groups would want representation (suppliers, consumers, etc.) and the result would be a hotch-potch board	

Source: H. Ramsay. Unpublished Ph.D. thesis.

Nationalisation was designed to improve the efficiency of predominantly capitalist economy, not to mark the beginning of its wholesale transformation. (Fox, 1985, p. 364.)

As Hinton adds, if the nationalized industries were designed to inaugurate a new form of democratic organization they could never have had a 'less suitable instrument'. They were, above all, instruments of planning and state control and:

> This view of public ownership as a mechanism of shifting class power within industry had always run counter to a view of nationalization as a means of increasing the efficiency across industries, a view which had gone along with a commitment to the retention within the new public corporations of traditional managerial hierarchies. (Hinton, 1983, p. 172)

The form of nationalization was also in some little way a reflection of trade unions who, threatened by 'real measures of workers' control', wished to secure their control over the membership by sticking to more traditional roles. As Dahl notes, the reasons for opting for management by experts responsible to parliament was, in part, to secure the independent function of the union, to forestall the situation in which the members have two bosses and to ensure policy direction external to the industry (Dahl, 1947). The outcome and the very real sense of workforce disappointment with nationalization are captured well in Plater's play *Close the Coalhouse Door* when on arrival at the pits on vesting day they find the same management, the same supervision, the same job and the same routines of subordination.

> The end product was that rapid alienation from nationalisation amongst large sections of the Labour electorate that has bedevilled the Labour Party ever since. (Coates, 1975, p. 54)

Joint consultation was to be the format for worker involvement. This format owed much to the wartime experience of joint production committees that did so much to increase production, morale and involvement. However, lacking the cement of common purpose that the fight against fascism provided, these committees tended not to live up to the promises achieved in wartime.

> The vast majority of councils had once more failed to produce the goods – for either side of industry. The co-operative spirit of the war could not be recreated nor could a genuine transfer of decision-making power to workers be achieved through a weak system of advisory committees. (Ramsay, 1977, p. 492)

In both the private and public sector works councils and joint consultation committees were established, although by 1953 the TUC was expressing 'disappointment and frustration' with the limitations of this form of participative machinery.

> Within months, disillusionment with nationalisation set in. A flood of trade union conference resolutions reflected a widespread feeling that the newly nationalised industries were no more the people's industries than they had been before the state takeover. By the late 1940s demands for workers' control in the nationalised industries were being made and the campaign had built up quite a head of steam when Labour left office in 1951. (Ramsay, 1977, p. 492)

THE IWC DEBATE

Ramsay explains that the revival of interest in worker participation can be dated to the mid to late 1960s (Ramsay, 1977). For him, the surge in productivity deals following the 'Fawley Experiments' marks the beginning of the new cycle of pressure for particpation. Undeniably from 1966 we see calls for industrial democracy emerge from a number of sources, important among which was the development in some European countries such as Sweden and West Germany, of longer-term institutional forms of industrial democracy (Forester, 1980; Elliot, 1978). The received wisdom from Europe was pointing to the benefits of worker representation through involvement in works councils and on the boards of enterprises. The growing importance of the EEC and its later directives on information disclosure (Vredling Proposals) and enhanced worker representation (5th Directive) has kept worker particpation as a major background feature of British industrial relations.

A second source of impetus towards industrial democracy was undoubtedly the rapid growth of the shop steward structure with its increased awareness of 'control' issues in industry. Plant-level collective bargaining in a period of sustained growth did not limit itself to instrumental issues of substance surrounding pay and conditions. The contesting of power within enterprises and its effect on the system of industrial relations, most visibly through increased use of the strike weapon, became the major focus of the Donovan Report of 1968 which, albeit negatively, identified the need for other sources of control.

The third source identified by Panitch was the development of a corporatist framework that represented the realignment by the state of its form of economic intervention. Corporatism, with its corresponding increase of trade union influence through such things as top-level representation on governmental committees, on the National Economic Development Board, through the deliberations of the TUC/Labour Party Liaison Committee and later in forming the Social Contract, represented a shift away from the previous separation of economics and politics enforced through 'labourism'. The trade unions, and more particularly their leaders, could now exercise some control at the macro-level and demand, in return for their co-operation, advances in the form of enhanced worker representation (Panitch, 1977). Another major source was the movement's re-evaluation of Labour in government and its failure to alter basic power structures, irrespective of nationalization. Hence the focus began to fall on the enterprise and the existence of the 'power gap' that held there. Trade union structures, shop stewards and plant bargaining essentially operated at a level and over a scope of issues in the enterprise that in effect left managerial freedom over a whole series of financial and strategic issues. From 1966 the TUC/Labour Party Liaison Committee specifically centred on this issue of the 'power gap'. Hence the TUC in their 1974 policy statement could declare:

> Some of the most basic aspects of the work situation and the security of that employment stems from decisions taken at extremely remote levels. . . . It is for this reason that any policy for the extension of industrial democracy must operate at all levels, from shop floor to board room and indeed, affect the process of national economic planning itself. (TUC/Labour Party Liaison Committee, 1974, p. 27)

This quote brings together the two-sided reappraisal of the concept of industrial democracy that was taking place, both as a macro-planning or corporatist device and as a method whereby the workforce could gain direct influence in the full range of decision-making within the enterprise. Observers of the revival of interest tend to divide into two camps when looking for the leading advocates and pressure groups of industrial democracy. For Elliot (1978) and Fatchett (1977) it was undoubtedly union leaders, Jack Jones, David Lea and members of the TUC/Labour Party Liaison Committee that forced the issue and kept it within a reformist debate regarding possible programmatic provisions of a macro kind. For Hyman and Ramsay, among many others, it was a grass roots issue springing out of the reality of workplace practice whose sustained pressure forced union leaders to catch up with their membership and place the issue back on the agenda. It was organizations like the Institute for Workers' Control that channelled and expressed some of the growing shop steward and lay opinion into a movement and a decade of agitation. The IWC, and more particularly Ken Coates, Tony Topham and Michael Barret Brown, were closely involved both polemically and academically with the promotion and spread of labour interest in workers' control. From the outset, they saw the ambiguity of the terms industrial democracy, worker participation and employee involvement. Yet they sought advance in the 'here and now' and were keen to overcome the confusion that was inherent in the concept of workers participation that could seriously threaten to split the movement that had arisen. For when discussing the idea of worker participation two views were discernible:

> [T]he idea is seen as a step on the road to full democracy and reflects the anxiety natural to reformers, to avoid any fundamentalism which might intensify the difficulties involved in securing change. However, it cannot be too strongly urged that, in its usual meaning, participation has the closest and ugliest relationship with a whole train of mean and sleazy predecessors in the sequence of devices for 'heading off' a growing working class demand for control. (Coates and Topham, 1968, p. 228)

What they did pursue was an alternative but less than precise concept of workers' control;

> Workers' control exists wherever trade union practice, shop stewards' sanctions and collective power constrain employers. . . . To take on a precise meaning for trade unionists this general view must be translated into actual plans, detailed programmes for particular industries. This does not mean that the overall plans (for opening the books, for the right of recall of workers' representatives and so on) are not crucially important. But if these slogans remain disembodied, they do not convey their own full significance, and they do not engage with the apparently 'practical' plans of the corporatists. (pp. 235–6)

The IWC began to publish and agitate around the 1960s, the conferences attracted increasing numbers of participants, they published their own bulletin and a range of pamphlets and books under the IWC and Spokesman imprint. They did not constitute themselves as a political party or tendency, rather the avowed aim of the institute was:

> [to] act as a research and educational body, to co-ordinate discussion and communication between worker control groups, and trade unions, to provide lists of speakers and to publish important materials on the subject of industrial democracy and worker control (IWC, 1968, pp. 104–5).

This format meant that the IWC was always a 'broad church' made up of revolutionary, sectarian and mainstream Labour movement members. If, as we have already seen, industrial democracy was a contested concept in general, then within the IWC this was indeed the case. At base it came from the supporters' widely differing philosophies for greater industrial democracy, rationale was piled on rationale, leading to various strands and competing definitions. William Morris' famous tenet 'no man is good enough to be another man's master' expresses one theme, the moralist–ethical grounds for extending democracy. Industrial democracy was also portrayed as a revolutionary overthrow of hierarchy and capitalist domination: at base about a power struggle and the transformation of relations of production. Yet in other tracts the reformism of its members shows through. Here industrial democracy is about efficiency through greater workforce involvement, forms of participation become adjuncts to the rational use of resources. The worker/management relation will as a result proceed more smoothly and enhance productivity. Allied to this was the view of industrial democracy framed by the Oxford School analysis as a regulating and stabilizing form of authority distribution, some extension of democratic regulation aids the good government of industry (see especially Flanders, 1970). In addition to these clear lines of advocacy other, supplementary rationales, can be detected. Participation was often seen as a personal means of handling change, enhancing worker satisfaction by direct means of individual and workgroup involvement. Most of all, the focus led by the core advocates of workers' control was that it was a progressive power redistribution mechanism, allowing industry to be changed from the inside, leading eventually to a dual power situation. All of these views could be held without dissonance because of the notion of equating any constraint on employers with workers' control. The broadness of this concept was a way of maximizing support and at the same time a refusal to dictate correct doctrine. It was, however, also a weakness, for in the end the IWC was never sure which form of industrial democracy it was pushing. Poole's research (see Table 6.2) indicates this extended range with IWC support possible for virtually all of those categories with the possible exceptions of modern capitalism and state socialism.

Even given this diversity there was a core of strategic thinking underlying the IWC's outlook. This contained three main areas. The first was the

Table 6.2 The main institutional forms of industrial democracy

Various ideological positions	Modern capitalism	Managerialism	Corporatism	Liberal pluralism and social democracy	Democratic socialism	State socialism	Syndicalism
Initiating agents	Employers, Management	Management	The state	Trade unions, political parties	Political party	Political party and the state	Trade unions, workers
Principal objectives and operational concepts	Productivity and efficiency	Human growth and development	System integration	Representative industrial democracy, power sharing, workers' rights	Limited self-management	Organizations for fulfilment of plans	Workers' ownership and self-management
Institutional forms	Co-partnership and employee shareholding	Employee involvement and joint consultation	Planning agreements, incorporation of unions at enterprise and society levels via integrative machinery	Worker-directors, co-determination, works councils, and producer co-operatives	Yugoslav workers' councils and other self-management organs	Participation in management and union organization in USSR and most eastern countries	Workers' control programs (often delegated rather than representative)

Source: M. Poole, 1986.

development of IWC industrial groups that could produce plans for their enterprise or industry. This used the shop steward support that the IWC had in a number of industries, especially in the docks, mining, steel, motor and transport industries. The notion of alternative planning was dependent on increasing the scope and quality of information coming to the stewards. Hence the call for 'opening the books' emerges both as a propaganda slogan and as a building block in devising other visions of what the enterprise could become. An extension of these demands into the 'social audit' came later and was effectively used to look at the impact that the loss of Upper Clyde Shipbuilders would have on the workers and the local economy. This used social criteria and wider measures of 'community health' to show the destructive effect that narrow capitalist-based accounting was having on that enterprise and area. However, as Bodington later admitted, too often such audits and plans were of a transitory and limited nature:

> The struggle for alternatives to policies devised by some hundreds of thousands of administrators and research and planning bodies working full time in the service of the existing order of capitalism needs the support of more than *ad hoc* collections for a few days of a few specialists ready to argue the case from the standpoint of the workers and the ordinary people. (Bodington, 1973, p. 65)

The bulletins of the IWC were always largely given over to the different industry groups and their plans did reach some degrees of sophistication, but in reality the function of those plans tended to be limited to a pedagogical one or as symbols in the absence of any grounds for their inauguration.

The second element in IWC thinking was the development of trade union strategies within the enterprise based upon encroaching 'control'. The 'control bargain' was advocated as a way of channelling existing trade union activity into positive rather than instrumental areas. By extending the collective bargaining practice within enterprises it was felt that one could overcome the problems of incorporation that the management-inspired participation schemes were prone to. Further, the control bargain drew on and incorporated many of the key themes that had animated the revival of interest in industrial democracy: it was firmly based on shop steward activity with which they were familiar, it built on activity at the plant and enterprise level and therefore could proceed irrespective of state action. It also appealed to those trade union impulses to gain control in management, especially control of a procedural kind being advocated by the Oxford School. For Topham, the main architect, it also signalled a tactical breakthrough by which means trade unionists could exercise positive rather than defensive/instrumental controls. He asked why not a control bargain instead of the then fashionable productivity bargains? This bargain would be qualitatively different for it would discuss and ask such questions as:

> What aspects of workers' control do we want to advance, what areas of managerial authority do we wish to challenge and acquire for the workers, what reductions in

top executive salaries do we seek and what restrictions on information do we wish to challenge? What wage structure and overall wage increase will we settle for? What research into the firm's profit structure, monopoly links, and alliance with the state, is needed? (Topham, in Coates and Topham, 1968, pp. 424–5)

This bargaining is mounted on a basis which goes on to challenge authority rather than to make accommodations with it:

The bargain then proceeds, until or unless the proposals are rejected by the representatives of the employers. . . . Imagine such a bargain. Imagine what happens if the workers' proposals are rejected. Assuming a real industrial democracy, what would the workers' do? (p. 425)

In practice the attempts to put such bargains forward in such explicit terms were not made, or if they were, the material and ideological power of capital and management quickly overruled them. Instead, the evidence that the IWC pointed to in order to support its claims that advances *were* being made was that of Turner (1963) and the Workplace Industrial Relations Survey (Parker, 1974). This evidence broke down collective bargaining issues into wages, working conditions, employment issues and disciplinary matters. The IWC's contention was that the patterns of bargaining were already showing a movement towards the contestation of employment and disciplinary issues that were themselves control-based, including hiring and firing, allocation of work, selection of overtime workers, pace of work, and so on.

The proportion of strikes about wage matters 'other than demands for increases', or about 'working arrangements', 'rules and discipline' rose from one-third to three-quarters of the total. This gives us a measure of the changing mood of the worker. (Coates, 1975, p. 99)

In effect they saw that the encroachment of control was happening. But this was *ad hoc* and needed moulding into a conscious strategy, whether this was sanctioned by the official union movement or not was deemed irrelevant.

The third leg of the IWC strategy was the inauguration of a movement for industrial democracy as a free-standing pressure group not necessarily tied to Labourism and state reform, which could use, but not be dominated by, parliamentarism. An analysis of the membership of the IWC does show a fair cross-section of the Labour movement with significant numbers of MP's and union leaders. During the 1970s' debate about Bullock's proposals for worker directors many of these members were firm advocates of the TUC line for 50–50 representation and the vesting of veto powers with workforce representatives. However, the Bullock debate did test the IWC's coherence as it became more and more sucked into a debate about the correct legislative line. For many the IWC had done its job by placing the issue of industrial democracy on the Labour Party agenda and subsequently, post-Bullock, the movement tended not to have the same vitality. Hyman extracts some of the reasons for the IWC's 'failure', a term that he uses with some reservation (Hyman, 1975). The initial problem he raises is that of their perspective on control and rightly asks what control was sought. Was it a largely pedagogic/consciousness-raising exercise where 'unattainable' demands are made but the process of their articulation then involves critical thinking, the extension of perspectives and the re-evaluation of the status quo? In a second perspective, control is seen as a contestable issue which could 'extend collective bargaining into forms of "joint control over traditional managerial prerogatives"' (p. 249). Hence, in this view, workers' control could be institutionalized into the very structures of industrial regulation. The third perspective he puts forward is the one that sees the contestation of control as signalling a 'real shift in the balance of industrial power' (p. 249), but a shift based on the unstable foundation of dual power. The diversity of IWC supporters meant that each of these perspectives were held simultaneously. The second major point he raises is the role of trade unions in the IWC strategy and the handling of the inherent conflict between spontaniety and discipline. This was discussed in Chapter 4 and refers to the limits of official trade unionism as a vehicle for social advance. Whilst the IWC may be feeding off and encouraging the spontaneous expression of workers' desire to gain control over their working environment, how far are they implicated at the same time in the 'officialization' of those struggles, being drawn into setting a new form of 'industrial legality' (Gramsci, 1977) that accords with the needs of stable industrial relations?

> When stable industrial relations are threatened, union officials may be expected to react in ways which *restrict* rank-and-file self-activity. (Hyman, 1975, p. 263)

Because of its need for support from the union movement, especially trade union leaders, Hyman saw that the IWC would inevitably succumb to a subordinate position and recast their strategy in a fashion acceptable to that of the official Labour movement. The subsequent events and the splits that developed within the IWC over the Bullock recommendations did highlight these tensions and the pressure to conform to a programme that could be kept within the well-policed framework of 'industrial legality'. Furthermore, the politically-induced recession of the Thatcher administration highlighted the political fragility of the role of the plant as the key one in strategic control terms, for the debate and issues of moment did change and with it withered the faith in achieving workers' control through such voluntaristic methods. However, what cannot be denied is that the IWC achieved through sheer activity and force of will an enormous amount, but the structures of authority and the institutions that give them power were deeply entrenched and resistant to such activity. Moreover, the IWC approach underestimated the strength of worker indifference and the contradictions in working class and trade union responses to control and power issues.

The resurrection of worker-directors as a method for industrial preferred democracy came in 1966 with the formation of the joint liaison committee. The re-nationalization of steel in the 1960s, however, presented the first opportunity for testing the idea on a long-term and on a closely monitored basis. In post-war experience, worker-directors have been largely a public sector phenomenon, fortunately research teams have focused on both of the long-running British Steel Corporation and Post Office experiments. These have been supplemented by research in the private sector by Chell, Cox and Towers that refers to a sample of seven instances of worker-directors.

This section draws heavily upon the research of Brannen *et al.* (1979) who carried out a model study of the BSC experiment. The work of Jones (1977), Batstone *et al.* (1983) and Tower *et al.* (1981) is also relevant and well worth consulting.

Public sector experiments

The BSC programme began in 1968 for an initial three-year period. Twelve directors were appointed to divisional boards, these were to be the crowning point of a participation programme that also included expanded collective bargaining and extensive consultation at plant and company level. Directors were nominated by the trade unions but then selected by the BSC board, each was paid £1,000 and a condition of their acceptance was their renunciation of all trade union offices. The four divisional boards on which the directors sat had only advisory powers in relation to the central board of the corporation; it was this latter that held policy-making and strategic planning authority.

Much of the criticism that Brannen *et al.* detected was based on two grounds: the separation of worker-directors from their trade union and the fact that it was an advisory function they performed. The longer the experiment proceeded the more the workforce saw a widening gulf between their original aims and the actual experience. The worker-directors, being non-elective, had an indistinct chain of accountability, they had no real power, nor was there, on the basis of board-room practice, any evidence that they affected decision-making within BSC. Even after the changes to allow trade union links and access for the directors to the main policy board, the researchers continued to identify serious problems which led to the failure of the experiment. For Brannen *et al.* these included: a failure at the outset to specify the roles and objectives of worker-directors, this vagueness they saw as largely deliberate in as much as it avoided the crystallization of opposing interests prior to the experiment proceeding; and the refusal to face up to potential problems of dissociation, accountability and the authority of worker-directors, all of which seriously undermined the project. However, other equally serious problems emerged in the practice of such representation. Minority representation on boards did little or nothing to alter the routines, values or authority relations within the board. The worker-directors were placed under severe social pressure to 'conform to normal board room procedure'. With no clear function they accepted a largely passive role within the board, limited in scope. Their expertise, if accepted at all by other members, was seen in the area of workforce attitudes, they became a sounding board for potential opposition to certain plans. Brannen *et al.* vividly describe the process of socialization that the worker-directors underwent: how they were educated, coached and fitted into acceptable board room roles. In the context of increasingly serious rationalization moves that reduced employment substantially there was little indication that they would then put forward any alternatives or social criteria that could mollify such programmes:

> This was not the case: during our period of observation of board meetings there was no instance in which the assumption behind any closure was challenged, the economic data presented by the directors appeared to be invested with impartiality and objectivity. (Brannen *et al.*, 1979, p. 173)

Their analysis of the project generally shows a massive underestimation of the forces at play within the board room constraining an oppositional stance of worker-directors. The experiment was ill-thought through and structurally problematic from the outset. It took place in a period of rapid restructuring within which the worker-directors became known as 'hatchet men' for management. Once in place, the unions failed to support the directors adequately. There had been no thought given to how, at an enterprise level, the workforce could use them. There was little training or educational support for them and the problem of 'expertise' was hardly confronted. Socialization was a powerful tool especially in the context of their virtual isolation, the failure to challenge head-on the existing board-room procedures meant that they opted instead for a marginal role as personnel experts, one that was at least validated by the other members of the board.

The Post Office experiment which was inaugurated later corrected some of the mistakes identified in the steel experiment. Their format allowed for trade union links to be kept throughout, although worker-directors could have no part in the collective bargaining machinery. The number of worker-directors was similar in proportion to the $2x + y$ formula proposed by the Bullock report with equal numbers of management and union representatives plus an independent set of members including two consumer representatives. In this case the researchers saw that the worker-directors did not, as the management had feared, bring conflict into the board room. Whilst there were some attempts to challenge board decisions this never developed into a frontal assault upon the procedures and norms of board-room activity. As a group, the worker-directors did constitute an independent force with less reliance upon management. However, there were similarities between their activities and behaviour and that of the steel worker-directors. Here, too, there tended to be a focus upon 'workforce' rather than strategic issues, with them being perceived as experts only in the area of workforce and industrial relations. They had little to contribute to general board discussions, and their influence was regarded as small both in affecting worker attitude and in shaping board-room decisions:

> Few board decisions were different as a result of trade union nominees' pressure and the extent to which they affected management and union behaviour was limited. (Batstone *et al.*, 1983, p. 165)

The unions had additional problems that Snell and Taylor point to regarding disagreement between unions and again a failure to support, train or resource them properly (Snell and Taylor, 1984).

Private sector

Research in the private sector had great difficulty in finding any extant schemes to analyse. After a nationwide search, eight functioning schemes were identified and seven made the object of study (Towers *et al.*, 1988). Two of these were schemes from the 1940s initiated as part of a share ownership scheme rather than as an effort to enhance representation. The five remaining schemes were conceived and established by management. As Chell *et al.* say, this meant they were based within a 'unitary' frame of reference which aimed for the suppression of conflicts of interest. Worker-directors were used essentially as a tool to strengthen managerial control and authority. Only two schemes had formal union involvement. The overall finding suggested a lack of strategic use of this high-level representation, an inability to use information/procedures adequately, an exclusion from the informal network of control, and by and large indifference to the schemes from the workforce and unions within the companies.

Evidence on broader attitudes to worker-directors has come from two other studies conducted by the Department of Employment. The Dowling *et al.* study in the North West found total hostility from management to Bullock-style proposals, but also highly ambiguous responses from unionists and trade union officers (Dowling *et al.*, 1981). Of fourteen unions only one reported rank and file support for progress to industrial democracy, and only three of the unions supported the proposals encased in the Bullock Report.

> [The role of the worker-director was felt to be] compromised by over-association with management and participation in managerially-based policy decisions may be unpopular with the workforce. (p. 30)

In the eyes of trade union officers, worker-directors are a potential threat to workforce power and the structures of trade union organization in enterprises.

The survey of Scottish enterprises by Cressey *et al.* shows clearly the hostility of management and the ambivalence of shop stewards to worker-directors (Cressey *et al.*, 1981). Figure 6.1 details what Cressey *et al.* describe as the 'evaporation of enthusiasm' of both managers and workforce representatives as participation of different forms are suggested.

Managers saw their rights to manage directly infringed by such moves; moreover, such moves challenged the hierarchical structure of the enterprise, crossing functional lines of authority because of what managers saw as the operation of 'pure ideology'. Nor did they see any workforce enthusiasm for this, with the addendum that shop stewards would suffer the confusion and frustration of not being able to bargain in the board room. The shop stewards

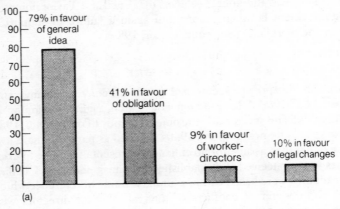

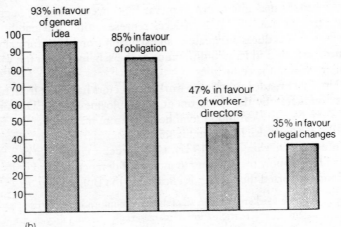

Figure 6.1 Managers' (a) and representatives' (b) views on industrial democracy and participation.
Source: Cressey *et al.* 1981.

were, as Figure 6.1 suggests, split down the middle over worker-directors. On the one side the scheme offered early information and some prospect of influence in strategic discussions, whilst on the other they doubted if share-holders would allow 'real involvement', so that they would be left in the middle carrying responsibility but having no real power or control over the terms of the decision-making. They also doubted whether the board was in fact the site of control in enterprise terms. This latter point seems justified as most evidence points clearly to the widespread existence of informal networks of decision-making: executive boards, managerial committees, and so on (Cressey et al., 1981, pp. 37–47).

Overall, the research evidence on worker-directors results in a surprising unanimity, portraying in turn a wholesale management hostility, trade union ambivalence and workforce indifference. The long-running experiments in steel and the Post Office, both since terminated by the Conservative govern-ment, did not break this mould: instead they highlighted a series of deficiencies that add up to a pessimistic picture for the extension of industrial democracy through the medium of worker-directors. In sum, the analysis emphasized the strength of capitalistic norms and the difficulty of installing other criteria for the operation of an enterprise.

> Within the board room in a market society the dominance of market over other forms of discourse is already established and constantly reinforced by organisational practice. (Brannen et al., 1979, p. 114)

There is a logic to capital, its institutions and its organization that an isolated group of workers' representatives, placed within it, cannot break. The experiments also highlight the acceptance in Britain of a form of reactive trade unionism that shies away from joint responsibility. This flight from enterprise responsibility negatively validates managerial legitimacy in the areas of busi-ness policy, financial planning, design and technology, essentially in the areas of the strategic direction of the enterprise. Bound up with this flight from responsibility is a refusal to put forward other options in terms of either planning, representation or objectives. In their absence, of course, capitalistic/managerial perspectives do dominate. This defensive posture also means that productivity, creativity and experimentation become associated with managerial action and initiatives, so much so that it reaffirms the voluntaristic nature of the system that states that participation is best left to management to inaugurate, unfettered by statutes and regulation. It shows participation as, at best, 'needs driven' and orientated to marginal forms of organizational problem-solving. Lastly, the analysis of worker-directors shows at base the conflict of interest and expectations that these actors have, the more detailed studies highlighting how the aims, values, imagery and even vocabulary of participation is different. (See the opening chapter in Brannen et al., 1979, for a discussion of the 'vocabulary of participation'.) Irrespective, then, of the political debate or the analytic problems, empirically, at least, there was unanimity regarding the problems of this format. Even without Thatcherism, the concept of worker-directors was already tarnished and would have posed serious questions and difficulties of inauguration had the Labour Party won the 1979 election and proceeded with the reforms in the White Paper *Industrial Democracy* (HMSO, 1977).

AN ALTERNATIVE INDUSTRIAL DEMOCRACY?

With the victory of the Conservatives in May 1979 the whole political land-scape regarding industrial democracy changed. The Department of Employment was now identifying voluntarism as the only sensible way of proceeding towards 'industrial participation'. Any research undertaken was orientated towards the merits of freely-agreed joint consultation or increasingly em-phasizing financial participation whether by profit-sharing or wider share ownership. Rather than be a programmatic, national-level issue for progress-ive reform forwarded by the state, it became a matter for the parties, driven by their specific needs, at the enterprise level. As such, participation came ultimately to reflect the new power balance. Whilst the rhetoric of participa-tion remained, the will to legislate, inaugurate frameworks or to issue guidelines was quietly dropped, with only one minor area of reform legislated for. This was a part of the Employment Act, 1982, which called for the inclusion of employee involvement statements in companies' annual reports: a mechanism intended to improve employee involvement but which has since been shown to be a failure (IRRR, 1987a, b; McHugh *et al.*, 1987).

Research conducted by numerous groups has identified joint consultation as the main participative format at play within voluntarism. There is some broad measure of agreement regarding the distribution of committees with sectors such as food and drink, chemicals and engineering having a high incidence, with the larger plants more likely to have a functioning committee in existence. Overall, the figures range from 34 per cent in all establishments to over 60 per cent of establishments having some form of joint consultation. Politically such figures have tended to be used to illustrate the fact that legislation is not needed to underpin the provision of participation. (For further discussion see Daniels *et al.*, 1983; Millward and Stevens, 1986; Marchington, 1987; Cressey *et al.*, 1985.) However, the figures are highly sensitive to the methods of drawing the sample and analysis used. For instance, if one looks at a time series analysis as MacInnes (1985) does, then the apparent renaissance of this form of participation claimed by many government and academic figures does not seem to have occurred. He challenges the overall figures and the rate of growth in consultation that has been claimed. More important is the debate surrounding the changing purpose of joint consultation in the context of crisis. For Cressey *et al.* (1985), the recession has highlighted the inherent weaknesses of joint consultation. Marginal as it was at the best of times to enterprise decision-making, it still had a function for both workforce representatives and management. For the former it was a flexible way of influencing management, gaining information, and of pursuing workforce interests and articulating them directly to management. For the latter it was a controllable form of 'participation': one that had a strong ideological, educative function of teaching the workforce representatives the capitalist ABC, that introduced them to the problems of running an enterprise. In recession, the fragile unity of interests that supported joint consultation changes, and where the consultation committees survived they often did so on a changed basis with reordered functions. For instance, the committees became for the workforce a forum within which job guarantees and redundancy protections were sought. For management, rather than seeking legitimacy for their decisions through, at worst, a passive form of consent, joint consultation reinstates a unitarist conception of the enterprise and offers one-dimensional solutions to the problems facing it. The workforce can now participate in as much as they are more efficiently solving those problems visited on them by the recession.

As for the rest of the participative provisions found, they tend to be based on the communication of information from the top, primarily exhortational in character. Alongside these has been the fashion for quality circles, some direct workgroup participation and a growing concern to integrate small group activity into larger technological changes. In general, the United Kingdom, along with most of Europe, has seen since the mid 1970s a sharp movement away from 'programmatic' statutory provisions towards 'issue based' participation (Cressey *et al.*, 1988.). It is now more common to see participative initiatives focused upon definable changes – to do with new technology, work organization, quality improvements and specific problems, rather than inaugurating institutional schemes that cover enterprises, whether by works councils, joint committees or legislation for statutory rights at a national level.

A SOCIALIST ALTERNATIVE

In the aftermath of three consecutive political defeats there had to be a rethink regarding the conceptual basis and the method of installing industrial democracy. The core question of control within enterprises and its linkage to overall political control have been the basis for this rethink and have led to the discussion of industrial democracy alongside extended and 'popular' planning. The Alternative Economic Strategy (Conference of Socialist Economists, 1981) placed industrial democracy at the centre of its plans for changing the dynamic of an economy in decline. This strategy drew eclectically from pre-existing strands of thought on industrial democracy. From Bullock and the earlier debate it repeated the need to close the 'control gap' in enterprises. It also drew on other notions of democratic planning from three main sources: the IWC and their advocacy of workers' company and industry plans; from the Lucas Aerospace experiment where the plans established the social criteria that ought to guide production; and from previous Labour Party practice in establishing a National Enterprise Board with directive planning power in the private sector. Their act of synthesis was at the same time an attempt to overcome the schism inherent in Labourism between the political, economic and social levels of action (Miliband, 1973). Enterprise activity should not be isolated from macro-politics, nor social criteria from productive activity. George describes the different criteria upon which popular planning was based and the independence sought from managerialist aims:

> [Workers plans] are about (i) seeking appropriate and effective forms of union organisations to deal with vastly changed corporate structures, (ii) using knowledge and information obtained through the labour process for getting a handle on those corporate decisions which affect jobs and other employment matters, (iii) using this knowledge and information to build up an independent bargaining position based firmly on the workers' views of what they require from the enterprise, (iv) extending the boundaries of collective bargaining and related activities, not accepting managements' view of what is or is not negotiable, (v) overcoming traditional divisions between industrial, economic and social policy, partly through production proposals to meet social needs in communities, partly through demands on company taxation, government grants and the rest. (George, 1981, pp. 93–4)

The previous problems of macro-, meso- and micro-activity were to be overcome by a thorough-going restructuring of democratic planning that interlinked plans and levels in the following way:

Macro political direction
National investment board
|
Industry planning agreements
Sectorally-based plans
|
Workers' control struggles
Workers' alternative plans

The publication in 1982 of the Labour Party/TUC Liaison Committee document *Economic Planning and Industrial Democracy* also followed closely this line of development. They proposed that worker involvement had to occur in the planning of economic and industrial policy at each level of the economy:

> Planning will only be effective in the UK if the government's economic and industrial strategy is coherent with the strategies pursued by companies and vice versa. Two main lessons stand out. First, there must be firm links established between national planning and company planning: and, second, workers must be involved at all levels of the planning system. These lessons are central to our thinking. (p. 6)

The format proposed for local level involvement was to be firmly single-channel, based around the extension of collective bargaining, the building of strong trade union representation and the gradual encroachment of worker influence into key and strategic areas of enterprise decision-making. Such extensions provided the basis upon which local initiatives could be built – local plans, local enterprise boards would then complement the macro- and industrial-level planning undertaken by government and its quangos.

The Liaison Committee proposed a number of supportive or enabling measures to underpin this structure. The first was the development of an extensive planning agency that could advise enterprises and oversee the signing of agreed development plans. Such plans would cover important issues in enterprises – purchasing policy, import levels, investment plans, pricing strategies and training policies. For effective trade union involvement, rights to enhanced information, consultation and representation were promised linked directly to these areas (pp. 24–5). These rights included the creation of joint union committees and in some cases the possible inauguration of worker-directors (p. 29). The debate raised by the alternative economic strategy and the Liaison Committee document was cut short by the political defeat of 1983, but not before criticism of some of these ideas, especially of the linkage between those three areas of planning activity: the workplace, the industry and the state. For underpinning this structure there was seen to be an implicit and explicit reliance upon an unproblematic worker interest and, more importantly, mobilization. The following quotes indicate this:

> In the development of planning suggested by the AES, the involvement of workers at the point of production, and of workers and their families in localities, would enable planning to be democratised from the outset. (Conference of Socialist Economists, 1981, p. 85)

> Mobilisation will need to have some clear point of application if it is not to be frittered away in ineffective gesture. The development of more democratic forms of policy-making through planning agreements and local struggle is one channel for this. Another channel is the development of the political role of working class organisations, both through existing trade union structure and through new forms of organisation. *Both have developed considerably in recent years.* [our emphasis] (Labour Party/TUC Liaison Committee, 1982, p. 139)

Such formulations, however, tend to be stating requirements, the 'ought to be' rather than the realities of trade union and political mobilization in the 1980s. The problems with these formulations and the later Labour Party/TUC Liaison Committee document are threefold. Firstly, the problem of the Labour Party and parliamentarism. Both post-war and recent experience has seen the continual breakdown of policies that extended beyond accepted parliamentary practice. Fiscal and monetary measures, legislation on employer and unions, nationalization and public ownership have been the acceptable methods for economic planning and intervention. Where this was breached or over-extended – in the case of George Brown's Ministry for Economic Planning, in the Chrysler intervention, or in trade union plans at Lucas – such experiments or proposals were quickly dropped in favour of more controllable measures. Extra-parliamentary activity of the kind proposed has never been the basis of Labour's policies. Where the mobilization of workers or trade unions in such plans becomes a necessity for the success of parliamentary/state action then such plans have been and continue to be rejected by the Labour leadership. Secondly, it has to be asked whether such a mobilization was a possible, coherent and reliable force. The evidence would indicate that it is in fact unreliable, unstructured and prone to sectionalism. Much of the supporting analysis of the potential for such mobilization has been pinned on the 'leading edge' of the British trade union movement. Lucas and Vickers (Wainwright and Elliot, 1982) have a status of 'icons' for the wider workforce but cannot be said to be representative of the mass of enterprise situations. The detailed evidence of post-war practices and experiments relating to participation (even those of a low key character from worker-directors through to job redesign teams) shows the difficulties of nurturing and sustaining their operation. This is not only due to the indifference of workforce, which has been a consistent factor, but importantly because of trade union representational weakness, sectionalism and ambivalence towards an extended role in enterprise decision-making. Bodington emphasizes as a precondition the need for a workforce to have unanimity of purpose and a thorough knowledge of organizational objectives and practice in order for workers' plans to succeed (Bodington, 1973). Lane has repeatedly pointed out that a reliance upon trade union involvement at plant, company, sector and national level demands 'capacities and competencies' that are as yet not present either in terms of orientation, skills or structure (Lane, 1985, p. 322). Lane especially emphasizes the lack of an adequate 'intelligence function' that can provide real grounds for planning, for directing and reforming an organization. He supports Tomlinson's contention that:

> The Left has not dirtied its hands by examining all these gritty but crucial problems about financial control, information systems, organisational hierarchies, accounting methods, etc. which any serious proposals for enterprise reform would have to deal with. (Tomlinson, 1982, p. 3)

The third major problem relates to the workforce representational structures that exist in enterprises. Without a strong basis of such representation the whole superstructure of the alternative economic strategy and the reforms in the Liaison Committee document would have little foundation upon which to rest. Evidence from research does not give rise to optimism about this foundation being in place. There is a lack of what might be called 'grounded proposals' here to deal with problems clearly identified by the

Bullock Committee. The committee saw wholesale involvement in the enterprise as demanding some mechanism for total enterprise representation and for the internal resolution of workforce differences. The proposed solution for Bullock was the Joint Representation Committee: this straddled the different union groupings and formed in essence an effective combine committee (Bullock Report, 1979, pp. 109–27.) This recognized and attempted to reconcile trade union sectionalism and admitted that enterprise complexity, multi-union, multi-plant and multi-product groupings do pose difficulties in creating a workforce identity and in allowing effective workforce agreement to be reached never mind concerted planning to take place. Hirst points to the growing fragmentation and heterogeneity of enterprises:

> British firms are increasingly multi-industry, multi-plant and multi-locational groups of companies – often with no apparent economic rhyme or reason. Such firms offer intractable difficulties to effective industrial democracy, or even to inter-site union action. (Hirst, 1982, p. 2)

If popular planning and tiered arrangements for democratic planning are to succeed then one fundamental building block – that of overall enterprise representation and organization – has to be secured. Combine committees have been one of the cornerstones upon which the possibility of company plans are founded, but unfortunately the recent evidence points to a patchy incidence of their existence, with little over one-third of sampled companies having some form of joint shop steward committee in place. (For further discussion of combine committees see Friedman, 1976; Cressey and MacInnes, 1982; Lane, 1982; George, 1981; Terry, 1985.) This figure should not, however, be taken at face value for it is based on establishments rather than enterprises and therefore overstates the existence of such committees. Furthermore it does not distinguish between single and multi-plant enterprises, nor does it indicate anything about the strength or significance of such joint committees.

When one does look at the findings regarding combines functioning there are a number of points that indicate their current infeasibility as straightforward vehicles of advance towards industrial democracy. Combines tend to be used predominantly as channels for extended negotiation up to, but not exclusively at, the enterprise level, especially where the company has multi-plant bargaining. However, the authority or representation of the stewards involved remains firmly plant-based; Cressey et al.'s study (1981) of large Scottish enterprises revealed a similar level of combine existence to the one mentioned above (34 per cent). However, of those seventeen committees with representatives from more than one union, only eight appeared to operate beyond the boundaries of an individual plant. Of these only four were organized at an enterprise-wide level, with the remaining four pitched at other levels within the larger enterprise (i.e. either subsidiary company, division or product grouping). Most were found in company environments that were not very complex. All were located in manufacturing industry, with the engineering sector accounting for half. As regards their normal function, if one looks beyond the modest negotiations around pay equalization then it appeared that most combine committees operated on a basis of contact, chiefly as information bureaux. However, as Baldry *et al.* (1981) point out, this provides a flimsy basis for contesting corporate power. In crisis, such committees may crumble when attempting to handle issues of substance. With little organizational basis they mistake 'communication for organization'. Where the committees were based on negotiation and bargaining structures there was little indication that they took on issues affecting the whole enterprise or strategic or long-term plans. Beyond seeking equalization of pay rates the evidence suggests that, at present, to the extent that combine committees go beyond information exchanging to negotiation functions, they do so not to challenge the overall structure of control in the enterprise or to take up the negotiation of 'business decisions', but to undertake on an enterprise-wide basis, the negotiation of much the same range of issues as union organization at plant level currently tackles. If one puts these caveats with the long-standing hostility of many unions to the growth of combines and the 'company unionism' that they represent, then one can see the wide gap between the polemic about workers' plans and their empirical possibility. The first steps in installing basic structures capable of promoting such a national framework of plans and initiatives have hardly been taken. Mobilization on this basis is bound to be patchy and in the end self-defeating. Thus Lane's critique of the Labour Party/TUC Liaison Committee's document is well aimed. There is little emphasis on unions' intelligence function detectable, there are few structures extant to sustain workers' plans and there is an absence of thought-out strategy regarding the enterprise level. It appears that the result would once again be a reversion to macro-level fiscal policies at the expense of 'failed' popular planning.

MUNICIPAL SOCIALISM

The failure to think through the problems involved in generating a committed and active workforce in pursuit of such desired aims can be illustrated in the later attempt by Greater London Enterprise Board to use its financial purse strings to enforce enterprise 'good practice' in relation to employee democracy. The 1980s had left the British Left with little influence at the national political level; the tripartite or corporatist forums were quickly evacuated of trade unionism, and the major experiments and legislative moves towards greater industrial democracy were at an end. At the same time shop stewards and union workplace influence were being challenged by adverse market and legislative effects. As a result, those municipal enclaves of socialism became more important as a basis for developing democratic ideas centred on popular planning. In 1982 the Greater London Council, alongside the West Midlands, Lancashire, Merseyside and West Yorkshire, sought a more interventionist role in the local economy by starting enterprise boards. The most developed ideas were those of the GLC and West Midlands who saw the enterprise boards as vehicles for promoting industrial democracy through enterprise planning (Hasluck, 1987, p. 191). Enterprise planning had a number of components, but essentially:

> Any intervention by GLEB in pursuit of any of its investment functions will be conditional upon agreement between GLEB, the enterprise concerned and the unions concerned, covering in particular future patterns of employment and investment in the enterprise. (Ball, 1986, pp. 131–2)

The financing by the GLC of any industrial or corporate venture now had to measure up to those priorities encased in the London Industrial Strategy as well as to defined standards of industrial relations and democratic procedures. For instance, the enterprise would have to pay the going rate for the job, comply with health and safety standards and recognize trade unions, in addition to installing a mechanism for enterprise planning. This mechanism was to be agreed with the GLEB and would prescribe the enterprise's:

1. Product and market strategy.
2. Future investment and technological change.
3. Location.
4. Pricing policy.
5. Employment levels and conditions.
6. Skill mixture and training policy.
7. Equal opportunity policy.

This plan would not necessarily be separate from collective bargaining but could proceed at either a workplace or enterprise level depending on the form of representation. Aid would be forthcoming from GLEB for the parties in drawing up such plans, and a planning support unit was formed to this end. In all, the enterprises were committed to fulfilling certain basic conditions on investment strategy, job creation, location, condition of work, equal opportunities policy and tendering. Ball analysed 102 projects funded by the GLEB in order to see how the reality of enterprise planning measured up to its promise. His conclusions are pessimistic:

> It will surprise no one with a modicum of experience of industrial relations to learn that the system was quite unable to operate as it had been initially conceived. Had the Enterprise Board restricted its investment to medium to large sized companies, where trade union organisation was well developed, where shop stewards had an abundance of experience in dealing with the grittiest of industrial relations problems, and had sought to understand and 'shadow plan' the company over an extended period, and had managements adopted the most forthcoming

co-operative attitudes imaginable, *it would still have been difficult to fulfil the initial expectations of enterprise planning. The reality was much worse.* Many of the companies that GLEB dealt with – particularly in its earliest stages of operating – were small, with poor or even non-existent trade union organisation, crude and unsophisticated approaches to dealing with industrial relations, and managements that were not in the least committed to 'airy fairy' notions of industrial democracy. Moreover, the companies concerned often had the most serious of commercial operating problems – why else should they come to GLEB after all? The reality was that as a 'test bed' for ideas about industrial democracy, GLEB projects were very poor laboratory conditions indeed – unless, that is, one takes the view that adverse circumstances are a useful test of any theory. [our emphasis] (pp. 131–2)

Of 102 companies assisted, only 4 eventually produced an enterprise plan. Half of them recognized unions but only 19 put in place basic industrial relations procedures. Because the enterprises involved employed less than two hundred people and had rudimentary industrial relations, Ball concludes that this put an enormous strain upon the GLEB to make good the lack of trade union and management organizational skills. No real planning took place without considerable support from the external unit. However, where this was achieved Ball did see that a positive contribution was made to the commercial success of the company. As most of the companies were under the whip of financial exigencies, though, this was a poor sample in which to test the notion of enterprise planning. The central problems that Ball alerts us to again are the capabilities of the workforce, their structure and motivation to secure and operate such plans. To take this route it appears that a long process of preparation is necessary, involving the building of legal rights, appropriate structures, industrial attitudes and a political culture that could overcome basic attitudes of indifference:

> The message for trade unions is surely that they must not only look outside themselves for new workers rightly in order to advance industrial democracy, they must also look within themselves at their own industrial strategies and leadership, if industrial democracy is to live in the minds of workers rather than in paper pronouncements. (Ball, 1986, p. 142)

Ball sees a much longer time span and gradual strategy emerging in which trade unions, if they are committed to industrial democracy, must first seek procedural agreements between trade unions and employers, securing consultative and information rights before moving on to dealing with specific problem areas by agreed joint action, beginning only then to think of shadow planning and possibly corporate plans. The clear message from Ball's case studies is that any reliance upon collective bargaining as the main tool of enterprise planning is misguided in that it is a restrictive tool based on a defensive consciousness that limits rather than breaks down boundaries of possible activity.

CONCLUSION

This review of the post-war history of British thinking on industrial democracy has highlighted both the political and the empirical debate. In tracing their course, what appears strongly is a sense of cycles – but not cycles of the character described by Ramsay. Rather we seem to have here two separate cycles, one polemically-based that deals in moral, ethical and political prescriptions, visions of what industry could be, given changes in attitudes, power structures and vested interests. This debate has had high spots with the development of manifestos, statutory or programmatic frameworks of the Bullock and White Paper kind. However, this cycle appears to have been at a low point, not only in Britain but also in many of the European countries, with few political proposals or debates being generated since the mid 1970s. Only in the very recent past has there been some stirring in Europe related to the developments around the Single European Act and its call for greater 'social dialogue' and as a result of the push towards a completed internal market by 1992.

The other cycle apparent is one based on close observation of actual practice in industry, and which uses empirical evidence on the existence, aims and rationales for 'participation'. Such evidence shows participation to be a set of relations that is continually sought and also responsive to cycles but of a different order. In this perspective the term industrial democracy is hardly ever used, and the 'participative practices' that are found are dismissed as micro-level, 'needs driven' participation or simply as managerial strategies to gain commitment. There is, however, a danger in dismissing this area as merely incorporative devices as it has provided for long periods the only context in which the contestations of authority are played out, showing why the parties in enterprises seek to exercise control over what issues to implement and their effects (see also Cressey *et al.*, 1985).

Overall, the crisis of industrial democracy that one finds tends to be related to the polemical debate: it is essentially a crisis for the institutions of the Labour movement as they in their pronouncements appear further and further detached from the empirical reality that might underwrite their programmes. Hence in our view the 'crisis' is characterized by these 'cycles' being out of synchronization, by an ignorance of the real sources and demands for industrial democracy, and by an underestimation of the structural and representational problems facing the proposals put forward in the polemical debate.

Industrial sociology becomes an actor in this drama only to the extent that it provides the necessary corrective to polemical debate by supplying hard evidence that debunks myths and applies critical thought to 'fashionable' argument. It has no function to question the vision but it might be able to advise on whether that vision is within grasp and to advise on the likely problems that will have to be faced; to that extent much of the material used in this chapter does go some way to answering the question 'whatever happened to industrial democracy?' – it still remains in the utopian future so long as the hard work of analysis, programme building, persuasion, resourcing and realization is postponed.

7

DOES CLASS MATTER ANY MORE?

Alas, just as our generation inherited a legacy of old industrial buildings,
so too, I fear, have we inherited a legacy of old industrial relationships
Lord Young of Graffham (1986)

THE CONCEPT OF CLASS

Many people argue that modern Britain is a class-ridden society, but the
argument ranges from those who, like Lord Young, the then Conservative
Secretary of State for Employment, see outdated, irrelevant and irrational
class prejudice as a contributor to industrial conflict and poor economic
performance, to those who see such a view as 'a narrow and trivial' concept of
class, and see the main issue as being the 'hard core of class . . . the substance
and structural sources of inequality' (Westergaard and Resler, 1976, pp. 1–2)
which remain largely unaltered in essence since the previous century. From
this perspective, what requires explanation is the passivity within Britain of
those who suffer most from the maintenance of such inequality. Such an
approach is not confined to Marxists, but as Goldthorpe (1984) points out, has
been studied by American social scientists studying the social roots of political
authority (e.g. Nordlinger, 1967). For supporters of the first view, class
no longer has any substance but as an ideologically-based identity whose
persistence is a puzzle. For the second it is the relative absence of such an
identity, in the face of the persistence of material class inequalities, which
needs explaining.

Class as economic position

The meanings given to the word class vary widely, but there are three common
features. The first, and most fundamental to the concept, is the idea of an
economically defined position in society, usually associated with the ideas that
there is a range of different positions and some definite hierarchy or inequality
between them connected with the division of labour in society and ownership

175

of property. But the way such positions are conceptualized and defined varies tremendously: a simple comparison of wealth and income to give poor and rich; taxonomies of occupations which describe a place in the division of labour at work; or place in the social relations of production such as worker and employer. Classifications based on occupations have often combined the nature of the work itself (manual/non-manual, skilled/unskilled) with the relations of employment and authority within which it is carried out (employed/self-employed/professional, supervisory/managerial), usually in a pretty eclectic way (Marshall *et al.*, 1989). The most relevant for us are the categories used by the Registrar General, which have been modified by Goldthorpe for his work on social mobility (see Table 7.1).

Although the Registrar General's schema may not be logically consistent it provides observers or analysts of class with a reasonably continuous set of data over time from the decennial census. An important feature is that it gives a particular set of possible functional definitions of the term working class. Usually this is taken to mean classes 4 and 5: manual occupations. This might indeed give us a class of workers with broadly similar jobs, working conditions and even life styles, but it does assume a definition of class in terms of the division of labour at work, rather than in terms of the social relations of production. For if we wished to define working class in terms used by Marx (and indeed Weber) of those people who sold their working abilities for a wage because they did not otherwise have access to the means of production and subsistence, then we would surely have to include most of classes 3 and 4, and probably some professional workers too. Conversely, we might find that many people in all four of these classes exercised some functions of authority at work – nominally on behalf of the employer. Does this therefore mean that these people ought to be seen either as part of the employing rather than working class, or as occupying some form of contradictory class location? A number of theorists have pursued this issue, but most of the attempts (such as those of Wright (1985)) to come up with other taxonomies have run into problems at least as severe as the drawbacks they have sought to overcome.

In much of the discussion here we refer to the categories developed by Goldthorpe. He uses the census material to allocate people to three main

Table 7.1 Registrar General's class categories

Class	
1	Professional, etc. occupations
2	Intermediate occupations
3	Skilled occupations non-manual
4	Skilled occupations, manual
5	Unskilled occupations

classes as shown in Table 7.2. As a rough guide, about one-quarter of the population are in Goldthorpe's service class, and between one-third and two-fifths in each of the intermediate and working classes.

Most of these approaches to class have seen formal employment as central to the idea of class. However, a person's position in the labour market is not the only important determinant of their economic position: their relationship to the household in which they live will be significant too. This will strongly influence their access to resources and therefore their market position as a consumer. Secondly, it is in the household that economically important but unpaid, non-waged work takes place, embracing both the care and main-tenance of waged workers and the rearing of children (which can be seen as the reproduction of the labour force) as well as the care of dependent adults. In addition, if we are interested in the issue of social mobility and the extent to which people inherit the class positions of their parents, then the household must be a focus of the analysis. As we shall see, the issue of how economic positions can be grouped into classes and the issue of whether class is best thought of as a characteristic of a person or a household, are contentious ones.

Class as identity and action

The second dimension of class is the idea that a common economic position is bound up with other aspects of social life and gives (at least potentially) a significant common identity to those sharing the same class position. This gives rise to concepts like working class culture or studies of the relationship between 'economically' defined class and political behaviour, such as voting for political parties. Classes are, therefore, not just static classifications of people with various common characteristics, they are to some extent groups of people with common interests and the potential to pursue these interests through common action, often in conflict with other classes. Marx, for example, drew a distinction between what he termed class-in-itself (a collection of

Table 7.2 Goldthorpe's class categories

Service	I	Higher-grade professionals, administrators, managers, officials and proprietors
	II	Lower-grade professionals, administrators, managers, officials; supervisors of non-manuals; higher-grade technicians
Intermediate	III	Routine non-manuals; personal service workers
	IV	Small proprietors, farmers, fishermen; artisans
	V	Lower-grade technicians; supervisors of manuals
Working	VI	Skilled manuals
	VII	Semi- and unskilled manuals

people in a similar economic position) and class-for-itself (a class which had come to recognize and act upon its common material interests). What is a matter for analysis and debate is the nature of the relationship between material position, ideology or identity, and action. An analysis which asserts that an individual's or household's class position is objectively determined by their economic position, and that their identity and action could be seen as 'caused' by this is too simplistic. At least we could allow that their ideas and actions could also influence their material economic position. But if an economic determinist analysis is unsatisfactory, and we recognize the influence of ideology and action to influence economic development, then classes and class structure become rather fluid categories. Do people belong to a class by virtue of believing that they do? And if classes are about a style of life or conceptions of status do we not arrive at a point where we take as our starting point – common identity and action – that which we want to explain?

The use of class has often been extended beyond the idea of the existence of classes to that of a class system or societies analysed in terms of class relations, describing the way in which people in different economic positions, and therefore classes, relate to each other. Thus the historian E. P. Thompson has emphasized that class ought to be seen as a process rather than a static category:

> Sociologists . . . find a multitude of people with different occupations, incomes, status-hierarchies, and the rest. Of course they are right, since class is not that part of the machine, but *the way the machine works* once it is set in motion – not this interest, and that interest, but the *friction* of interests – the movement itself, the heat, the thundering noise. Class is a social and cultural formation (often finding institutional expression) which cannot be defined abstractly, or in isolation, but only in terms of relationship with other classes; and ultimately, the definition can only be made in the medium of *time* – that is, action and reaction, change and conflict. When we speak of a class we are thinking of a very loosely defined body of people who share the same categories of interests, social experiences, traditions and value-system, who have a *disposition to behave* as a class, to define themselves in their actions and in their consciousness in relation to other groups of people in class ways. But class itself is not a thing, it is a happening. (Thompson, 1965, p. 85)

Thirdly, there is usually a normative element in the analysis of class, in the sense that in so far as class is concerned with fundamental inequalities and hierarchy of social position (which need not be inevitable) then class is something that it is often thought desirable to abolish. Of course, just as definitions of class vary so too will definitions of classlessness. Some theorists who were impressed by the apparent convergence of different industrial societies, increasing equality of opportunity and 'the end of ideology' saw class as becoming a historical feature. For example, Blau and Duncan (1967) argued that in a modern industrial capitalist country like the United States, economic decision-making was characterized by rationality and efficiency which in turn maximized social mobility and rewarded ability and achievement rather than background or status. It was therefore becoming a society which, as Goldthorpe summarizes it:

> has no inherent tendency to give rise to distinguishable collectivities of any kind with which individuals might identity or which could provide a basis for socio-political mobilisation (Goldthorpe, 1987, p. 16).

In other words, a classless society. Conversely, other theorists have argued that, even if it did exist, which was empirically questionable, such equality of opportunity only placed people in an economic system whose main features were determined by private ownership of the means of production, the search for profit and the market forces that created it. In such a structure definite class positions with inequalities of decision-making power and income and wealth remained, even if the people who occupied them might now come from a wider range of class backgrounds.

Marx and class

Each of these three aspects of class can be seen in Marx's approach. For Marx all of history could be understood as the process of class struggle in so far as history was the development of human labour in the widest sense. Labour is inevitably social, and the social production relations thus created when men and women work give rise to different forms of property and ownership of the means of production, and therefore give rise to different classes, such as wage-labourers and capitalists within capitalism. This gives to waged workers an ultimate identity of interest with each other (beyond immediate differences in their work or market position) and fundamental antagonism of interest to capital or those who manage it. The resolution of this conflict would abolish the wage-labour system, and eventually produce a classless society.

There have been two main areas of debate over how useful Marx's theories are in understanding modern capitalist society. The first concerns the nature of production and therefore how broadly we define the realm of economics. If we define economics and production narrowly (for example, as the production of goods and services for sale on the market) then we will certainly find the wage-labour/capital relation dominant, but we could not conclude from this alone that class conflict was the most important determinant of the development of society because large areas of social life would lie outside 'economics': for example, domestic labour in the household or areas of production not directed at a market. Conversely, if we argue that production ought to be more broadly defined (as Marx often does) as the 'production of social life in general', including not just the production of commodities but also the raising of children, the organization of religion, the development of cultural life and personal identity, then it might be possible to argue for the pervasiveness of class relations in understanding society, but these class relations would themselves need to be seen as far more complex than just that of the relation between wage-labour and capital.

The second area of debate concerns the precise nature of the capital/wage-labour relationship. Marx's theory has been taken by many to imply that the working class will tend to become more homogeneous and relatively powerless economically as capital accumulation develops. This is certainly the view developed by Braverman (1974) in his analysis of the development of the labour process, and by Wright *et al.* (1982) in their work on class. They argue that as the control of the employer over the worker has become stronger, the economic position of one worker as against another, in the sense of both job content and levels of wages has in essence become more homogeneous. These developments reflect Marx's argument that the working class in capitalist society was fairly powerless. Any ability of particular groups of workers to bargain with capital over the content of work or wages would be strictly temporary and exceptional.

However, other theorists have argued that the inequalities of bargaining power between labour and capital need not be so dramatic and one-dimensional (see for example, Cressey and MacInnes, 1980; Friedman, 1977). In practice, considerable differences of market position, job content, wage levels and ability to organize unions could and did exist. This is important because it makes problematic not just the concept of a homogeneous and potentially united working class, but also how members of that class will come to define their material interests. It could be that they see their interest not in terms of all wage earners against all employers, but in terms of one group of wage earners against other competing groups, or indeed in terms of individual endeavour and advancement. For example, Parkin (1972) has emphasized the importance of strategies of 'social closure' for classes in Britain: that is to say, developing ways to restrict participation in a market to particular groups so as to give them more bargaining power and a better economic position. Such strategies by definition are sectional and enhance the position of one group relative to others.

As well as sectional interests pursued by particular groups of workers, the possibility of alliances between workers and employers in a particular firm, industry or area against other competing firms, industries or areas opens up. In other words, unless it can be argued that beyond all the competing private interests in a capitalist market society lies a more substantial and immediate opposition of interest between employer and worker, overriding everything else, then the lines of class conflict will be more complex than Marx appeared to suggest. So, too, will be the nature and meaning of such conflict. Workplace conflict could represent the clash of labour and capital, and signify the contradictions and instability of the capitalist system, or it could simply represent the normal functioning of the market through different interest groups in different market positions bargaining robustly with each other about what they are really worth. In fact Marx conceded in some of his writings that classes were in reality 'fragmented' into many different interests and ranks, but smuggled into his approach is the assumption that ultimately these gradations are secondary to the fundamental cleavage based around ownership of the means of production.

Thus to answer 'does class matter any more?' we have to look at the empirical development of workplace social relations in Britain, what their wider significance has been, and what relationship they have to other relevant social relations (such as gender, relations, the household, the development of the state). We also have to keep aware of the relationship between economic position, consciousness and social action and try to avoid the pitfall of economic determinism (arguments that an economically defined class position must inevitably lead to a certain behaviour) but keep in focus the relationship in class between ideas and behaviour and material forces. We will also have to look at economic position empirically, focusing on particular types of worker (such as male and female, skilled and unskilled, manual and white collar, production industry workers and service sector workers, public and private sector workers) without assuming either a basic communality of interest or total heterogeneity between these various cross-cutting groups. To do this we can briefly review some of the debates about the history of class formation in Britain, debates about the impact of economic change on class, about changing class identity and behaviour, and about the overall importance of class.

ACCOUNTS OF CLASS FORMATION IN BRITAIN

Britain was the first industrial nation. This important feature of British capitalism has been the subject of heated argument about its implications for class formation. Anderson (1964) argued that the capitalist revolution in Britain had never really been pushed through to a conclusion, the rising capitalist class had compromised with the feudal landed aristocracy in the aftermath of the English Civil War, frightened by its own more radical elements like the Levellers and the Diggers; the bourgeoisie itself was infatuated with status, the pursuits of the landed gentry, careers in church, state or in the empire, rather than developing a modern capitalist economy. This legacy contributed both to Britain's relative economic stagnation in the 1960s (its capitalists were less innovative than their foreign counterparts) and also to the reformist, constitutional and quiescent character of its labour movement and its avoidance of Marxist theory or revolutionary activity: one could not expect a socialist revolution in a country which had yet to complete its bourgeois one, so to speak. Anderson's theory was, therefore, an attempt to explain both Britain's economic crisis and the failure of a radical response to this crisis by the working class, which a traditional Marxist analysis might have predicted.

Thompson (1965) argued against this that the landed aristocracy were themselves largely a capitalist class; that the history of the British working class movement, from the Chartists through to the Communist Party, was neither quiescent nor exclusively constitutionalist, that the genteel style of the British capitalist revealed little about the content of class relations and that Anderson and Nairn were in any event comparing British experience with a highly abstract and mechanical idea of how capitalist societies developed.

Fox, who focuses on the development of British industrial relations, goes over some of this ground, paying particular attention to the way relations between private capitalists, the state and the working class developed. Fox wants to explain the paradox that whilst workplace relations between the workforce and management have been marked by conflict and adversarial postures, at the political level British society has seen little class warfare. On the contrary, both the industrial and political arms of the British Labour movement have espoused constitutionalism and collaboration, whilst the state and employers too have avoided any attempt to wage war on the movement as a whole (Fox, 1985, p. 17). He argues that in Britain those who developed the new capitalist forms of organizing production wished to combine the maximum private individual freedom to produce for the market as they saw fit (to trade freely, to hire and fire labour as they required it, for example) with as limited a role as possible for the state in economic and other affairs. They feared a strong state might mean the return of royal absolutism and greater encroachment in their economic affairs. They emphasized the importance of the rule of law as the best defence of individual economic freedom against encroachment either from the state or from attempts by workers to organize collectively to defend their interests against market forces. Later in the course of the Industrial Revolution these ideas became known as a policy of *laissez faire*.

Just as important as the economic effects of such an approach were its social and political implications. The emphasis on the rights of private property, sovereignty of the market and the perils of state interference with market forces meant that neither the state nor individual employers pursued any active social policy towards the emerging proletariat. In Britain, as in all other industrializing countries, the proletariat was seen as a new and potentially dangerous political factor. Elsewhere both state and employers tended to pursue a mixture of paternalist social policies providing guaranteed minimum living and welfare standards, combined with fierce repression of independent working class economic or political activity. But in Britain both these measures were precluded by the strength of economic individualism and weakness of the state. Thus employers tended to see their obligations to the workforce as limited to providing adequate wages and conditions (leaving to the market the definition of adequate). Meanwhile the state's weakness precluded not only a paternalist social policy but also any comprehensive repression of early trade union organization. Working class organizations were hounded through the courts in the name of economic freedom, attacked by judges in the name of the freedom of private property from 'monopoly' restraints on its use, but the employers could not simply call in the state for action to eliminate them. And in more buoyant economic times, when the workforce enjoyed more bargaining leverage, employers could be forced to heed the early unions' claims, even if they preferred not to officially admit their existence. Until the late nineteenth century, then, unions existed in a legal limbo. In themselves they were not illegal (though the law on conspiracy was always a potential threat) but virtually any action they took to further their demands was liable to be so. However, at times it would be in the immediate interests of either government or employer to avoid worsening relations by invoking the law. In the course of the nineteenth century unions gradually became more firmly established; the minds of employers and the state turned to how best to integrate unions, regulate them and steer their activities towards functions which the employers themselves saw as useful, such as wage bargaining, whilst resisting any union attack on managerial prerogatives over the management of business.

In a world where the economic and social distance between small master and craft workers was not always great, the cultivation of respectability, including moderate political attitudes and behaviour was important not only in defining and protecting the identity and interest of the craft but in blocking more radical lines of working class organization, or the development of a 'wider vision' either socialist or corporatist in character of the aims and nature of the Labour movement. The union movement was locally-based (although significant negotiations and agreements were developed at regional and national level in some trades, particularly between the two world wars) and the roots of organization often based around the struggle to control how work was done and who was eligible to do it. Such struggles were as much between worker and worker (between craftsman and unskilled, or between men and women) as between worker and employer. And the deep antagonism between employer and worker generated in the course of such struggles need not imply any wider conflict between labour and capital as such.

Fox's analysis illuminates many aspects of the structure and behaviour of employers and the Labour movement in modern Britain. The relative absence of repression and direct state involvement in the development of the British working class meant that the focus of worker organization was local employers, and its objectives overwhelmingly immediate and economic in character: 'a fair day's work for a fair day's wage'. Relations between employers and workers at local level were likely to be volatile, determined by the state of trade, characterized by mutual distrust and dependent on the ability of the union to restrict the supply of labour through enforcing unilaterally traditions of skill, access to jobs or apprenticeships, 'custom and practice' of the trade and exerting control over the work process. At any point employers might decide that the costs of attacking union organization were less than co-operating with it. However, such mutual antagonism was primarily economic rather than political. It was more about the terms of operation of market forces than whether they should operate. Especially in a local context the aims of the union could often best be met by restricting the supply of labour and thus organizing to keep other workers out of the labour market (strategies of social closure, described by Parkin) by, for example, defining work as skilled and open only to those who had completed apprenticeships in the trade. A social closure strategy of fundamental importance was that of denying access to some jobs to women. Sometimes this was under the banner of protective legislation, as in the mines; sometimes it was directly as a result of a formal or informal bar to the employment of married women. Allied to this was the union strategy of bargaining for 'family wages'. It was argued that if married women did not or could not work, then men should be paid wages sufficient to cover family rather than personal subsistence.

A fundamental outcome of this evolution was the distinctive relationship between the political and industrial sides of the Labour movement in Britain. In most countries, in a context of state paternalism and repression it was the social-ist political parties which set about trying to organize and win political freedom for trade unions. This tended to give them both a more national centralized nature and stronger political commitment. Conversely, in Britain it was the trade unions which emerged first, and then proceeded to create a political party with the aim not of struggling for a socialist society, but of securing greater economic and political freedom and security for the trade unions.

Two things are worth emphasizing in these accounts of class formation in Britain. The first is that they focus less on the purely economic component of class (that is positions in the social division of labour or ownership of property and means of production) and more on the relationship between these aspects and issues of identity and action. They examine how groups of workers and em-ployers came to define what they thought were their interests, and how they set about pursuing them in co-operation or conflict with other groups. The second important point is that these historical accounts do not suggest the existence of an earlier phase of class development in Britain when classes were monolithic in nature, pursuing strategies that subordinated divisions within classes to struggles between them. Whilst it makes sense to group together employers or waged workers as distinct classes, these classes were always composed of fragments formed from divisions such as those of trade, craft, region or gender.

THE POST-WAR SETTLEMENT AND CHANGES IN CLASS

The post-war settlement (discussed extensively in Chapter 2) had major implications for the development of class relations. Its authors saw it as softening or ultimately abolishing class differences and class conflict, not through pious appeals to reason and social responsibility, but through substantial material economic change. Full employment and rapid growth meant not only employment security but also greater shopfloor bargaining power which could mean better working conditions and ensure that a substantial share of increasing wealth went to wage earners, giving them greater access to the expanding markets for consumer goods. The Butskellite consensus about state responsibility for the economy and social welfare held out the prospect of more equal access to education, housing and health resources. Even as voters, classes now chose between two styles of running much the same consensus over economic and social policy.

These changes gave rise to the debate over whether 'class' was declining in importance or disappearing, and as part of the same process, capitalist society was changing its form into something else: that the post-war boom was witnessing the 'end of ideology' in social relations, in the sense that past class cleavages associated with visions of social transformation were now irrelevant. As we noted above some argued that the social relations of industrial societies worldwide were converging, shaped by the technological requirements of sophisticated modern economies. In order to examine this issue we need to look at the way in which the class structure was changing in terms of the economic positions available in the developing post-war economy, and in terms of the evidence of changing class identities and action.

Economic growth brought considerable changes in the occupational structure of the economy. Manual labour became less important, as did craft-based skilled jobs, whilst semi-skilled jobs dependent more on skills specific to a particular office or factory became more important. The decline of the working class in the sense of manual workers was a process as old as the century. From being three-quarters of the working population in 1911 they dropped to about one-half in the late 1970s and just over two-fifths by the late 1980s. Certainly the speed of change was faster after 1945 and accelerated after 1965 as employment in industry fell. By the start of the 1980s around one-quarter of the workforce worked in the public sector, and just under one-third worked in manufacturing industry – a proportion that was to fall to one-fifth in the course of the decade. Both Goldthorpe (1984) and Westergaard and Resler discovered considerable mobility between unskilled and skilled manual positions, suggesting a weakening of the distinction between craft and unskilled workers. The proportion of white collar jobs both routine clerical and professional managerial increased correspondingly, although the content of jobs changed so much with technological evolution that the line dividing manual and non-manual work has become hard to draw in a logically consistent fashion. If we use the occupational categories of the Registrar General, in 1931 about 8 per cent of all economically active men and women were self-employed or salaried professionals, technicians, managers or administrators. By 1971, 22 per cent of men were in these categories and 16 per cent of women (Goldthorpe, 1987, pp. 62–3). These figures demonstrate the great expansion of the service class.

The number of women in the labour force increased steadily, whilst the number of men started to fall after the mid 1960s. In 1965 there were over 14 million men in work and 8 million women. By 1990 there were under 12 million men and over ten million women. While young, unmarried women were as likely to work as before, older married women were much more likely to take jobs, because of changes in how women reared children:

> Women now marry earlier, but continue working until they are pregnant instead of stopping work at marriage; they have fewer children per family and return to work after childbirth sooner. (Dex, 1985, p. 4)

In 1931 one in ten married women worked, mostly in manual jobs in factories: in many white collar occupations an official or unofficial marriage bar operated: women who married had to leave work. By 1989 almost six out of ten married women worked. The rise in women's employment was also associated with expansion of public and private service sector jobs, many of them part-time. For example, most women's manual work in the health, education and social services is part-time work (Beechey, 1985, p. 12). Married women are particularly likely to work part time: 54 per cent did so in 1987, compared with 24 per cent for unmarried women and only 5 per cent for men (Labour Force Survey, 1988). Partly this results from employers' attempts to solve labour shortages by creating jobs which women with domestic responsibilities could fill, and partly from employers' desire to use part-time jobs to increase flexibility.

The expansion of non-manual employment implied substantial opportunities for upward social mobility out of the manual working class. If we look at this in terms of the experience of households across generations, people whose fathers were manual labourers, for example, might find jobs as clerical staff, teachers or technicians. There were, therefore, three sources of new working class affluence. Wages were higher and more regular, more households had two wages and more workers and their children had the prospect of intermediate or service class work.

Allied to this change in the structure of material positions we might expect corresponding changes in class identity and action. Some observers argued that working class 'embourgeoisement' was taking place. Rising living standards enabled working class households to adopt middle class lifestyles based around consumerism (washing machines, television, house ownership, holidays abroad) 'home centredness' (meaning more attention to the nuclear family than the wider community and extended family), and a new 'instrumental' attitude to work which focused on high wages rather than interest in the job itself or issue of power in the workplace. One feature of this was the rise of a new social group: the teenager with novel cultural and consumer interests, as well as attitudes to work. The argument was not that the new working class had become identical to, or identified with the middle class, but that its interests and aspirations had become less distinctive and in particular had become private and domestic in orientation rather than collectivist and public: 'a concern with limited and private achievement; a pragmatic conception of the politics of change, incapable of stretching much beyond the here and now' (Westergaard, 1972, p. 161). For example, Beynon contrasts the attitudes of Ford car workers to their factory to that of miners to their pit:

> The slogan 'the mines for the miners' meant something. That no similar slogan has come from the car workers is important, and is tied up with the fact that 'the car plants for the car workers' makes no sense to the lads who work on the line. They hate the car plant in a way the miners never hated the pit. They can see no obvious salvation in the nationalisation of the car industry, be it under workers' control or not. (Beynon, 1975, pp. 318–19)

One of the most famous industrial sociology projects of the 1960s, the Affluent Worker Study, examined the attitudes and behaviour of workers in Luton from a variety of production processes and skill backgrounds. It argued that regardless of their social and technical work environment these workers were overwhelmingly 'instrumental' in their outlook, seeing work purely as a means to an end and pursuing 'a privatized social life', these two features were 'mutually supportive aspects of a particular life style' in which work was no longer a central life interest for these men (Goldthorpe et al., 1968, p. 9).

These processes could also be seen as a weakening of common position and identity in the sphere of work, as the distinction between manual and non-manual work became progressively more blurred and the restructuring of capital obliterated old craft, industrial or regional identities; together with an increasing importance of new and quite different common positions and identity in the sphere of consumption. Perhaps those who owned their own homes or who owned their own cars had a keener sense of common identity, in contrast to those who still relied on collective public provision of housing and transport. The declining salience of class could also be seen to be connected with the development of the divorce of ownership from control in industry and the increasing institutionalization of industrial ownership, so that the owners of the means of production were less and less private shareholders and more and more the pension funds of workers themselves.

At the extreme, writers such as Gorz (1982) argued that continually rising productivity and material abundance must spell the end of work and production being an important focus of people's life experience and identity. He argues that the development of modern technology has meant that productivity increases allow vastly increased leisure time but that a substantial proportion of the work that remains necessary is inevitably unpleasant, intrinsically unsatisfying and alienating. This makes orthodox class analysis and the Marxist vision of liberation through workers' control redundant. The attempt to make work a central life interest in which people realize their potential and find happiness, by changing the social relations of work and realizing workers' control, is bound to fail. Instead, Gorz argues that 'post-industrial socialism' ought to be based on sharing out inevitably alienating work more equitably, and developing small-scale production and leisure activities as people's main source of creativity, possibly based on the household as much as the workplace.

If these issues concerned the empirical accuracy of the concept of class in a materially changing world, a second dimension of the debate over class concerned the theoretical adequacy of class as a concept because of the way class analysis had usually failed to integrate issues of gender and race. Whilst attention to cleavages of material position and identity based around the division of labour or ownership of the means of production might be important, it often overlooked the fact that just as deep clefts ran between men and women or between different ethnic groups either as workers with quite different jobs, incomes and chances of promotion, as family members with responsibilities for domestic labour, or as consumers of housing, education or welfare services.

GENDER AND CLASS

The opening section of this chapter noted the problems of defining the terms economic position or work when developing an account of class, and that 'economic position' has tended to be reduced to 'work' and that in turn 'work' has been reduced to wage labour or paid work in the market economy. Such a focus on paid work has come under two related lines of criticism. The first is that the nature of and changes in paid work cannot be understood simply in terms of relations between labour and capital, employer and employee, but depend critically, among other things on the *gender* of the workers involved. The second is that paid work in the market economy is only one aspect of work in capitalist society. Also of great importance for people's individual experience and for social change is unpaid work, chiefly the domestic labour of the daily care and maintenance of adults and their living environment (both partners, other family members or elderly relations) and the rearing of children.

Despite widespread assumptions about the marginal nature of women's labour market participation, or about the primacy of men's role as breadwinner, we have already noted how women are a major and increasing part of the workforce in their own right, and that relatively few are totally economically dependent on a partner. The fastest expanding areas of employment at present are jobs in the service sector, part-time jobs and white collar work, all areas where women are critical to the labour force.

Further evidence of the strength of women's attachment to paid work comes from work on 'careers'. Dex (1984), for example, has shown that women have 'careers' in the labour market just as much as men, except that their 'careers' involve a shift from better, more secure and full-time jobs prior to pregnancy to jobs which are less secure and more likely to be part-time afterwards. Dex has pointed to the importance of a corresponding division by age in the women's labour market, and Crompton has speculated that this may relate to the demand for younger women to work in 'display' related jobs. As well as having identifiable careers most other aspects of women's experience of, attitudes to, and behaviour in paid work are far more similar to their male counterparts than stereotypical ideas about women as wives and mothers would suggest. Dex (1985) reviews a range of literature that shows that women's orientation to work is similar: they want to do it for much the same reasons as men, they find similar sources of satisfaction and dissatisfaction in their work, and their experience of and reaction to redundancy is similar. It may be a greater threat to men's gender identity, and unlike men, women continued to be responsible for domestic labour, but Coyle (1982, p. 121) described the experience of unemployment of the women she studied as 'a crisis of autonomy, as a loss of independence, and here women's domestic role is no compensation'.

We cannot assume (as has been done in the past, see Dex (1985)) that the experience of male workers is that of all workers, or treat workers as though their gender was irrelevant. Women and men do not participate in paid work in the same way, and understanding the differences is essential for understanding the sorts of change that have been taking place in employment. Women are paid much less than men, despite some significant improvements brought by the Equal Pay and Sex Discrimination Acts and more recently by the impact of European 'equal pay for work of equal value' legislation. This reflects the different jobs that women do (not necessarily that they are worth less, but rather that they are *valued* less, which in turn relates to gender determined skill definitions); the different hours they work (about 45 per cent of women work part-time as opposed to 5 per cent of men) and the different industries in which they work: relatively more women work in the service sector.

Women do different jobs because large areas of work are defined as women's work or men's work. The extent of occupational segregation in the economy is startling. In 1983 women constituted 75 per cent or more of the workforce in the jobs of typists, secretaries, domestic servants, nurses, canteen workers, charwomen, office cleaners, sewing machinists, hairdressers, laundry workers, waitresses and kitchen hands (Dex, 1985, pp. 95 ff). At the level of the workplace segregation is much higher. Martin and Roberts (1984) found that 63 per cent of women were in jobs done only by women, and 80 per cent of men. This segregation also has a strong vertical component: more men than women gain access to promoted or supervisory posts. Thus Martin and Roberts also found that only two men in one hundred had a female supervisor or forewoman at work. Women are largely confined to jobs in which they receive orders and perform routine work.

Women's work in paid employment corresponds closely to their unpaid work: servicing, caring, clothing, feeding men and children. Conversely, women are conspicuous in their absence from work defined by employers and trade unions as craft work or skilled work. In order to explain this, theories have moved beyond simply examining the distribution of women to poorly paid places within the division of labour to examining the nature of these places themselves: arguing that skilled jobs, for example, have been developed in an explicitly gender-conscious way. Cockburn (1983) has studied the importance of masculinity in definitions of work in engineering and the printing industries. This has involved looking at the way gender has been socially constructed and used to emphasize the women's role as comforters and carers and men's role as masters of technology and muscle. Such identities not only reinforce women's domestic subordination but also shape their role in the labour market since jobs are themselves created and defined as appropriate to one gender. This goes beyond men organizing explicitly to exclude female competition in the labour market (although that was important in the nineteenth and early twentieth centuries) to the generation of a gender-specific culture around men's work which reinforces the economic disadvantages women face (in access to training or employment) with the ideology that by nature some tasks and roles are inevitably 'male'. Cockburn, in her study of compositors, comments:

> The occupation of composing is one of many 'male jobs' that has contributed to the construction of men as strong, manually able and technologically endowed, and women as physically and technically incompetent. . . . When a compositor talks of the greater physical strength of a man, the strength that enables him to carry a printing frame, of the affinity for technology that differentiates a man from a woman, we need not accept his claim that 'it's only natural'. . . . It has been a process parallel to that which has turned the biological fact that women bear children into the social fact that they also look afer them. (pp. 203–4).

Her description of the composing room resembles many other male workplaces:

> The social currency of the composing room is women and women objectifying talk, from sexual exploits and innuendo through to narrations of exploits and fantasies. The wall is graced with four-colour litho 'tits and bums'. (p. 134)

This point is reinforced by research on skill. Phillips and Taylor (1980) show that, far from being a purely economically defined category, skill itself is suffused with gender: it is not primarily the technical complexity or learning time associated with a task which explains its definition as skilled, but the gender of those who traditionally perform it. For example, work involved in sewing and associated tasks in electronic assembly requires as much technical competence and manual dexterity as many male crafts, but as women's work, is poorly organized and paid. Cockburn gives a graphic example of this process in the printing industry with the changeover from large but central linotype keyboards to typewriter style 'QWERTY' boards from the compositors. The compositors found the retraining and new fingering techniques involved difficult, but this technical problem was less important than the change of identity involved in moving to technology which had none of the associations with craft and muscle of the Linotype machines:

> The typewriter board seems cramped to ex-lino operators. The men feel it is fiddly. To our eyes, used to seeing women and girls sitting at typewriters, the men in their shirtsleeves, often quite heavy built men used to more strenuous manual work, do indeed seem out of scale with the new equipment.
>
> The operators barely reached half the speeds of a good touch typist, but continued to belong to a craft union and be paid craft rates.
>
> Some of the men reduced to a fumbling incompetence in a job that thousands of teenage girls could do better, felt fraudulent and ashamed. (Cockburn, 1983, pp. 96, 99)

Cavendish (1982) studying the competences needed and rewards given for different jobs in a car components factory concluded: 'It was obvious that the only qualification you needed for a better job was to be a man' (p. 79).

This suggests that it is important not to assume that the social construction of gender or the roots of patriarchal subordination of women to men lies in the family, whilst class is fashioned in the world of work. In turn this means that we cannot simply explain women's subordinate role in paid employment by reference to their disadvantaged terms of participation in the labour market because of their disproportionate responsibility for unpaid domestic labour or ideologies about appropriate roles for women. It seems that employment is important not just as a generator of income inequality or hierarchy of class positions in the traditional sense, but also as a site of the construction of gender relations and masculine identity in particular. For many men, sacrifice in work (whether through physical or mental exertion, long hours or hostile working conditions) often in the name of 'supporting the rest of the family' is a fundamental part of their identity not just as workers but as *men*.

Masculinity has been central to the development of the British Labour movement itself. In the nineteenth century one of its strategies of social closure for bargaining purposes was that of organizing to exclude women, especially married women, from particular labour markets. Its focus on work and the workplace, rather than embracing issues around the reproduction of the labour force has reinforced its masculine focus. In so far as it has embraced a 'family wage' bargaining strategy, it has been less able to argue consistently for 'equal pay' as the latter assumes the equal ability of men and women to gain waged work, whilst the former implies that a non-working or less well paid spouse must be supported out of the breadwinner's wage. Unions continue to be overwhelmingly staffed and controlled by men and continue to operate in ways which frustrate women's fuller participation (such as highly formal, bureaucratic and lengthy branch and committee meetings in the evening in pubs and clubs). The attitude of many union officials, full-time and lay, as well as that of their male membership, that 'if it is only women, it doesn't matter so much' still persists (Armstrong, 1982).

The relationship between paid and unpaid work, or the relationship between the home, family and workplace has come to be seen as more important as the vital nature of domestic labour has been appreciated. One line of debate looked at the nature of domestic labour by women and tried to define to what extent it could be seen as 'productive' for capital, thereby seen as contributing to the production of surplus value and so linking domestic work to class exploitation. Without covering the intricacies of this debate, it became clear that regardless of the link between domestic labour or reproduction and the sphere of employment and production, not only capitalists but all male family members (including working class ones) benefited directly from women's unpaid labour. Secondly, women themselves saw it clearly as work, even if it was unpaid. Dex (1985, p. 88) draws attention to the women and employment survey (Martin and Roberts, 1984) findings on women's perceptions of the similarities between paid and unpaid work and its implications for their self-perception of their employment status. 'The vast majority of women [who were not working] did not see themselves as unemployed; approximately two-thirds said that their reason was that they worked at home and were employed as a wife and mother'.

Another approach which has tried to link gender and class is to view women as part of the 'industrial reserve army' of marginal workers which capital can draw on to weaken the bargaining power of employed workers or to expand the labour force when necessary. But others have argued that the sexual division of labour and occupational segregation put severe limits on this process. Work on women's unemployment, including their experience in the current economic crisis, suggests that their domestic role does not simply turn women into a marginal, secondary or reserve labour force. Dex and Perry (1984) confirmed that women were not simply the 'first to go' in a recession, and that in so far as they did suffer greater unemployment, this was confined to specific sectors, or was more attributable to differences between part-time and full-time workers.

But just how the concepts of gender and class are best integrated is complex and controversial, covering both empirical and theoretical disputes. Cockburn (1983) has argued that it is best to approach the analysis of work in capitalism simultaneously with a class and 'sex/gender' perspective. Class is clearly a historical concept in that classes are subject to social change, and analyses and explanations of the existence of class relations can be offered in terms of relations of production, property, types of occupation and so on. But gender is both a social and a biological concept. In any society there will always be men and women, but not necessarily masculinity and feminity as presently socially constructed. Feminist analyses have emphasized the importance of the concept of patriarchy to describe male dominance and female subordination, but this faces the problem that this is a rather ahistorical concept. It can be argued that male dominance has empirically and historically been astonishingly universal (see Eldholm, Harris and Young, 1977), but unless this can be historically and socially rooted in theory there is always the danger of ending up with an argument which concludes that women are *naturally* inferior.

These debates on gender have affected the discussion of class and social mobility too, for two main reasons. The first is that the expansion of non-manual work (service and intermediate class jobs) has been bound up with the expansion of women's employment: it has not been a gender-neutral process because of the nature of the sexual division of labour at work. The second is that, as we noted in the introduction to this chapter, in so far as class is seen as a function of the position of households as well as individuals within them who have formal employment, we have to decide on how the class position of a household is determined. In conventional social mobility studies which examine class trajectories of people in terms of their occupation and family position there has been a debate over how best to analyse the class position of women and fit them into occupationally-based taxonomies. Goldthorpe has argued that the household as a whole is the best unit for analysis and that its class position ought to be defined by the member with the 'fullest commitment to the labour market' – in practice usually the male head of household. In effect he argues that, empirically, the household experience of women is more important for their mobility chances or class identity and behaviour than their own occupation or experience in the labour market. He argues that this is not just a sexist assumption on his part: it reflects male patriarchal power rooted in the household, and women's correspondingly more marginal participation in the formal economy. Marshall *et al.* (1989) illustrate his argument by pointing to the voting behaviour of women clerical workers in 1979. Those married to industrial workers gave Labour a 6 per cent lead; those married to professionals and managers gave the Conservatives a 45 per cent lead.

Conversely, Stanworth (1984) has argued that this approach simply obscures the differences in opportunity that men and women have in the labour market, which should itself be seen as an aspect of class, and the way in which this relates to labour market strategies that families adopt: if men have much better labour market opportunities it is not surprising that women end up having to put domestic obligations before their careers. Also, Goldthorpe's approach obscures the fact that women's own labour market position – in terms of their qualifications – seems to have more impact on their mobility chances than their husbands' class position. In other words, their own labour market experience does make a real difference. Moreover, Goldthorpe's position seems to take attention away from one of the fundamental changes in the workplace division of labour over the last three decades: the rise in women's employment and the decline in male employment.

Behind this debate lies two aspects of the issue we have already discussed about how to articulate gender and class. The first is the nature and origin of the sexual division of labour in the workplace. Criticism of Goldthorpe's 'labour market commitment approach' turns on the rather obvious and important point that the facts of horizontal and vertical occupational segregation by gender in the labour market mean that men and women do not compete on the same terms for occupational positions, and to a large extent do not compete *at all* for the same positions since so much employment is strongly socially defined informally as men's or women's work. In order to analyse this it is surely necessary to follow the occupational class positions of individuals rather than family units.

The second is the way we see the relation between men and women's household position and their positions in the formal economy in relation to patriarchy. If we were to see the household and family as the main locus of patriarchal relations, then we could analyse women's and men's occupational experiences in the sort of way Goldthorpe envisages: women's subordinate position in the occupational class structure could be seen as a question external to class analysis as such, explicable by their domestic oppression. Conversely, if we accept that patriarchal relations operate in the formal economy too, independently of the effects which domestic subordination has on the terms on which women enter the labour market, then the lines of class division can be seen to run through households, since the choices they make about the participation of members in the formal economy will be determined by, as well as determine, the gendered division of labour and rewards from it in the formal economy. For example, households may decide quite rationally to commit a male more fully to the labour market, since the rewards to his commitment will be greater than from investing comparable commitment from an equally well qualified female member. But such a decision-making process could be seen to result from the existing class and gender system rather than simply creating it.

RACE AND CLASS STRUCTURE

Another set of arguments has concerned the articulation of race and class. In 1951 there were about 200,000 people born in the New Commonwealth (mainly India, Pakistan, Africa and the West Indies) resident in Britain. By

1971 this figure had reached 1.5 millon (including children born in the United Kingdom) and by the mid 1980s stood at about 2.4 million. This has raised the question of the impact on the class structure of the development of these ethnic groups and their relationship to the white British population. As with the analysis of gender, there are strong empirical and theoretical reasons for trying to integrate an analysis of class with race. Empirically there are clear differences in the 'class position' of people in Britain from different ethnic backgrounds as measured by occupational taxonomies, as Table 7.3 shows.

In addition there is other evidence that people from different ethnic backgrounds have a different experience of other 'class' processes. Thus if we compare the incidence of unemployment among workers with similar qualifications or labour market experience we find that New Commonwealth immigrants and their children fare badly. The question which this raises is, of course, how these differences might be explained.

Theoretically, class processes have been seen as an important part of the explanation for New Commonwealth immigration and for the reaction to it in Britain. Castles and Kosack (1973) argued that the long and unprecedented post-war boom had brought a tremendous labour shortage throughout Europe. This forced employers to look abroad for labour. In turn, because of their migrant status, poorer economic position and qualifications (itself a legacy of the imperialist development of the world economy), immigrant workers were recruited to do the jobs the European working class could now avoid: the most mundane and the least well paid. These workers thus formed an underclass, a reserve army of labour which could always be sent 'back home' if the demand for labour slackened. Elsewhere in Europe this immigration took the form of contract migrant labour from less developed countries which had few political rights in the host nations. But in Britain, because of the legacy of Empire, it

Table 7.3 Job levels of employees by ethnic group (%)

	White	West Indian	Asian
Males			
Professional, employer, management	19	5	13
Other non-manual	23	10	13
Skilled manual and foreman	42	48	43
Semiskilled manual	13	26	34
Unskilled manual	3	9	6
Females			
Professional, employer, management	7	1	6
Other non-manual	55	52	42
Skilled manual and foreman	5	4	6
Semiskilled manual	21	36	44
Unskilled manual	11	7	2

Source: Brown, 1985.

was possible for employers to recruit labour from the colonies as citizens of the Commonwealth with rights to enter, work and live in Britain. It has been argued that despite this *de jure* difference, immigration into Britain was originally *de facto* temporary, work-related migration. It was only as restrictions on the rights of entry developed that immigration came to take on a more permanent character. In turn the development of ever tighter restrictions on immigration has been analysed both in terms of racial ideology (fears of being 'swamped' by an 'alien' culture) which has been legitimated by the state, and in terms of the economic self-interest of the host working class, who feared competition for both jobs and other resources.

However, a class-based explanation of the arrival of New Commonwealth migrants may not explain adequately their experience here or their impact on, or place in, the class structure. Firstly, it cannot explain why other migrant labour – from elsewhere in Europe, Australia, New Zealand, the United States – evoked so little response politically, despite the fact that the numbers involved were about as large or larger at times than those coming from the New Commonwealth (Sarre, 1989). It is difficult to avoid the conclusion that race itself was the issue. Secondly, neither the occupational position of those of New Commonwealth origin, nor their experience in other markets as consumers of housing or education can be explained simply by reference to their labour market status: after allowing for differences in jobs or income they do less well. The discrimination endured by New Commonwealth immigrants across all areas of social life is well-documented and does not seem explicable simply by virtue of their immigrant status, but by the colour of their skin and ethnic identity.

Thirdly, their origins in Britain as a migrant underclass does not tell us so much about the range of jobs and economic activity they now perform. Even to start with many had qualifications which set them apart from what we would normally think of as an underclass: such as doctors and other professionals. Significant numbers of Asian men and women are now self-employed: more than comparable white men and women. We cannot simply describe the non-white population in Britain as an industrial reserve army.

The drift of all these factors is that the race of the migrants has had a clear and distinct impact on their economic life chances over and above class position. Whilst they may have shared some common experiences with the white native working class, they have also been brought into conflict with elements of it in competition on the labour market and for other resources. Their experience may have been as powerfully shaped by their common ethnic identity and experience of racial discrimination and prejudice across class divides within their own ethnic communities than by a common class position with others across different ethnic groups. Thus writers such as Parkin (1979) and Rex and Tomlinson (1979) have argued that the systematic discrimination that New Commonwealth immigrants and their children suffer can be seen as a distinct type of social closure strategy practised by the white population to enhance its own access to the best jobs, houses, educational opportunities and so on. In this approach, race has to be taken as a distinct concept which is just as important as class; class may still matter, but the relative importance of class and race in analysing the life chances, identity or behaviour of different groups is an empirical question: class cannot claim priority.

Miles (1982, 1989) has elaborated the argument still further. He shares Parkin's and Rex and Tomlinson's dissatisfaction with the attempts to subsume questions of race into a class analysis. But he is equally unhappy with the proposition that race can be treated as a concept with equal explanatory power to that of class, because it both fails to answer the question of why race has become a socially important phenomenon in the first place and fails to integrate into the analysis an explanation of how it is that different ethnic groups have the resources to pursue strategies of exclusion in the first place. These two questions, Miles argues, take us back to considering colonialism, the world economy and migrant labour – in other words to questions of class. He thus arrives at the concept of 'racialized class fractions' in order to describe the distinct experience of New Commonwealth origin ethnic groups in Britain. Their members may occupy a variety of class positions, but will also share the experience of being a racialized fraction of that class – subject to discrimination and exclusionary strategies by the dominant fraction.

THE WITHERING AWAY OF CLASS POLITICS?

If the disintegration of class boundaries and identity was taking place with a switch in focus from production to consumption and new cleavages along gender and ethnic lines coming to be more salient, then this had ironical political implications for the author of the post-war settlement, given the dependence of the Labour Party on the manual working class for its votes. It faced two problems: the shrinkage in the absolute size of the working class, and the prospect of a weakening of their loyalty to Labour as their culture and life style changed. Hobsbawm argued that a 'common style of . . . British proletarian life' emerged in the 1880s and 1890s but began to be eroded from the 1950s onwards:

> I am thinking not only of the rise of the socialist movement and the Labour Party as the mass party of British workers, the changes in trade unionism, the enormous and unbroken increase in the number of co-op members from ½ million in 1880 to 3 million in 1914, but of non-political aspects of working class life; of the rise of football as a mass proletarian sport, of Blackpool as we still know it today, of the fish and chip shop. . . . (1981, p. 8)

> The number and percentage of Labour voters (including Communist ones) grew without interruption (except for 1931) between 1900 and 1951 when it reached a peak of 14 million, or just under 49 per cent of all votes . . . at the 1974 election it was well under 40 per cent. (1981, pp. 8, 16)

These considerations led some to argue that the triumph of Thatcherism should really be seen as the outcome of a deep-seated change in the British social and political structure which meant that a return to the sort of political and economic system which operated between 1940 and 1979 was quite unthinkable.

DOES CLASS STILL MATTER?

Despite such evidence pointing to the substantial changes in the nature of class structure in Britain and the recognition that members of a class are at the same time members of an ethnic group and gender, there has also been an increasing realization that many features of class have survived the post-war settlement and economic restructuring in a much less altered form than has often been assumed or asserted.

Firstly, social mobility, both intra- and intergenerationally, has not occurred because of any increase in equality of opportunity between people of different class backgrounds, but because of the rapid expansion of white collar and service class jobs. These could not be filled by the sons and daughters of the service class because there were simply not enough of them to staff the new positions. Conversely, the ability of the better-off to avoid downward social mobility has remained unchanged.

> While there can be little doubt that over recent decades the service class has been recruited from increasingly diverse social origins, there is no sign of any falling off in the capacity of its numbers to transmit social advantage to their offspring. (Goldthorpe, 1980, p. 286)

Parallel to this, most working class males still have working class fathers: manual work is intergenerationally 'a largely self-recruiting bloc' (Goldthorpe, 1980, p. 259). In this Britain differs from most other countries where often only about half the working class is 'second generation' because of the continuing importance of employment in agriculture. Thus one legacy of Britain being the first industrial capitalist nation which entailed the destruction of the peasantry and urbanization of the population in the nineteenth century has been that its working class in the twentieth century has been more homogeneous and long-established. Paradoxically, it was only the rate of growth achieved under the post-war settlement that concealed its *failure* to provide more equal opportunities for those of different class backgrounds. Despite increasing social mobility and rising incomes there was in this sense no material disintegration of the working class or opening up to many of its members of new life chances once in a manual job. In this context the survival of 'traditional' class attitudes at work should not surprise us.

Whilst relative inequalities changed only gradually, absolute inequality, in the sense of poverty also remained a stubborn problem. The 'safety net' of the social security system was set at an absolute level of subsistence: the minimum income level at which decency could be maintained, rather than related to general living standards. The low paid and those with restricted work opportunities – through domestic responsibilities, ill health or unemployment – were all especially vulnerable.

Since 1979, rising unemployment, falling real pay levels and increasing taxes for the low-paid have led to increases in the incidence of poverty. The EEC has proposed a decency threshold for measuring poverty. By 1987, 46 per cent of the British adult workforce earned less than this threshold, up from 36 per cent in 1979. In the same year a Low Pay Unit report revealed that low-paid male manual workers earned less relative to the average than their counterparts of a century earlier, whilst the highest paid had increased their differential over the average (Low Pay Unit, 1988). By 1986 the Child Poverty Action Group estimated (in the absence of government figures – whose failure to appear it alleged to be a cover up) that those in poverty (defined as eligible for Supplementary Benefit) numbered 13 million: about double the 1979 figure of 6½ million.

Lastly, the arguments made about changes in working class culture have to be treated cautiously. It is certainly the case that lifestyles changed and that close-knit working class communities were broken up by changes in the geographical location of industry and by new public sector housing programmes. Rising absolute incomes did mean that the market for consumer goods became far more significant in working class lives. The experience of consumerism provided a direct experience for most people of the democracy of individual consumer sovereignty and market freedom which was appealed to by Thatcherism, in contrast to the alienating, bureaucratic and impoverished face of public provision of social services. However, it would be wrong to overstate the nature of change. As we have seen in Fox's account for example, it would be a mistake to envisage the pre-war working class as homogeneous in its organization and collectivist in its outlook. Individualism, self-improvement and the pursuit of respectability had always been important elements in its behaviour and thinking. The pursuit of a 'family wage' strategy by unions, whereby it was argued that a male worker should be paid enough to provide also for wife and children, was an earlier manifestation of 'family centredness', so too was the emphasis on respectability. The 'instrumental' attitude to work, with robust bargaining over job control aimed at securing higher wages was also central to earlier workplace industrial relations as we have seen. Nor was the absence, after 1945, of any wider vision of social and economic change in the running of the economy as a whole or of individual factories, shops and offices a new phenomenon. Such a vision, Fox demonstrates, had always been marginal. British working class collectivism had also been instrumental, sectional and directed at immediate limited but concrete aims. From a quite different perspective and methodology, Marshall *et al.*

reach similar conclusions: 'sectionalism, instrumentalism, and privatism are not characteristics peculiar to the recent years of economic recession' (1989, p. 217). It could be argued then, that Britain's class structure remains a particular mixture of profound class antagonism in the sense of mistrust, conflict and presumption of opposition of interest between labour and capital, combined with the absence of any overall political challenge to the existing order. Class relations around the workplace remain rooted in the tradition of individualism in Britain, and in particular its economic development.

It is also premature to conclude that the 1980s saw a disillusionment with class solidarity, collectivism and state control, and a revolution in public attitudes towards individualism, self-reliance, private property and opportunity based on thirty years' experience of the benefits of consumerism. The facts that people have found new needs and desires to satisfy in individual consumption and that older forms of community have disintegrated does not mean that a rampant individualism is dominant. Public social services are still highly valued: Thatcherism has not been able to command support for rolling back the frontier of the state here.

Despite the rise in unemployment, trade union membership of those in work has fallen only slightly. There has been no managerial drive against unionism except in a few highly publicized sectors, notably in some of the nationalized industries (such as coal, steel and shipbuilding) where management has been able to depend on government resources to face out long strikes, and where a collapse in demand for the product has weakened union bargaining power. There have not appeared any 'sunbelt' areas of where non-unionism is the norm, as has occurred in the United States. The success of the trade unions in their political funds ballots, where every union won substantial majorities for maintaining funds to finance political campaigning and economic support to the Labour Party, demonstrated that despite the electoral disaster of 1983, the political arm of the Labour movement was not in terminal decline.

There is further evidence from attitude surveys and opinion polls that the major aims of the post-war settlement: full employment, a welfare state and greater equality of position and opportunity, are still overwhelmingly popular. SCPR's report of British social attitudes (Jowell and Witherspoon, 1985) found that only 5 per cent favoured a reduction in social service provision even if this was linked to tax cuts, almost half of the remainder favoured higher taxes to increase services, with health and education as the favourites for more expenditure. A large majority (including supporters of all parties) thought that the gap between those with high and low incomes in Britain was too large.

Lastly, it seems that class still matters in the sense that class remains an important and powerful explanation of people's life chances (in terms of immediate opportunities and future mobility prospects), their identity and their actions and beliefs. Marshall et al. concluded from their study, which reinforced Goldthorpe's conclusions about the contrast between the increase in *absolute* mobility and stability of *relative* mobility chances, that there was 'nothing in our data to suggest that collective identities and collective action of a class-based kind are in the process of long-term decline' (1989, p. 272).

CONCLUSIONS

Thompson has written in a number of different contexts about how difficult a concept class is to define and to use (Thompson, 1965, 1968). This chapter has illustrated some of the problems in its usage, covering empirical definitions and theoretical analysis of how class relates to social action and the nature of society. This should make it clear that no definitive answer is possible to such questions as, 'does class matter anymore?' or 'are class attitudes responsible for Britian's economic decline?' But it does allow us to rule out some simplistic formulations. It is hard to argue that Britain was a class society in the past but is not one now. The changes in the structure of people's economic positions and ideas or behaviour related to them has been more subtle and complex than that. It would be hard to argue that nothing has changed, unless an extremely rigid definition of class is taken (e.g. class equals the existence of wage labour as such) but as the arguments of Fox and others suggest, there are some remarkable continuities in Britain's workplace social relations which are central to class formation and outlook. In this sense, class certainly still 'matters', but in what way it matters is open to debate. The emphasis on the relationship between material circumstances and social action and consciousness which this chapter has stressed suggests that Lord Young's strictures about class attitudes are simplistic nonsense in so far as they assert that workplace conflict and its associated social relations are a function of historically outmoded, and therefore irrational, class 'prejudice'. But this does not mean that class has nothing to do with Britain's economic problems; on the contrary, it could be argued that it is indeed central both to poor economic performance and to the limited nature of social change towards greater equality of position and life chances.

How class relates to these issues depends heavily on how the relative power and influence of different classes in Britain is seen, or what the nature of the relationshp is. Lord Young's comments, and the thrust of arguments by monetarists, free marketeers and the New Right was that the working class in the form of organized labour had become much more powerful as a result of the state's commitment to full employment, to the extent that it was enforcing such restrictions on capital (directly at the workplace and through state taxation and public expenditure) that capitalism was being transformed into a bureaucratic and inefficient socialism. Low growth was the fault of this move towards collectivism. Conversely, traditional left wing positions – as advanced by Miliband, some of the critics of Hobsbawm and by many members of the Labour movement – argue that labour, despite some improvement in the terms of its bargaining power in the era of full employment, is still virtually economically and politically powerless and dominated by capital. This explains both the maintenance of social inequality because capital needs it and poor growth because capital diverts resources to fending off the struggle of labour for greater inequality, and denies itself access to the full productive potential that a non-alienated workforce would possess. It is therefore in everyone's interest that the demands of the working class are met.

Writers such as Fox (1985) and Cameron (1984) have argued that neither capital nor labour has dominated the other (though this does not imply equality in their relationship at any particular point or over time). What must be examined, then, are the forms of compromise, co-operation and conflict that have been adopted (which may change both over time and across different sections of the classes) under the influence of different historical conditions, and how they shape future developments. In this sense, class may well be central to poor economic growth or social reform, but the origins of class and changes in the class nature of society are seen to lie not in the success or defeat of particular class demands but in the nature of these demands themselves and the actual way that class has been constructed.

Thus to argue that class continues to matter, is not to argue that class relations are the same today as twenty, fifty or a hundred years ago. Nor is it to argue that class is obvious and straightforward: the nature of changes in class relations is often difficult to grasp definitively. Lastly, the extent to which class matters in the sense of explaining and understanding social change depends critically on what concept of economic position and class is being used. If class is to be defined without reference to gender or race it can embrace only one, limited, dimension of social relations. If, however, it is to be broadened to embrace concepts of gender, and the social construction of masculinity and femininity in the course of both paid and unpaid work, then it becomes a far more complex concept than has traditionally been deployed by social scientists.

8

INDUSTRIAL SOCIOLOGY – AN IDENTITY CRISIS?

Whatever happened to industrial sociology? This blunt question was posed by Hyman (1981). We take his approach to the question as our point of departure, and although we are not finally convinced by his argument, it is challenging and opens up a number of important issues. His account is primarily with reference to the United Kingdom which inevitably leaves unsaid some concerns relevant to the development of industrial sociology. We return to those later, but first let us attend to his inquiry.

In the early 1960s industrial sociology looked as though it had arrived. Its special task was the study of social relations in work situations and to develop an understanding of the links between industrial systems and the wider society. The sense of this comes through in Smith's UNESCO monograph (1961) and in the first textbook on the subject by British authors (Parker *et al.*, 1967). But by the late 1970s sociologists had come to speak about the demise of industrial sociology.

What had happened? According to Hyman there had been a theoretical collapse. The functionalist paradigm no longer held sway, a point which is illustrated in the changing editions of Parker *et al.* (which has been a best-selling text for many years). This demise of functionalism affected not only industrial sociology but also sociology in general. No longer could one neatly link individuals and their roles and statuses with groups, organizations and institutions and depict them as an interrelated set of sub-systems, all contributing to a functioning whole. In its place we have a fragmented, sometimes eclectic approach, notably expressed in neo-Weberian and phenomenological formulations, although these could vary in emphasis (compare, for example, the treatments of Fox (1971) and Silverman (1970)).

As Hyman sees it, then:

> The fragmentation of industrial sociology in the 1970s may be viewed in part as a reflection of the general crisis of western sociology, eloquently if belatedly proclaimed by Alvin Gouldner in 1970, and itself partly explicable in terms of the crisis of western capitalism. (Hyman, 1981, p. 88)

According to that position, a connection is postulated between what is happening in the real world of producing, distributing, buying, selling and consuming, and what this does to social scientists who try to make sense of it. We can see that the term crisis occurs twice in the same sentence: firstly with reference to western sociology (an intellectual crisis) and secondly in relation to western capitalism (a crisis in economy and society). For Hyman, the intellectual crisis was exemplified by the eclectic and diverse strands which replaced the dominant functionalist paradigm. But, he argues, this did not solve the intellectual crisis because these alternative approaches themselves did not deal adequately with such matters as class relations, the role of the state and the domination of capital over labour. Industrial sociology did not operate with these categories in any developed way and therefore was not equipped to analyse what was actually happening to industrial societies. What then was needed? In a word, a political economy grounded in Marx.

Did not such Marxist analyses exist? Examples could be cited, notably Braverman (1974), as well as Nichols (1980) and Clegg and Dunkerley (1980). Apart from specific criticisms of these contributions, Hyman insists that the theoretical tasks implied in moving from industrial sociology to political economy have scarcely begun and that we are left with little more than an agenda. This agenda is based upon the premise that the necessary task is to flesh out through the analysis of empirically-given circumstances a set of assumptions originally propounded by Marx in *Capital*:

> The specific economic form, in which unpaid surplus-labour is pumped out of direct producers, determines the relationship of rulers and ruled, as it grows directly out of production itself and, in turn, reacts upon it as a determining element. Upon this, however, is founded the entire formation of the economic community which grows up out of the production relations themselves, thereby simultaneously its specific political form. It is always the direct relationship of the owners of the conditions of production to the direct producers – a relation always naturally corresponding to a definite stage in the development of the methods of labour and thereby its social productivity – which reveals the innermost secret, the hidden basis of the entire social structure, and with it the political form of the relation of sovereignty and dependence, in short, the corresponding specific form of the state. This does not prevent the same economic basis – the same from the standpoint of its main conditions – due to innumerable different empirical circumstances, natural environment, racial relations, external historical influences etc., from showing infinite variations and gradations in appearance, which can be ascertained only by analysis of the empirically given circumstances. (Marx, 1959 edn, pp. 791–2.)

What this amounts to is an invitation to begin the study of the relationship between economy and society in a particular way. Yet just as functionalism might have problems within its paradigm so, perhaps, might this view. In so far as it focuses on class relationships – between the ruler and the ruled – instead of assuming a natural harmony of interests in equilibrium, it can with reason be regarded as more likely to throw light on crisis situations. But whether it suffices as theory or method is not self-evident. Let us press the matter a little by looking at how Marx saw the study of industry as contributing towards a theory of crisis in capitalist societies.

It is, of course, a famous analysis which seeks to identify both the productive power of capitalist societies and the contradictions and instabilities which accompany its development. The new forms of co-operation upon which these societies necessarily depend are, at the same time, shot through with antagonisms and conflict. We may take as a point of departure Marx and Engels' recognition that:

> The bourgeoisie, during its rule of scarce one hundred years, has created more massive and more colossal productive forces than have all preceding generations together. Subjection of Nature's forces to man, machinery, application of chemistry to industry and agriculture, steam-navigation, railways, electric telegraphs, clearing of whole continents for cultivation, canalisation of rivers, whole populations conjured out of the ground – what earlier century had even a presentiment that such productive forces slumbered in the lap of productive labour? (Marx and Engels, 1957, pp. 55–6)

Marx and Engels underline the decisive character of this extraordinary activity:

> Constant revolutionising of production, uninterrupted disturbance of all social conditions, everlasting uncertainty and agitation distinguish the bourgeois epoch from all earlier ones. . . . All that is solid melts into the air. (pp. 52–3)

In a dramatic metaphor Marx and Engels liken this new bourgeois society to a sorcerer who, having conjured up the mighty means of production and exchange, is not able to control its power. The primary point of reference is the new system of manufacture based upon the factory system. Consider how Marx spells this out:

> The factory system's tremendous capacity for expanding with sudden immense leaps, and its dependence on the world market, necessarily give rise to the following cycle: feverish production, a consequent glut on the market, which causes production to be crippled. The life of industry becomes a series of periods of moderate activity, prosperity, overproduction, crisis and stagnation. The uncertainty and instability to which machinery subjects the employment, and consequently the living conditions, of the workers becomes a normal state of affairs, owing to these periodic turns of the industrial cycle. Except in the periods of prosperity, a most furious combat rages between the capitalists for their individual share in the market. This share is directly proportional to the cheapness of the product. Apart from the rivalry this struggle gives rise to in the use of improved machinery for replacing labour power, and the introduction of new methods of production, there also comes a time in every industrial cycle when a forcible

reduction of wages beneath the value of labour-power is attempted so as to cheapen commodities. (Marx, 1976 edn, pp. 580–2)

According to Marx the self-valorization of capital (i.e. the creation of surplus value) is the determining and overriding purpose of the capitalist. The labour process is the instrument of the valorization process. How can this subordination of labour to capital be accomplished? After all, social labour brings individual labourers together and can surely make them aware of their collective power *vis-à-vis* their employer. One answer has to do with the mystification implicit in the relations of capital – the reality of the situation is hidden by the appearance. In the chapter on co-operation in *Capital*, Marx notes:

> Their co-operation only begins with the labour process, but by then they have ceased to belong to themselves. On entering the labour process they are incorporated into capital. As co-operators, as members of a working organism, they merely form a particular mode of existence of capital. Hence the productive power developed by the worker socially is the productive power of capital. The socially productive power of labour develops as a free gift to capital whenever workers are placed under certain conditions, and it is capital which places them under these conditions. Because this power costs capital nothing, while on the other hand it is not developed by the worker until his labour itself belongs to capital, it appears as a power which capital possesses by its nature – a productive power inherent in capital. (p. 451)

Socially productive labour is, as it were, gifted to capital because in the immediate process of production it comes to be defined as the productive power of capital. It is as though the capitalist is giving things to the worker yet these things, including machinery and the applied sciences, are the embodiment of dead labour without which he would have nothing to offer:

> Hence the interconnection between their various labours confronts them, in the realm of ideas, as a plan drawn up by the capitalist, and, in practice, as his authority, as the powerful will of a being outside them, who subjects their activity to his purpose. (p. 450)

All of this is a way of speaking about alienated labour since the rule of the capitalist over the worker is 'the rule of things over man, of dead labour over the living, of the product over the producer' and it leads Marx to comment on the ideological nature of control in capitalist relations with its inversion of subject into object and vice versa:

> Viewed *historically* this inversion is the indispensable transition without which wealth as such, i.e. the relentless productive forces of social labour, which alone can form the material base of a free human society, could not possibly be created by force at the expense of the majority. (p. 990)

Still this ideological control is not to be seen as complete or permanent – how could it be if the free human society is to be realized?

As the number of the co-operating workers increases, so too does their resistance to the domination of capital, and necessarily, the pressure put on by capital to overcome this resistance. The control exercised by the capitalist is not only a special function arising from the nature of the social labour process and peculiar to that process, but it is at the same time a function of the exploitation of a social labour process, and is consequently conditioned by the unavoidable antagonism between the exploiter and the raw material of his exploitation. (p. 986)

This is why Marx writes of the despotism of the workplace and likens the workforce to an army which has to be controlled by officers and NCOs, that is managers and foremen. The labour process is commanded by them in the name of capital. The analogy of the army was of course taken up without irony by early management theorists such as Urwick – ideas of staff and line management are directly derived from the army. The concept of unitary management, with commands flowing from the top downwards, is in accord with this image. By the same token, views of what leadership and managerial prerogatives entail are also built in. In *Capital* Marx goes into considerable detail on the issue of control. There is not only the general requirement of the capitalist to secure continuity of work but also the need to control the quantity and quality of production through appropriate methods of supervision, discipline and wage systems:

> He must make sure that the process of production is not interrupted or disturbed and that it really does proceed to the creation of the product within the time allowed for by the particular labour process and its objective requirements. (p. 986)

We can see, incidentally, that as Marx contemplates the growth in the scale of capitalist industry, systems of control embrace not only the direct control of the owner or his manager over the worker, but technical controls embedded in the production system itself and bureaucratic controls stemming from organizational growth. Bureaucracies are manifestly hierarchical and are the instruments of the owners of capital – representing and reinforcing their power and emphasizing their legitimacy. Still, resistance to domination is present even if a strategy to overcome capitalism is not. Hence the emergence of social labour makes possible the development of collective activity, notably in the form of trade unions. Such collectivities will seek to bargain over the terms of the labour process and to put limits on the degree of labour intensification. This may indeed give rise to interruptions or disturbances in the flow of production in the form of strikes, sabotage, output restriction, go-slows and the like. In *Wages, Price and Profit* Marx concludes:

> Trade unions work well as centres of resistance against the encroachments of capital. They fail partially from an injudicious use of their power. They fail generally from limiting themselves to a guerrilla war against the effects of the existing system, instead of simultaneously trying to change it, instead of using their organised forces as a lever for the final emancipation of the working class, that is to say, the ultimate abolition of the wages system. (Marx, 1968 edn, p. 229)

Resistance within a capitalist framework is one thing, revolution to over-throw it is another. The relationship between the two is highly problematical. Berman has asked, for example, why the social labour which has been formed in capitalist industry should necessarily generate the kind of community which can overthrow capitalist social relations. He suggests that their solidarity, however impressive in particular instances, might be as transient as the machines they operate or the products they make:

> The workers may sustain each other today on the assembly line or the picket line, only to find themselves scattered among different collectivities with different conditions, different processes and products, different needs and interests. Once again the abstract forms of capitalism seem to subsist – capital, wage labour, commodities, exploitation, surplus value – while their human contents are thrown into perpetual flux. How can any lasting bonds grow in such loose and shifting soil? (Berman, 1982, p. 104)

Built into a Marxist theory of crisis is the concept of a class-conscious revolutionary proletariat, which will by its action transform the social relations of production and resolve the crisis. As Lockwood has pointed out, this theory of action is itself unstable. There is, he suggests, a tendency to shuttle back and forth between positivistic and idealistic explanations of working class radicalism and acquiescence. 'The positivistic type of explanation makes it possible, for example, to hold to the belief that the next economic crisis will provide the occasion for the leap into consciousness that fuses the immediate and fundamental interests of the proletariat. At the same time, the idealistic reaction to this utilitarian conspectus can lead to the opposite, pessimistic theory that the working class is sunk in a chronic, an almost irremediable, false consciousness' (Lockwood, 1981, p. 457). Lockwood holds that both these explanations are found in Marx and that modern Marxism continues to live with this problem of interpretation. In this sense it is not just an abstract theoretical problem because writers referring to the same society at the same point in time can come to very different conclusions as to the radical potential of the working class. This can lead to different practical and political pro-gnoses, and Lockwood cites by way of example the work of Miliband (1969) and Glynn and Sutcliffe (1972). We have more to say about Lockwood's argu-ments elsewhere; what is challenged, however, is any thought that assumes Marx's theory is so unproblematic that it simply has to be restated, with appropriate quotations, to provide an adequate basis for analysing advanced industrial societies in the late twentieth century. If industrial sociology has an identity crisis then that, in fact, is something it shares with Marxism.

If, therefore, we do not share Hyman's confidence in his solution to the crisis of industrial sociology, it is nevertheless instructive to compare his position with that of another Marxist writer, Burawoy. The opening chapter of Burawoy's *Manufacturing Consent* (1979) is entitled 'The demise of industrial sociology'. Burawoy's point of departure is an American one and begins, as most American accounts do, with reference to the famous Hawthorne plant studies at Western Electric. The main account is found in Roethlisberger and Dickson (1964).

The Hawthorne studies contributed to the human relations school of management and in that respect need to be differentiated from Taylorism. Faunce has reminded us of the deep controversy that this generated among industrial sociologists and students of industrial relations in the United States during the 1940s and 1950s (Faunce 1967). It centred on such matters as the manipulative character of the human relations movement. The distinction (derived from a particular use of Pareto's categories) between logical managers and non-logical workers, the neglect of trade unions in the analysis, the attribution of restrictive practices to the workforce, whose irrational behaviour needed to be superseded and whose productive capacities needed to be harnessed to managerial interests. The scepticism of the sociological critics was humorously captured by the title of Lewis Carliner's polemic, cited by Faunce – 'Deep therapy on the assembly line: moo, moo, moo, say the cow sociologists, but they don't even give skimmed milk'. On this rendering it was the workers who were really being milked. The interest in individual therapy, which constitutes a large section of *Management and the Worker*, and the neglect of the structural problems of control, provided the key to critique of the approach and the 'cow sociologists' stood condemned as the servants of managerial power.

Burawoy, not surprisingly, is sympathetic to such critiques. Yet he wants to rescue what he regards as the partial truths of this plant sociology which the critiques tend to overlook. His own empirical work was, after all, a participant observation study in an engineering plant in Illinois during the 1970s. Burawoy saw his task as placing studies of the social relations of production in a different context to that of 'traditional' industrial sociology and he expresses his position as follows:

> Rather than highlight the absurdity of isolating the factory from its environment, I shall try to pin down the precise nature of its isolation or relative autonomy – an autonomy that allowed the earlier researchers to make so many contributions to the understanding of industrial organisations. Rather than argue that conflict between management and worker is endemic or 'structural', I shall show how both conflict and consent are organised on the shopfloor. Rather than continually harp on the manipulativeness and inefficacy of the human relations attempt to elicit greater co-operation from workers, I shall stress its essential truth, namely, that activities on the shopfloor cannot be understood outside the political and ideological realms of the organisation of production. While the view that workers are somehow irrational in their responses to work is an untenable position, the notion that they lean towards economic rationality is equally unsatisfactory. In this study I shall show how rationality is a product of the specific organisation of production and is part and

parcel of the factory 'culture'. In short, rather than dismiss the findings of industrial sociology, I shall move beyond them by placing and sometimes incorporating them into a broader perspective. (Burawoy, 1979, p. 4)

What, then, constituted the demise of industrial sociology for Burawoy? The burden of his argument is that with the decline of shopfloor studies industrial sociology has been subsumed under organization theory. Whilst he welcomes the interest (or perhaps the renewal of interest since it was not a new theme in sociology) in bureaucratic structures which this represented, his criticism is that in its elaboration of general and abstract concepts, organization theory has lacked concreteness and historical specificity. Consequently:

It has substituted formal rationality for substantive rationality and has underplayed the essential feature of the capitalist labour process – the transformation of nature or raw materials into useful things, on the one hand, and into profit, on the other. (p. 7)

Moreover, in Burawoy's view, the ahistorical way in which organization studies proceeded rested either on harmonistic assumptions about organizations or, in contradistinction, on views about the necessity of social control. Burawoy's contention is that those who emphasize the underlying harmonistic assumptions of consensus have great difficulty in not treating conflict as deviant or pathological and in accounting for the empirical presence of coercive controls. Those who do take seriously the issues of control do not properly explore the specific historical origins and forms of social control. What some might have claimed to be a development in industrial sociology is, in Burawoy's view, the source of its demise. What then is to be done?

It is necessary . . . to break with the transhistorical generalities and partial perspectives of industrial sociology and organisation theory and to dispense with metaphysical assumptions about underlying conflict or harmony. Conflict and consent are neither latent nor underlying but refer to directly observable activities that must be grasped in terms of the organisation of the labour process under capitalism. Conflict and consent are not primordial conditions but products of the particular organisation of work. We must avoid being trapped in the various debates between 'consensus theory' and 'conflict theory' and move the discourse into an entirely different terrain. To do this we must restore historical context to the discussion. Our first task, therefore, is to comprehend the specificity of the capitalist labour process as one that is distinct from pre-capitalist and post-capitalist labour processes. (p. 12)

For Burawoy, it is important to identify and analyse what goes on at the point of production. For this reason the case studies of the earlier generation of industrial sociologists were valuable precisely because they did observe closely what was going on and in that crucial respect had the advantage over more formal ahistorical organization studies. It was indeed an extraordinary coincidence that Burawoy's own case study was, he later discovered, the same plant where Donald Roy had done his shopfloor participant observation studies, in 1944–5, some thirty years earlier (Roy, 1952a, 1952b, 1953, 1954, 1960). What Roy did, on the basis of his fieldwork, was to challenge the human relations position which attributed restriction of output to the irrationality or 'non-logical' behaviour of the workers. Their rationality was grounded in different interests and assumptions from those of management. In some respects this could provide the basis for an answer to the question of why workers do not work harder. According to their own canons they worked hard enough to get the kind of take-home pay they were looking for.

But there was another question posed by Roy's research and taken up by Burawoy, namely: why do workers work as hard as they do? Both Roy and Burawoy were impressed with the intensity of the work activity they and their fellows were engaged in. The puzzle was why they pushed themselves so hard that sometimes they even exceeded the expectations of management. As Burawoy wryly reflects, he moved from a position where he was both in contempt and awe of what the workers were doing to one in which he too was 'breaking my back to make out, to make the quota, to discover a new angle, and to run two jobs at once – risking life and limb for that extra piece. What was driving me to increase Allied profits? Why was I actively participating in the intensification of my own exploitation and even losing my temper when I couldn't? (p. xi).

Burawoy's theoretical strategy, then, is to draw on the insights and empirical strengths of plant-based studies of the earlier industrial sociologists and to relocate them in a Marxist perspective. In relation to shopfloor studies this is done in his analysis of the labour process as games that individuals and groups of workers play to 'make out'. These games are not wholly independent of managerial controls and the playing of the game in Burawoy's view both obscures and secures surplus labour. This, he argues, is what Roy's own findings point to. Roy's own comments on the activity are as follows:

> Could 'making out' be considered as 'an end in itself'? It might be suggested that the attainment of 'quota' marked the successful completion of an 'act' or 'task' in which the outcome was largely controllable by the operator; although the 'chance' factors were also important determinants. 'Making out' called for the exercise of skill and stamina; it offered the opportunities of 'self-expression'. The element of uncertainty of outcome provided by ever-present possibilities of 'bad breaks' made 'quota' attainment an 'exciting game' played against the clock on the wall, a 'game' in which the elements of control provided by the application of knowledge, skill, ingenuity, speed and stamina heightened interest and lent to the exhilaration of 'winning' feelings of 'accomplishment'. Although operators constantly shared their piecework experiences as a chief item of conversation, and always in terms of 'making money', they were, in reality, communicating 'game scores' or 'race results', not financial success or disappointments. It is doubtful if any operator ever thought that he had been 'making money'. It is likely that had anyone been able to communicate accurately such a conviction, he would have been laughed out of the shop. (Roy, 1952b, cited in Burawoy, 1979, p. 83)

The function of these games, according to Burawoy, is to generate consent to the social relations in production that provide the framework within which the games are played and serve to obscure those same relations. The games do not represent some pre-established value consensus between management and workers: it is through playing the game itself that consent is generated. Providing the rules of the game are observed by all concerned, involvement in the game can displace wider considerations of the property and power relations in which they are grounded. The processes of socialization at the point of production are seen as constituting the hegemony of the culture of the factory.

If, in Burawoy, there is critical respect for plant-based empirical studies of industrial sociology, there is also the judgement that a political economy grounded in Marxism is required to explain the significance of the labour process to which these studies, sometimes unwittingly, had drawn attention. Yet he is unwilling to align himself with neo-Marxist crisis theory available in the works for example of O'Connor (1973) and Habermas (1975). To distinguish between systems crises and social crises, between political crises and economic crises is one thing, but to show how one leads to another is something else. How and when, moreover, are people to become conscious of these crises as crises of capitalism? Burawoy's scepticism appears to be partly theoretical and partly empirical – these neo-Marxists do not take seriously enough the labour process as a site of domination and the workplace as a source of hegemony. Hence, from his socialist perspective, there is a pessimistic strain at the end of *Manufacturing Consent*:

> Crisis theory is a blossoming area of Marxist discourse. Indeed, it seems that the more stable capitalism appears, the more we lament the gap between what is and what could be and the more desperately we search for new crises. In this study, however, I have resisted the temptation. Instead, I have suggested that the prospects of a local crisis – that is, one emerging at the point of production – are bleak indeed. Others have persuasively argued that capitalists can buy peace in the economy only at the price of externalising or displacing struggles into the wider political arena, where they become fiscal or legitimation cries. Unfortunately, these are abstract crises, as much a product of the Marxist imagination, as of the real world. Moreover, as Marx points out, crises present opportunities to the dominant classes as well as to the dominated classes. They are the means by which capitalism is able to restore stability and save itself from itself. Nowhere is this more clear than in the crisis of transition from competitive to monopoly capitalism. (pp. 202–3)

We cannot quite leave the matter there, and this for several reasons. Firstly, whilst Burawoy focuses on the paradox of consent, he is clear that hegemony in the workplace is not a uniform phenomenon. This is true for different sections of industry in advanced capitalist societies and also as between different societies. There may be elements of despotism and hegemony in factory organization depending upon the market situation for labour and the product among other things. Secondly, there may be different relationships between the state and industry – the politics of production and the politics of the state. Thirdly, whilst he is sceptical of the empirical adequacy of Marxist crisis theories, Burawoy is prepared to argue that when local or global crises actually occur then hegemonic systems may break down. At such a time 'the consciousness people carry in their heads and the characters they have formed become critical in the shaping of activities' (p. 202).

Despite his reservations about some neo-Marxism and his sympathy towards plant-based empirical industrial sociology, Burawoy is clear in the end about the primacy to be accorded to class analysis and, in particular, to the industrial working class.

> The industrial working class still represents the most fundamental point of critique, both of advanced capitalism, dominated by private appropriation of the product of direct producers, and of state socialism, dominated by central appropriation of the product of direct producers. (Burawoy, 1985, p. 9)

This he defends against the charge from Marxists and non-Marxists that such an approach is anachronistic and irrelevant. It certainly tackles head-on some of the problems raised by Lockwood, which we discussed above. Burawoy claims that a focus on the industrial working class has a methodological and a theoretical rationale:

> For the industrial working class is at once the most fundamental and the most suspect link in the Marxian schema. The reconstruction of Marxism must examine how the process of production shapes the industrial working class not only objectively – that is, the type of labour it carries out – but also subjectively – that is, the struggles engendered by a specific experience or interpretation of that labour. (p. 8)

This does not make any assumptions about the historical agency of the working class, nor on the other hand of its necessary quiescence. It does raise questions about what kinds of factory regime are found in capitalist and socialist societies, at what times and in what places. So a comparative study whereby factory regimes are situated in their historical contexts of specific economies and states is pursued. Here, then, is an imaginative response both to Marxism and industrial sociology. Both are the subject of critique but both serve as a resource for studying the organization of work and the politics of production.

Within the sociological tradition it is not only Marxism which emphasizes the inherent instability of industrial capitalism. The core of Durkheim's own diagnosis of the character of industrial societies in the nineteenth and early twentieth century was that they had a tendency to incipient disorder. The absence of effective forms of social regulation signified a condition of anomie. And he did not hesitate to write in terms of crisis. But this could be manifested in times of abrupt change – hence there could be a crisis of prosperity as well as a crisis of economic depression. In this sense Durkheim was a precursor of those who see economic growth as problematical rather than thinking of abundance as the solution to social problems. As he pointed out, this was no reason that humanity should not seek to improve its material condition and nor did he suppose that the question of social regulation was insoluble. What is interesting is the way in which an essentially functionalist analysis is nevertheless shot through with moral and normative considerations. Moreover, there is a prevailing theme that whilst some kind of social equilibrium (with explicit moral connotations concerned with reducing social inequality) might be desirable and even possible, the pervasive reality, pathological though it may be, was quite different. Writing about crises brought about by abrupt changes, Durkheim describes this as a situation in which a scale is upset, without another being put in its place because of the rapidity of the change:

> Time is required for the public conscience to reclassify men and things. So long as the social forces thus freed have not regained equilibrium, their respective values are unknown and so all regulation is lacking for a time. The limits are unknown between the possible and the impossible, what is just and what is unjust, legitimate claims and hopes and those which are immoderate. Consequently there is no restraint upon aspirations. If the disturbance is profound, it affects even the principles controlling the distribution of men among various occupations. Since the relations between the various parts of society are necessarily modified, the ideas expressing these relations must change. Some particular class especially favoured by the crisis is no longer resigned to its former lot, and, on the other hand, the example of its greater fortune arouses all sorts of jealousy below and about it. (Durkheim, 1952, p. 253)

The language which Durkheim uses is in terms of appetites that have been stimulated but are incapable of satisfaction, of agitation that is unresolved, of violent, painful and uncontrolled competition. The sphere of life which he described as being in a chronic state of anomie was that of trade and industry, and the reason for this is explicitly related to vast extension of the market:

> So long as the producer could gain his profit only in his immediate neighbourhood, the restricted amount of possible gain could not much over-excite ambition. Now that he may assume to have almost the entire world as his customer, how could the passions accept their former confinement in the face of such limitless prospects? (pp. 255–6)

Durkheim continues his diagnosis in a way which manifestly invites comparison with the medical analogy. The pathology of the economic sphere penetrates and contaminates the whole of society. Indeed, it is in the economic sphere that he judges the state of crisis and anomie to be so endemic that it is 'normal'. His comments on the situation do not have the cool detachment a reading of his *Rules of Sociological Method* might lead us to suppose:

From top to bottom of the ladder, greed is aroused without knowing where to find ultimate foothold. Nothing can calm it, since its goal is far beyond all it can attain. Reality seems valueless by comparison with the dreams of fevered imaginations; reality is therefore abandoned when it in turn becomes reality. A thirst arises for novelties, unfamiliar pleasures, nameless sensations, all of which lose their savour once known. Henceforth one has no strength to endure the least reverse. The whole fever subsides and the sterility of all the tumult is apparent, and it can be seen that all these new sensations in their infinite quantity cannot form a solid foundation of happiness to support one during days of trial. . . . Weariness alone, moreover, is enough to bring disillusionment, for he cannot in the end escape the futility of an endless pursuit. (p. 256)

So it is that for Durkheim our very concept of social reality is thrown into disarray as a result of structural changes. Insatiable appetites, fevered imaginations, the quest for excitement, produce weariness and disillusionment are the enemies of happiness and well-being. This is scarcely the sterilized language of a positivist sociologist. We are, in fact, being invited to consider the dark side of modernity, the erosion of solid foundations, the impact of economic materialism on cultural life and individual identity. The absence of effective constraints in the conduct of economic life is depicted as having cumulative, reinforcing consequences:

When there is no other aim but to outstrip constantly the point arrived at, how painful to be thrown back! Now this very lack of organisation characterising our economic condition throws the door wide to every sort of adventure. Since imagination is hungry for novelty, and ungoverned, it gropes at random. Setbacks necessarily increase with risks and thus crises multiply, just when they are becoming more destructive. (p. 257)

If we refer back to Hyman's account of industrial sociology, then scrutiny of his paper reveals that Durkheim is assigned only a small walk-on part. Yet there is a considerable preoccupation with the character, consequences and extent of anomie in industrial societies. Commenting on Tawney's well-known book *The Acquisitive Society*, Elton Mayo remarked: 'Actually the problem is not that of the sickness of an acquisitive society; it is the acquisitiveness of a sick society' (Mayo, 1946, p. 153). Referring to this, Merton observed:

Mayo deals with the process through which wealth comes to be the basic symbol of social achievement and sees this as arising from a state of anomie. My major concern is with the social consequences of a heavy emphasis upon monetary success as goal in a society which has not adapted its structure to the implications of this emphasis. A complete analysis would require the simultaneous examination of both processes. (Merton, 1956, p. 135)

Merton's essay dwells upon the significance of the cultural goal of success in American society, the celebrated American dream. This goal is itself elusive since there is no defined stopping point. Moreover, there is a discrepancy between the goal and the institutional means to achieve it. This is the American version of the anomie of prosperity and Merton's general position is this:

> To say that the goal of monetary success is entrenched in American culture is only to say that Americans are bombarded on every side by precepts which affirm the right or, often, the duty of retaining the goal even in the face of repeated frustration. Prestigeful representatives of the society reinforce the cultural emphasis. The family, the school and the workplace – the major agencies shaping the personality structure and goal formation of Americans – join to provide the intensive disciplining required if an individual is to retain intact a goal that maintains elusively beyond reach, if he is to be motivated by the promise of a gratification which is not redeemed. (1956, pp. 136–7)

Merton then goes on to outline the modes of individual adaptation to this situation but that need not detain us here save to notice that it is a serious, if preliminary, attempt to sketch out the relationship between character and social structure. It may, for example, offer an interpretative reference point to those who want to make sense of ethnographic data about factory life and experiences and reactions to work situations (Eldridge, 1971, pp. 119ff)

Although Merton focuses upon the anomie of success, other versions of anomie generated by technological and/or economic depression are found in the American literature and not least in industrial sociology (for example, Cotrell, 1965, pp. 234–43). Essentially, Cotrell gave an account of how a community whose economic existence was based on the servicing of steam engines, was undermined by the advent of dieselization. The changes were implemented in the name of progress, but there were social and personal costs. 'The story is an old one and often repeated in the economic history of America. It represents the "loss" side of a profit-and-loss system of adjusting to technological change' (p. 237). The losses were carried by the workforce, the local merchants, bondholders and house owners. Those who represent the morality of the 'American way' are those who experience the disintegration of their community and the disruption of their social and work relationships. What follows is a process of *demoralization*. At such a time questions are raised about the justice of a system which permits such things to happen, when the forces of the market or the 'law of supply and demand' result in human casualties who feel that they have done nothing to deserve their lot. In more general terms we might add that if relatively small numbers of people experience the negative effect of economic changes in the name of progress and economic necessity, when we come to contemplate the effects of widespread unemployment brought about by technological change or widespread deindustrialization, the anomie perspective would suggest extensive demoralization, sometimes accompanied by a sense of apathy or fatalism.

There are, then, two rather different images of the social consequences and character of anomie. The anomie of economic depression is thought of in terms of passive resignation; the anomie of prosperity is described in terms of actively pursuing unattainable but changing goals in a restless, insatiable way. But both these images are in their turn derivative upon an image of society as a system of social relationships dependent upon competitiveness in the market. The moral economy of the rat race, as Burns has crisply called it, represents a transition 'from a market economy embedded in a social order to a social order embedded in a market economy' (Burns, 1983, p. 81). He argues that this did not just happen:

> It was made to happen by the social action of groups and individuals moved by values and purposes more in accordance with the latter order than the former, covered by infringements of the law as well as of traditional moral principles, and eventually by political decisions which changed the law so as to promote conditions favourable to the operation of free competitive markets and to the new values of maximising profit and promoting competitive enterprise. (p. 81)

Both Marx and Durkheim saw industrial capitalism as unstable and both offered explanations of the crises, present or impending, which they detected. Marx offers us a class analysis which both identifies and expresses the internal contradictions of capitalism. And, of course, he points to the transformation of capitalism into communism – as the resolution of the contradiction and the solution of the crisis in unbridled, unregulated competition – leading to cumulative collapse of the system (the centre cannot hold) and accompanied by the destruction of the social individual. The alternative to which he points is an organic division of labour in which unjust inequalities are not present. His programmatic statement of social reconstruction points to a liberal social democracy with all the pluralist connotations that that implies. The danger that he is indicating and wanting to avoid is that of a mass society in which the atomized individual replaces the truly social individual.

Even so, the instability of industrial capitalism is one thing; its demise is something else. The point has been well made by Burns:

> One of the more distinctive features of industrial capitalism is its ability to take on new life when its obituary has been written, as it has so frequently been since 1848, up to the Second World War (out of which the last thing we expected was the emergence of a resurgent, even triumphant capitalism, creating economic miracles in one country after another, and an affluent society even, so we were told, in Britain). The point, of course, is that it is a different capitalism which emerges out of these crises from that which suffered them; and what emerges is not a capitalism one step nearer the grave, or a capitalism with a new mask, but a regenerated capitalism, one with a new, or at least reconstructed, *modus operandi* and structure. (Burns, 1983, p. 82)

Burns' work, here and elsewhere, has reflected a preoccupation with the institutional nature of industrialism, the processes it embodies and the changing character of the societies in which it is embedded and to which it contributes (see, especially, Burns, 1962). Burns points out that industrialism is the product of techniques of social organization linked with techniques of manufacture. In the early stages of manufacture, the machines and techniques were compatible with what Burns terms the primitive social technology of the factory system, or indeed with forms of subcontracting and domestic industry connected with central workshops. By the second half of the nineteenth century, however, the factory system is extending into a range of industries beyond textiles, including engineering, iron and steel, chemicals, food manufacture and clothing, alongside technical developments in transport and communications. The social technology which accompanies this is bureaucracy. This in turn served to facilitate the growth in the scale of industrial and business undertakings. As a social technology, bureaucracy sought to deal with problems of control, planning, monitoring and coordination.

This part of Burns' exposition is consistent with, and derivative upon Weber's well-known account of bureaucracy. Indeed, for him the phenomenon of bureaucratization was so pervasive in the late nineteenth and early twentieth century, when he was writing, that it forms a central part of his social analysis. It is not only the worker who is separated from the ownership of the means of production, as identified by Marx, but the soldier from the ownership of the means of violence, the civil servant from ownership of the means of administration, the scholar from ownership of the means of knowledge and the manager from ownership of industrial property. Weber maintained that it was primarily the capitalist market economy which required that official business be conducted precisely, unambiguously and with speed. He claimed that 'normally, the very large capitalist enterprises are themselves unequalled models of strict bureaucratic organisation' (Weber, 1978 edn, p. 974). The emergence of bureaucratic forms of administration has important consequences for social structure and the exercise of power in industrial society:

> Once fully established, bureaucracy is among those structures which are the hardest to destroy. Bureaucracy is *the* means of transforming social action into rationally organised action. Therefore, as an instrument of rationally organising authority relations, bureaucracy was and is a power instrument of the first order for one who controls the bureaucratic apparatus. Under otherwise equal conditions, rationally organised and directed action is superior to every kind of collective behaviour and also social action opposing it. Where administrations have been completely bureaucratised, the resulting system of domination is practically indestructible. (p. 987)

Bureaucracy can, therefore, be an instrument for containing crisis and managing conflict. It is as though just at the point where class struggle might have intensified in capitalist societies, as in a Marxist analysis, or collapsed through unregulated competition, as in Durkheim's discussion of anomie, the bureaucratic form of administration maintains organizational stability and blunts the capacity for resistance, both practically and ideologically. Moreover, the bureaucratic form of administration, with its essentially hierarchical principles, permeates and weakens the ethos of democratic communities. More particularly, it incorporates the official secret and the role of the expert, both of which present problems in relation to the ideal of an open, democratic community.

Nevertheless, the idea of crisis is not absent from Weber's account. One crucial reason for this is that there are constraints on formal business rationality within the individual enterprise. Weber refers to certain features of finance capitalism as 'outside interests':

> The fact that such 'outside' interests can affect the mode of control over managerial positions, even and especially when the highest degree of *formal* rationality is attained constitutes a further element of *substantive* irrationality specific to the modern economic order. . . . The influence exercised by specialist interests outside the producing organisations themselves on the market situation, especially that for capital good, is *one* of the sources of the phenomena known as the 'crisis' of the modern market economy. (p. 140)

At the end of his paper Burns writes:

> The practice of sociology is criticism: to criticise or to raise questions about claims and assumptions concerning the value or meaning of conduct and achievement. It is the business of sociologists to conduct a critical debate, in this sense, with the public about its equipment of social institutions. (Burns, 1962, p. 211)

In this respect the sociological voice is only one among many. With its intrinsic regard for evidence and logical argument sociology has always been the enemy of dogma; but the practice of sociology is inescapably interpretative. We have seen, however, that the idea of crisis, with different emphases, has accompanied sociological discussions of industrialism. This remains the case today as the term is put through a variety of conceptual filters: legitimation crisis, cultural crisis, economic crisis, political crisis, a crisis of modernization and so on. These lead on to debates about social values and human purposes. Sociology in general, and industrial sociology in particular, will avoid such debates only at the cost of professional sterility. But a critical voice must certainly hear what other voices are saying. Touraine, for example, observes:

> A crisis is being declared on all sides: by the defenders of the capitalist economy, themselves uneasy as they see the sources of capitalist industrialisation – the propensity to sound long-term investment in productive activities and the stability of currency – threatened by a consumer society, that is, a consuming society; and in a more spectacular manner, by those who oppose unsatisfied real demands to oversatisfied, artificially stimulated demands. The latter ask, how can one not be sensitive to a crisis in societies that respond to needs only when such responses increase profits? (Touraine, 1981, p. 317)

Touraine's own critical sensitivities lead him to question too ready a use of the term crisis because he thinks that the notion of crisis has an ideological function. Thus:

> When we speak of crisis, we are looking at society from the point of view of the ruling forces; when we speak of transformation, we imply that we are studying the formation of a new cultural field, new relations, and new social conflicts. This directs our attention not only to the birth of new social movements but also to the shaping of new forms of power. (p. 339)

Yet, in spite of this, he returns to the notion:

> We must speak of crisis when we see some populations abandoned to hunger and death, while others speak only of relaxation, identity and pleasure. (p. 340)

And he concludes:

> We are being threatened with the loss of our capacity to imagine, prepare, and build the future. A crisis is not a situation; it is an incapacity to act. (p. 340)

To identify this incapacity to act is the first step in moving from crisis to transformation. To show what possibilities may exist for political choices in an active democracy is to exercise the sociological imagination. If this is so, then industrial sociology itself is in crisis only when it fails to embrace this challenge.

BIBLIOGRAPHY

ACAS. 1985. Annual Report.

Adeney, M. and Lloyd, J. 1986. *The Miners' Strike 1984–85: Loss without limit.* Routledge & Kegan Paul.

Altmann, N. and Dull, K. 1988. *Participation in Technological Change: Company strategies and participation.* European Foundation for the Improvement of Living and Working Conditions, Dublin.

Anderson, P. 1964. 'Origins of the present crisis', *New Left Review*, no. 23, pp. 26–53.

Anderson, P. 1967. 'The limits and possibilities of trade union action', in R. Blackburn and C. Cockburn (eds), *The Incompatibles.* Penguin.

Anderson, P. 1987. 'The figures of descent', *New Left Review*, no. 161.

Armstrong, P. 1982. 'If it's only women it doesn't matter so much', in J. West (ed.), *Work, Women and the Labour Market.* Routledge & Kegan Paul.

Ascherson, N. 1981. *The Polish August: The self-limiting revolution.* Penguin.

Atkinson, J. 1984. 'Manpower strategies for flexible firms'. *Personnel Management*, August.

Atkinson, J. and Meager, N. 1986. *Changing Patterns of Work: How companies introduce flexibility to meet new needs.* IMS.

Baddon, L., Hunter, L. C., Hyman, J., Leopold, J. and Ramsay, H. 1989. *People's Capitalism? A critical analysis of profit sharing and employee share ownership.* Routledge.

Bahro, R. 1978. *The Alternative in Eastern Europe.* New Left Books.

Bain, G. S. and Price, R. 1984. 'Union growth: dimensions, determinants and destinies', in G. S. Bain (ed.), *Industrial Relations in Britain.* Basil Blackwell.

Baldry, C., Haworth, N. and Ramsay, H. 1981. 'Multi-national capital in Scotland. The closure of the Massey-Ferguson plant', *BSA conference (Scotland) paper.*

Ball, C. 1986. 'Experiments and innovations in industrial democracy: enterprise planning at the GLEB' in G. Spyropoulous (ed.), *Trade Unions Today and Tomorrow Vol. II. Trade Unions in a Changing Workplace.* European Centre for Work and Society.

Barnett, A. 1984. 'The failed consensus', in J. Curran (ed.), *The Future of the Left.* Polity Press.

Batstone, E. 1984. *Working Order.* Basil Blackwell.

Batstone, E. 1985. 'International variations in strike activity', *European Sociological Review*, vol. 1, no. 1.

Batstone, E., Ferner, A. and Terry, M. 1983. *Unions on the Board*. Basil Blackwell.

Beaumont, P. 1987. *The Decline of Trade Union Organisation*. Croom Helm.

Beechey, V. 1985. 'The shape of the workforce to come', *Marxism Today*, August.

Bendix, R. 1956. *Work and Authority in Industry*. Harper & Row.

Berman, M. 1982. *All That Is Solid Melts Into Air*. Verso.

Beynon, H. 1975. *Working for Ford*. Penguin.

Beynon, H. (ed.). 1985. *Digging deeper: Issues in the miners' strike*. Verso.

Blau, P. M. and Duncan, O. D. 1967. *The American Occupational Structure*. Wiley.

Blumberg, P. 1968. *Industrial Democracy*. Constable.

Bodington, S. 1973. 'Workers control as a movement', *Bulletin of the Institute for Workers Control*, no. 10. Nottingham.

Brannen, P. 1983. *Authority and Participation in Industry*. Batsford.

Brannen, P., Batstone, E., Fatchett, D. and White, P. 1979. *The Worker Directors: A sociology of participation*. Hutchinson.

Braverman, H. 1974. *Labour and Monopoly Capital*. Monthly Review Press.

Brown, G. 1977. *Sabotage*. Spokesman Books.

Brown, W. (ed.). 1981. 'Trade union organisation in the workplace', in *The Changing Contours of British Industrial Relations: A survey of manufacturing industry*. Basil Blackwell.

Bullock Report. 1979. *Report of the Committees of Inquiry on Industrial Democracy*. Cmnd. 6706. HMSO.

Burawoy, M. 1979. *Manufacturing Consent*. University of Chicago Press.

Burawoy, M. 1985. *The Politics of Production*. Verso.

Burns, T. 1962. 'The sociology of industry', in A. T. Welford *et al.* (eds), *Society: Problems and methods of study*. Routledge & Kegan Paul.

Burns, T. 1971. 'Mechanistic and organismic structures', in D. S. Pugh (ed.), *Organisation Theory*. Penguin.

Burns, T. 1983. 'The moral economy of the rat race', in E. Goodman (ed.), *Non-conforming Radicals of Europe*. Duckworth.

Burns, T. and Stalker, G. 1961. *The Management of Innovation*. Tavistock.

Cairncross, A. 1989. 'Is there a cure for unemployment?' *Adult and Continuing Education Occasional Publication*, no. 3.

Cameron, D. R. 1984. 'Social democracy, corporatism labour quiescence and the representation of economic interest in advanced capitalist society', in J. H. Goldthorpe (ed.), 1984, *op. cit.*

Castles, S. and Kosack, G. 1973. *Immigrant Workers and Class Struggle in Western Europe*. Oxford University Press.

Cavendish, R. 1982. *Women on the Line*. Routledge & Kegan Paul.

Chandler, Jr, A. D. 1962. *Strategy and Structure*. MIT Press.

Chell, E., Cox, D. and Towers, B. 1988. 'The worker director and participative machinery', Department of Employment research paper, no. 29.

Child, J. 1969. *British Management Thought*. Allen & Unwin.

Child, J. 1972. 'Organisational structure, environment and performance: the role of strategic choice', *Sociology*, vol. 6, no. 1, pp. 1–22.

Clegg, H. 1960. *A New Approach to Industrial Democracy*. Basil Blackwell.

Clegg, S. and Dunkerley, D. 1980. *Organisation, Class and Control*. Routledge & Kegan Paul.

Coates, D. 1975. *The Labour Party and the Struggle for Socialism*. Cambridge University Press.

Coates, K. 1975. 'Democracy and workers control', in J. Vanek (ed.), *Self Management*. Penguin.

Coates, K. and Silburn, R. 1970. *Poverty: The forgotten Englishmen*. Penguin.

Coates, K. and Topham, T. 1968. 'Participation or control', in K. Coates (ed.), *Can the Workers Run Industry?* Sphere.

Coates, K. and Topham, T. (eds). 1970. *Workers Control*. Panther Modern Society.

Coates, K. and Topham, T. 1986. *Trade Unions and Politics*. Basil Blackwell.

Cockburn, C. 1983. *Brothers: Male domination and technological change*. Pluto.

Cohen, S. (ed.). 1971. *Images of Deviance*. Penguin.

Conference of Socialist Economists. 1981. *Alternative Economic Strategy*. CSE Books.

Coopers and Lybrand. 1985. *A Challenge to Complacency: Changing attitudes to training*. Coopers and Lybrand.

Cotrell, W. F. 1965. 'Death by dieselization', in N. J. Smelser (ed.), *Readings on Economic Sociology*. Prentice Hall, Inc.

Coyle, A. 1982. *Redundant Women*. The Women's Press.

Cressey, P. 1986. 'Recasting collectivism: non-unionisation in two American branch plants', in G. Spyropoulos (ed.), *Trade Unions Today and Tomorrow Vol. 2. Trade Unions in a Changing Workplace*, pp. 63–87. European Centre for Work and Society.

Cressey, P., Bolle de Bal, M., Trea, T., Di Martino, V. and Traynor, K. 1988. 'Participation review', *European Foundation for Living and Working Conditions Research on Participation*. European Foundation.

Cressey, P., Eldridge, J., MacInnes, J. and Norris, G. 1981. 'Industrial democracy and participation: A Scottish study', Department of Employment research paper no. 28.

Cressey, P., Eldridge, J. E. T. and MacInnes, J. 1985. *Just Managing: Authority and democracy in industry*. Open University Press.

Cressey, P. and MacInnes, J. 1980. 'Voting for Ford', *Capital and Class*, no. 11.

Cressey, P. and MacInnes, J. 1982. 'The modern capitalist enterprise and the structure of control', in D. Dunkerley and G. Salaman (eds), *International Yearbook of Organisation Studies*, Routledge & Kegan Paul.

Cronin, J. 1979. *Industrial Conflict in Modern Britain*. Croom Helm.

Crosland, C. A. R. 1956. *The Future of Socialism*. Jonathan Cape.

Cross, M. 1985. *Towards a Flexible Craftsman*. IDS study, no. 360. Technical Change Centre.

Cross, M. 1988. 'Changes in working practices in UK manufacturing, 1981–88', *Industrial Relations Review and Report*, no. 415, pp. 2–10.

Dahl, R. 1947. 'Workers control of industry and the British Labour Party',

American Political Science Review, vol. 41.

Dahrendorf, R. 1959. *Class and Class Conflict in Industrial Society*. Routledge & Kegan Paul.

Dalton, M. 1959. *Men Who Manage*. Wiley.

Daniels, W. and Millward, N. 1983. *Workplace Industrial Relations*. Gower.

Davis, H. and Scase, R. 1985. *Western Capitalism and State Socialism*. Basil Blackwell.

Department of Employment. 1986. 'International comparisons of industrial stoppages for 1984', *Department of Employment Gazette*, July.

Dex, S. 1984. 'Women's work histories: an analysis of the women and employment survey', Department of Employment research paper no. 46.

Dex, S. 1985. *The Sexual Division of Work*. Wheatsheaf.

Dex, S. and Perry, S. M. 1984. 'Women's Employment Changes in the 1970s' in *Department of Employment Gazette*, vol. 92, pp. 151–64.

Donovan Commission. 1968. *Royal Commission on Trade Unions and Employers Associations*. HMSO.

Dowling, M., Goodman, J., Gotting, F. and Hyman, J. D. 1981. 'Employee participation: practice and attitudes in the north west manufacturing industry', Department of Employment research paper no. 27.

Dubois, P. 1979. *Sabotage in Industry*. Penguin.

Dunlop, J. 1948. 'The development of labor organisations: a theoretical framework', in R. Lester and J. Shister (eds), *Insights in Labor Issues*. Macmillan.

Durcan, J. W., McCarthy, W. E. J. and Redman, G. P. 1983. *Strikes in Post-war Britain*. Allen & Unwin.

Durkheim, E. 1952. *Suicide*. Routledge & Kegan Paul.

Durkheim, E. 1982. *The Rules of Sociological Method*. Macmillan.

Earl, M. J. 1983. *Perspectives on Management*. Oxford University Press.

Edwards, P. 1981. *Strikes in the United States, 1881–1974*. Basil Blackwell.

Edwards, P. K. 1986. *Conflict at Work*. Basil Blackwell.

Edwards, P. K. and Scullion, H. 1982. *The Social Organisation of Industrial Conflict*. Basil Blackwell.

Edwards, P. K. and Sisson, K. 1989. 'Industrial relations in the UK: change in the 1980s', ESRC Research Briefing.

Edwards, R. C. 1980. *Contested Terrain*. Basic Books.

Eldholm, F., Harris, O. and Young, K. 1977. 'Conceptualising women', *Critique of Anthropology* nos. 9/10.

Eldridge, J. E. T. 1968. *Industrial Disputes*. Routledge & Kegan Paul.

Eldridge, J. E. T. 1971. *Sociology and Industrial Life*. Nelson/Joseph.

Elliot, J. 1978. *The Growth of Industrial Democracy – Conflict or Co-operation*. Kogan Page.

Fallick, L. and Elliott, R. F. 1981. *Incomes Policies, Inflation and Relative Pay*. Allen & Unwin.

Fatchett, D. 1977. *Industrial Democracy: Prospects after Bullock*. University of Leeds and University of Nottingham Press.

Faunce, W. (ed.). 1967. *Readings in Industrial Sociology*. Appleton–Century–Crofts.

Feinstein, C. (ed.). 1983. *The Managed Economy*. Oxford University Press.

Ferner, A. 1985. 'Political constraints and management strategies: the case of working practices in British Rail', *British Journal of Industrial Relations*, vol. 23, pp. 47–70.

Fidler, J. 1981. *The British Business Elite*. Routledge & Kegan Paul.

Flanders, A. 1970. 'What are trade unions for?' in *Management and Trade Unions*. Faber & Faber.

Forester, T. 1980. 'Whatever happened to industrial democracy?' *New Society*, July.

Fox, A. 1971. *A Sociology of Work in Industry*. Collier–Macmillan.

Fox, A. 1974. *Man Mismanagement*. Hutchinson.

Fox, A. 1985. *History and Heritage: The social origins of the British industrial relations system*. Allen & Unwin.

Fricke, W. 1986. 'New technologies and German co-determination', *Economic and Industrial Democracy*, vol. 7, no. 4.

Friedman, A. L. 1977. *Industry and Labour*. Macmillan.

Friedman, H. 1976. 'Multi-plant working and trade union organisation' *Studies for Trade Unionists*, vol. 2, no. 8. WEA.

Fulcher, J. 1987. 'Labour movement theory versus corporatism: social democracy in Sweden', *Sociology*, vol. 21, no. 2.

Galbraith, J. K. and Salinger, N. 1981. *Almost Everyone's Guide to Economics*. Penguin.

Gallie, D. 1978. *In Search of the New Working Class*. Cambridge University Press.

George, M. 1981. 'Developments in combine organisations', K. Coates (ed.). *How to Win*. Spokesman Press.

Gerth, H. H. and Mills, C. W. (eds). 1970. *From Max Weber*. Routledge & Kegan Paul.

Giddens, A. 1973. *The Class Structure of the Advanced Societies*. Hutchinson.

Gilmour, I. 1988. Speech to King's College (London) Tory Reform Group, 18 November 1988. Reprinted in *The Guardian*, 24 November.

Glynn, A. and Sutcliffe, B. 1972. *British Capitalism, Workers and the Profits Squeeze*. Penguin.

Goldthorpe, J. H. 1977. 'Industrial relations in Britain: a critique of reformism', in T. Clarke and L. Clements (eds), *Trade Unions under Capitalism*. Fontana/Collins.

Goldthorpe, J. H. 1980. *Social Mobility and Class Structure in Modern Britain*. (first edition), Clarendon Press.

Goldthorpe, J. H. (ed.). 1984. *Order and Conflict in Contemporary Capitalism*. Clarendon Press.

Goldthorpe, J. H. 1987. *Social Mobility and Class Structure in Modern Britain* (second edition), Clarendon Press.

Goldthorpe, J. H., Lockwood, D., Bechager, F. and Platt, J. 1968. *The Affluent Worker: Industrial attitudes and behaviour*. Cambridge University Press.

Gorz, A. 1969. *Reforme et Revolution*. Editions du Seuil.

Gorz, A. 1982. *Farewell to the Working Class?* Pluto.

Gospel, H. F. and Littler, C. R. (eds). 1983. *Managerial Strategies and Industrial Relations*. Heinemann.

Gouldner, A. W. 1971. *The Coming Crisis of Western Sociology*. Heinemann.

Gouldner, A. W. 1973. *For Sociology: Renewal and critique in sociology today*. Penguin.

Gramsci, A. 1971. *Prison Notebooks*. Lawrence & Wishart.

Gramsci, A. 1977. *Selections from Prison writings, 1910–20*. Lawrence & Wishart.

The Guardian. 1986. 'Engineers look to more single union agreements', 30 July 1986.

Guest, D. 1987. 'Human resource management and industrial relations', *Journal of Management Studies*, vol. 24, no. 5, pp. 503–22.

Habermas, J. 1975. *Legitimation Crisis*. Beacon Press.

Hain, P. 1986. *Political Strikes: The state and trade unionism in Britain*. Penguin.

Hall, S. 1988a. 'Brave new world', *Marxism Today*.

Hall, S. 1988b. *The Hard Road to Renewal*. Verso.

Hall, S. and Merlin J. (eds). 1983. *The Politics of Thatcherism*. Lawrence J. Wilbert.

Hammond, E. 1985. Article in *The Financial Times*, 14 December 1985.

Haraszti, M. 1977. *A Worker in a Workers' State*. Penguin.

Hasluck, C. 1987. *Urban Unemployment*. Longmans.

Hinton, J. 1983. *Labour and Socialism*. Wheatsheaf.

Hirst, P. 1982. 'Does industrial democracy have a future?' Mimeograph.

HMSO, 1967. *Workplace Industrial Relations Survey*. Department of Employment.

HMSO, 1977. White Paper, *Industrial Democracy*.

Hobsbawm, E. (ed.). 1964. 'Economic fluctuations and some social movements since 1800', in *Labouring Men*. Weidenfeld & Nicolson.

Hobsbawm, E. 1981. *The Forward March of Labour Halted?* Verso.

Hunter, L. C. and MacInnes, J. 1991. Forthcoming. 'Case studies of employers' labour use strategies', Department of Employment research paper.

Hyman, R. 1975. 'Workers' control and revolutionary theory', in *Socialist Register 1975*. Merlin Press.

Hyman, R. 1981. 'Whatever happened to industrial sociology?' in D. Dunkerley and G. Salaman (eds), *International Yearbook of Organisation Studies, 1981*, pp. 84–104. Routledge & Kegan Paul.

Hyman, R. 1982. 'Pressure, protest and struggle: some problems in the concept and theory of industrial conflict', in G. M. J. Bomers and R. B. Peterson (eds), *Conflict Management and Industrial Relations*. Kluwer–Nijhoff.

Hyman, R. (ed.). 1984. 'Trade union structure, policies and practices', in G. S. Bain, *Industrial Relations in Britain*. Basil Blackwell.

Hyman, R. 1988. *Strikes*. Fontana.

Hyman, R. and Fryer, R. H. 1975. 'Trade unions: sociology and political economy', in J. McKinley (ed.), *Processing People*. Holt, Rinehart & Winston.

IDS. *Flexibility at Work*, IDS study no. 360.

Industrial Relations Review and Report (IRRR). 1987a. No. 395 (July), p. 16.

Industrial Relations Review and Report. 1987b. No. 396 (July).

Ingham, G. K. 1984. *Capitalism Divided.* Macmillan.

Institute for Workers Control. 1968. *IWC Bulletin*, no. 1.

Jones, K. 1977. *Worker Directors Speak.* Gower.

Jowell, R. and Witherspoon, S. (eds). 1985. *British Social Attitudes. The 1985 Report.* Gower.

Kardelj, E. 1976. 'Socialist self-management in Yugoslavia', *International Review of Admin Sciences*, vol. 42, no. 2.

Kavanagh, D. 1987. *Thatcherism and British Politics: The end of consensus?* Oxford University Press.

Kelly, J. 1988. *Trade Unions and Socialist Politics.* Verso.

Kerr, C. 1960. 'Changing structures of the labour force' in C. Kerr (ed.) 1964. *Labor and Management in Industrial Society.* Doubleday.

Kerr, C., Dunlop, J. T., Harbison, F. and Myers, C. A. 1960 (first edition). *Industrialism and Industrial Man.* Heinemann.

Kerr, C., Dunlop, J. T., Harbison, F. and Myers, C. A. 1973. *Industrialism and Industrial Man* (second edition). Penguin.

Kerr, C. and Siegel, A. 1954. 'The inter-industry propensity to strike: an international comparison', in A. Kornhauser (ed.), *Industrial Conflict.* McGraw-Hill.

Keyes, David and the Labour Party Research Department. 1983. *Thatcher's Britain: A Guide to the Ruins.* Pluto Press.

Knowles, K. G. (1952). *Strikes: A study in industrial conflict.* Basil Blackwell.

Kolaga, J. 1965. *Workers' Councils: The Yugoslav experience.* Tavistock.

Kondratiev, N. D. 1935. 'The long waves in economic life', *Review of Economic Statistics*, vol. 17.

Korpi, W. 1981. 'Unofficial strikes in Sweden', *British Journal of Industrial Relations*, vol. 19, no. 1.

Korpi, W. 1983. *The Democratic Class Struggle.* Routledge & Kegan Paul.

Korpi, W. and Shalev, M. 1979. 'Strikes, industrial relations and class conflict in capitalist societies', *British Industrial Sociology*, vol. 30.

Labour force survey. 1988. '1987 Labour force survey – preliminary results' in *Department of Employment Gazette*, March.

Labour Party/TUC Liaison Committee. 1982. *Economic Planning and Industrial Democracy.*

Lane, T. 1982. 'The unions: caught on an ebb tide', *Marxism Today*, vol. 26, no. 9.

Lane, T. 1985. *The Union Makes Us Strong.* Oxford University Press.

Lenin, V. 1921. *What is to be Done?* Progress Press.

Lewis, R. 1984. 'Collective labour law', in G. S. Bain (ed.), *Industrial Relations in Britain.* Basil Blackwell.

Leys, C. 1985. 'Thatcherism and British manufacturing: a question of hegemony', *New Left Review*, no. 151, pp. 5–25.

Lloyd, J. 1988. 'The sparks are flying', *Marxism Today*, March.

Lockwood, D. 1981. 'The weakest link in the chain? Some comments on the Marxist theory of action', in Richard L. Simpson and Ida Harper Simpson (eds), *Research in the Sociology of Work.* Vol. 1. Jai Press.

Low Pay Unit. 1988. *The Poor Decade Wage Inequalities in the 1980s*. Low Pay Unit.

Lozovsky, A. 1972. 'The role of trade unions in the general class struggle of the proletariat', in W. MacCarthy (ed.), *Trade Unions*. Penguin.

Lukes, S. 1974. *Power: A radical view*. Macmillan.

MacGregor, I. 1986. *The Enemies Within: The story of the miners' strike 1984–5*. Collins.

MacInnes, J. 1985. 'Conjuring up consultation: The role and extent of joint consultation in post-war private manufacturing industry', *British Journal of Industrial Relations*, vol. XXIII, no. 1.

MacInnes, J. 1987. *Thatcherism at Work*. Open University Press.

McCarthy, W. E. J. and Ellis, N. D. 1973. *Management by Agreement*. Hutchinson.

McGregor, A. and Sproull, A. 1991, forthcoming. 'Employers' labour use strategies: analysis of a national survey', Department of Employment research paper.

McHugh, A., McIlwee, T. and Walby, N. 1987. 'A survey of company employee involvement statements', Ealing College of Higher Education School of Business and Management Occasional Paper Series, no. 4.

McKinley, J. (ed.). 1975. *Processing People*. Holt, Rinehart & Winston.

Mallet, S. 1963. *La nouvelle classe ouvrière*. Editions du Seuil.

Mann, M. 1973. *Consciousness and Action among the Western Working Class*. Macmillan.

Marchington, M. 1987. 'A review and critique of research on developments in joint consultation', *British Journal of Industrial Relations*, November.

Marginson, P., Terry, M., Martin, R., Sisson, K. 1988. *Beyond the workplace: managing industrial relations in the multi-establishment enterprise*. Basil Blackwell.

Marglin, S. 'What do bosses do?', *Review of Radical Political Economics*, vol. 6, no. 2.

Marsden, D. 1973. 'Industrial democracy and industrial control in West Germany, France and Great Britain', Department of Employment research paper no. 4.

Marshall, G., Rose, D., Newby, H. and Vogler, C. 1989. *Social Class in Modern Britain*. Unwin Hyman.

Marshall, T. H. 1950. *Citizenship and Social Class*. Cambridge University Press.

Martin, J. and Roberts, C. 1984. *Women and Employment: A Lifetime Perspective*. HMSO.

Marx, K. 'Resolution of the international working man's association on trade unions, Geneva 1866. Quoted in Lozovsky, 1972, *op. cit.*

Marx, K. 1959 edn. *Capital*. vol. 3. Foreign Languages Publishing House.

Marx, K. 1968 edn. 'Wages, price and profit', in *Marx, Engels: Selected Works*. Lawrence & Wishart.

Marx, K. 1976 edn. *Capital*. vol. 1, Penguin.

Marx, K. 1977. 'Capital and Labour' quoted in Clarke, T. and Clements, I. *Trade Unions under Capitalism*. Fontana.

Marx, K. and Engels, F. 1957 edn. *Manifesto of the Communist Party*. Foreign Languages Publishing House.

Marx, K. and Engels, F. 1968. *Selected Works in One Volume*. Lawrence & Wishart.

Massey, D. and Meegan, R. 1981. *The Anatomy of Job Loss*. Methuen.

Mayo, E. 1946. *The Human Problems of an Industrial Civilisation*. Routledge & Kegan Paul.

Merton, R. 1956. *Social Theory and Social Structure*. Free Press.

Metcalf, D. 1989. 'Water notes dry up', *British Journal of Industrial Relations*, vol. 27, no. 1.

Miles, R. 1982. *Racism and Migrant Labour*. Routledge & Kegan Paul.

Miles, R. 1989. *Racism*. Routledge.

Miliband, R. 1969. *The State in Capitalist Society*. Weidenfeld & Nicolson.

Miliband, R. 1973. *Parliamentary Socialism*. Merlin.

Mills, C. W. 1963. *Power, Politics and People*. Oxford University Press.

Millward, N. and Stevens, M. 1986. *British Workplace Industrial Relations 1980–84*. WIRS 2.

Milton, D. 1986. *Economic and Industrial Democracy*, vol. 7, no. 3.

Moore, B. 1979. *Injustice: The social bases of obedience and revolt*. Macmillan.

Morgan, K. O. 1985. *Labour in Power 1945–51*. Oxford University Press.

Nichols, T. 1969. *Ownership, Control and Ideology*. Allen & Unwin.

Nichols, T. (ed.). 1980. *Capital and Labour*. Fontana.

Nichols, T. 1986. *The British Worker Question*. Routledge & Kegan Paul.

Nordlinger, E. A. 1967. *The Working Class Tories: Authority, deference and stable democracy*. MacGibbon & Kee.

Nove, A. 1983. *The Economics of Feasible Socialism*. Hutchinson.

O'Connor, J. 1973. *The Fiscal Crisis of the State*. St Martins Press.

O'Connor, J. 1984. *Accumulation Crisis*. Basil Blackwell.

O'Connor, J. 1987. *The Meaning of Crisis*. Basil Blackwell.

Ouchi, W. 1981. *Theory Z: How American business can meet the Japanese challenge*. Addison-Wesley.

Pahl, R. E. and Winkler, J. T. 1974. 'The economic elite: theory and practice', in P. Stanworth and A. Giddens (eds), 1974, *op. cit.*, pp. 102–22.

Panitch, L. 1977. *Social democracy and Industrial Militancy: The Labour Party, Trade Unions and Incomes Policies, 1945–1974*.

Parker, S. R. 1974. *Workplace Industrial Relations 1972*. HMSO.

Parker, S. R., Brown, R. K., Child, J. and Smith, M. A. 1967. *The Sociology of Industry*. Allen & Unwin.

Parkin, F. 1972. *Class, Inequality and Political Order*. Palladin.

Parkin, F. 1979. *Marxism and Class Theory. A Bourgeois Critique*. Tavistock.

Partridge, H. 1986. 'Italy's Fiat in Turin: labour struggles and capital's responses', PhD thesis, University of Durham.

Pelling, H. 1972. *History of British Trade Unionism*. Penguin.

Phelps Brown, H. 1983. 'What is the British predicament?' in C. Feinstein (ed.), 1983, *op. cit.*, pp. 207–25.

Phillips, A. and Taylor, B. 1980. 'Sex and skill: notes towards a feminist economics', *Feminist Review*, no. 6.

Piore, M. and Sabel, C. 1984. *The Second Industrial Divide: Possibilities for prosperity*. Basic Books.

Pollard, S. J. 1965. *The Genesis of Modern Management*. Edward Arnold.

Poole, M. 1986. 'Participation through representation: a review of constraints and conflicting pressures', in R. N. Stern and S. McCarthy (eds), *The Organisational Practice of Democracy*. Wiley.

Poole, M., Mansfield, R., Blyton, P. and Frost, P. 1982. 'Managerial attitudes and behaviour in industrial relations: evidence from a national survey', *British Journal of Industrial Relations*, vol. 20, pp. 285–307.

Pouget, E. 1910. *Le Sabotage*.

Prais, S. J. 1976. *The Evolution of Giant Firms in the UK*. Cambridge University Press.

Ramsay, H. 1977. 'Cycles of control: worker participation in sociological and historical perspective', *Sociology*, vol. 11, no. 3.

Rex, J. and Tomlinson, S. 1979. *Colonial Immigrants in a British City: A Class Analysis*. Routledge & Kegan Paul.

Riddell, P. 1983. *The Thatcher Government*. Martin Robertson.

Roethlisberger, F. J. and Dickson, W. J. 1964. *Management and the Worker*. Harvard University Press.

Rose, M. 1988. *Industrial Behaviour*. Penguin.

Roy, D. 1952a. 'Do wage incentives reduce costs?' *Industrial Labour Relations Review*, vol. 5.

Roy, D. 1952b. 'Quota restriction and gold bricking in a machine shop', *American Journal of Sociology*, vol. 57.

Roy, D. 1953. 'Work satisfaction and social reward in quota achievement', *American Sociological Review*, vol. 18.

Roy, D. 1954. 'Efficiency and the "fix": informal inter-group relations in piecework machine shop' *American Journal of Sociology*, vol. 60.

Roy, D. 1960. 'Banana time: job satisfaction and informal interaction', *Human Organisation*, vol. 18.

Rutherford, M. 1983, 'Review of *The Politics of Thatcherism*', *Marxism Today*, July.

Samuel, R., Bloomfield, B. and Boanas, G. 1986. *The Enemy Within*. Routledge & Kegan Paul.

Sarre, P. 1989. 'Race and the class structure', in C. Hamnett *et al.* (eds), *Restructuring Britain: The Changing Social Structure*. Sage.

Sayles, L. R. 1964. *Managerial Behaviour: Administration in complex organisations*. McGraw-Hill.

Shell, K. L. 1957. 'Industrial democracy and the British labour movement', *Political Science Quarterly*, vol. 72, no. 4, pp. 513–39.

Shorter, E. and Tilly, C. 1974. *Strikes in France, 1830–1968*. Cambridge University Press.

Silverman, D. 1970. *The Theory of Organisations*. Heinemann.

Singleton, F. 1970. 'Workers' self-management and the role of trade unions in Yugoslavia', *Socialist Register*.

Smelser, N. 1959. *Social Change in the Industrial Revolution*. Routledge & Kegan Paul.

Smith, C. T. B., Clifton, R., Makeham, P., Creigh, S. W., and Burn, R. V. 1978. *Strikes in Britain*, Department of Employment, Manpower Research Paper, no. 15.

Smith, J. H. 1961. *The University Teaching of Social Sciences: Industrial Sociology.* UNESCO.

Smith, N. 1988. 'Politics, industrial policy and democracy: the Electricians Union 1945–1988', PhD thesis, Glasgow University.

Smith, S. A. 1983. *Red Petrograd: Revolution in the factories 1917–18.* Cambridge University Press.

Snell, W. and Taylor, D. 1984. 'Experimenting with industrial democracy: the impact on financial control in the UK Post Office', CRIDP Discussion Paper no. 11, Glasgow University.

Stanworth, M. 1984. 'Women and class analysis: a reply to Goldthorpe', *Sociology*, vol. 18, pp. 159–70.

Stanworth, P. and Giddens, A. 1974. *Elites and Power in British Society.* Cambridge University Press.

Stewart, R. 1983. 'Managerial behaviour: how research has changed the traditional picture' in M. J. Earl (ed.), 1983, *op. cit.*, pp. 82–98.

Stewart, R., Blake, J., Smith, P. and Wingate, P. 1980. *The District Administrator in the National Health Service.* King Edwards Hospital Fund for London.

Storey, J. 1990. 'Management development in Britain: which way forward?' *IRRU Research Review*, no. 2, University of Warwick.

Streeck, W. 1984. 'Co-determination in the fourth decade', in Wilpert B. and Sorge A. (eds), *International Yearbook of Organisational Democracy.* Vol. 11. *International Perspectives on Organisational Democracy.* Wiley.

Tawney, R. H. 1961. *The Acquisitive Society.* Fontana.

Terry, M. T. 1985. 'Combine committees developments of the 1970s', *British Journal of Industrial Relations*, vol. 23, no. 3.

Thompson, E. P. 1965. 'The peculiarities of the English', *Socialist Register.*

Thompson, E. P. 1967. 'Time, work discipline and industrial capitalism', *Past and Present*, vol. 38, pp. 56–97.

Thompson, E. P. 1968. *The Making of the English Working Class.* Penguin.

Thompson, E. P. 1978a. *The Poverty of Theory.* Merlin.

Thompson, E. P. 1978b. 'Eighteenth century English society: class struggle within classes?' *Social History*, vol. 5, pp. 183–221.

Tomlinson, J. 1982. *The Unequal Struggle? British Socialism and the Capitalist Enterprise.* Macmillan.

Topham, T. 1968. 'Productivity bargaining and workers control'. Quoted in K. Coates (ed.), 1968, *op. cit.*

Touraine, A. 1965. *Workers' Attitudes to Technical Change.* Organization for Economic Cooperation and Development.

Touraine, A. 1966. *La conscience ouvrière.* Editions du Seuil.

Touraine, A. 1981. 'The new social conflicts: crisis or transformation?' in C. C. Lemert, *French Sociology.* Columbia University Press.

Touraine, A. 1983. *Solidarity: Analysis of a social movement 1980–81.* Cambridge University Press.

Towers, B., Cox, D. and Chell, E. 1988. 'Do worker directors work?' *Depart-*

ment of Employment Gazette, September.

TUC/Labour Party Liaison Committee. 1974. *Industrial Democracy.*

TUC Consultative Document. 1980. *Industrial Relations Legislation*, January. p. 4.

Turner, H. A. 1963. *The Trend of Strikes.* Leeds University Press.

Undy, R., Ellis, V., McCarthy, W. and Halmos, A. M. 1981. *Change in Trade Unions.* Hutchinson.

Wadwhani, S. 1989. 'The effect of unions on productivity growth, investment and employment: a report on some recent work', *Discussion Paper*, no. 356, August, Centre for Labour Economics, London School of Economics and Political Science.

Wainwright, H. and Elliot, D. 1982. *The Lucas Plan: A new trade unionism in the making.* Allison & Busby.

Watson, T. J. 1986. *Management Organisation and Employment.* Routledge & Kegan Paul.

Weber, M. 1949. *The Methodology of the Social Sciences.* The Free Press.

Weber, M. 1978 edn. *Economy and Society.* University of California Press (2 vols).

Wells, J. R. 1988. 'Uneven development (manufacturing–services) and de-industrialisation in the UK since 1979'. Memeograph. Faculty of Economics, Cambridge.

Westergaard, J. H. 1972. 'The myth of classlessness', R. Blackburn (ed.), *Ideology in Social Science.* Fontana.

Westergaard, J. H. and Resler, H. 1976. *Class in a Capitalist Society.* Penguin.

Williams, K., Cutler, T., Williams, J. and Haslam, C. 1987. 'The end of mass production?' *Economy and Society*, vol. 16, no. 3.

Williams, R. 1989. *Resources of Hope.* Verso.

Wood, Sir John. 1985. 'The principles of "last offer arbitration"', *British Journal of Industrial Relations*, vol. 23, pp. 416–24.

Woodward, J. 1969. 'Management and Technology' in Burns, T. (ed.) *Industrial Man.* Penguin, pp. 196–231.

Wright, E. O. 1985. *Classes.* Verso.

Wright, E. O., Hacken, D., Costello, C. and Sprague, J. 1982. 'The American class structure', *American Sociological Review*, vol. 47, pp. 709–26.

INDEX